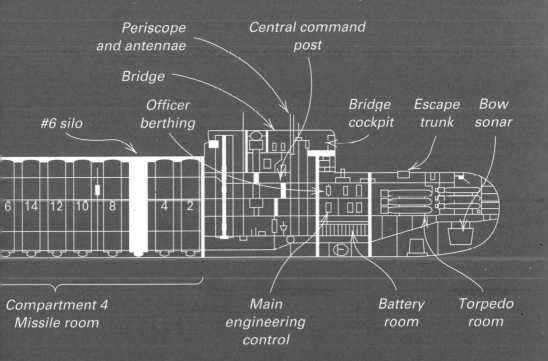

Periscope
and antennae

Central command
post

Bridge

Officer
berthing

Bridge
cockpit

Escape
trunk

Bow
sonar

#6 silo

6 14 12 10 8   4 2

Compartment 4
Missile room

Main
engineering
control

Battery
room

Torpedo
room

HOSTILE WATERS

HOSTILE

WATERS

Captain PETER HUCHTHAUSEN, USN (ret.),

Captain First Rank IGOR KURDIN, Russian Navy,

and R. ALAN WHITE

ST. MARTIN'S PRESS   NEW YORK

Design by Brian Mulligan

Library of Congress Cataloging-in-Publication Data

Huchthausen, Peter A.
    Hostile waters / Peter Huchthausen, Igor Kurdin, R. Alan White.
      p. cm.
    ISBN 0-312-16928-0
    1. K-219 (Submarine) 2. Submarine disasters—Soviet Union.
  3. Submarine disasters—North Atlantic Ocean. I. Kurdin, Igor.
  II. White, Robin A. III. Title.
  VA575.K14H83   1997
  363.17'99—dc21   97-13264
                                             CIP

First Edition: July 1997

10 9 8 7 6 5 4 3 2 1

A NOTE TO
THE READER

The ordeal of the *K-219* took place at the very height of the cold war. Much of its story is still shrouded in secrecy. Operations involving American submarines are simply not discussed by the United States Navy.

Ironically, it proved easier to obtain information from the Russians. Events portrayed in this book reflect that difference. Acts taken by, conversations held between, even the private thoughts of the crew of the *K-219* are taken directly from their testimony or from the submarine's log.

Actions inside and maneuvers made by the American sub present at *K-219*'s ordeal were reconstructed from Russian observations, American reports, interviews with many American naval officers and experts, and the authors' long experience in naval affairs. Conversations and commands portrayed in the book may not be the actual words spoken, the commands sent, or the orders received.

Like any intelligence analysis, the authors had to reconstruct this story from multiple sources. Sometimes they disagreed on the details. Their substance, however, is true.

Lord God, our power ever more, whose arm doth reach the ocean floor.

Divine with men beneath the sea; traverse the depths protectively.

Hear us when we pray, and keep them safe from peril in the deep.

Lord, guard and guide the men who man the submarines that guard our land.

Be with them always, night and day, in quiet depths and roaring spray.

O hear us when we cry to Thee, for those in peril on the sea.

—FROM THE UNITED STATES NAVY HYMN

FOREWORD
by TOM CLANCY

Nicholas Monsarrat called it "The Cruel Sea" because as unfeeling as it has always been, the works of man made it crueler still. The dawn of the nuclear age didn't help, sending men to sea for a longer time, under harsher conditions, and for the darkest of purposes.

With the end of the cold war and the demise of the Soviet Union, some new chapters have been revealed. This is one of them.

For years the Soviet Navy sent nuclear-powered fleet ballistic missile submarines to patrol off the American coast. Invariably shadowed by American fast-attack submarines, their mission was, if called upon, to launch their missiles against our country. The mission of the American submarines in trail was, if called upon, to prevent that from happening, and so there was a covenant of death between the ships and men moving invisibly beneath the sea while other ships plied the surface.

The Soviet submarines were technically inferior, and their crews knew it. Yet they did their jobs as best they could, ever wondering if there might be an unfriendly neighbor nearby. The Russian sailors' more immediate task, however, was to keep their ships operating. Far from home, they endured hazards unknown to their American counterparts, doing the jobs they were drafted to do.

K-219 was one of the losses in the cold war. Just a few hundred miles from the vacation island of Bermuda, the sub suffered a major casualty, endangering the crew as well as the ship. At the time of the incident I remember feeling little pity for the Russians aboard. That was wrong of me. Enemies, perhaps, but they were people, and there was no war at the time. Alone, thousands of miles from home or help, they faced dark death as many have done over the centuries. Their only purpose then was survival, and while American ships raced to the scene, the Russians were ordered not to accept assistance from any but their own.

This, then, is a tale of a cruel sea and crueler circumstances, of men trapped by duty into a duel with fire and water, which some of them did not survive. The cold war is over now, and over the coming years we'll total up the numbers of men and women who lost their lives, and if we are to value the peace we've earned, let it be in recognition of the price paid in buying it for ourselves and our children. The Russians paid, too. And this is one chapter in that story.

Hostile Waters is one of the most fascinating true submarine stories I have ever encountered.

—April 1997

INTRODUCTION

When fragments of the *K-219* story broke in the press in 1986, I was on my way to Moscow for what would become a three-year tour of duty as United States naval attaché. It was normal for a story like this to fade quickly from the public record; the Soviets suppressed details of their military accidents and the United States government refused to discuss submarine operations in general, and special "black" operations most of all. But my curiosity was aroused when I read an account in the *Washington Post* of a Soviet skipper who refused orders to leave his crippled submarine.

During my years in Moscow, the *K-219* incident was never officially raised by either side. It was only after pursuing the story, meeting the survivors and their families, interviewing the commanding officer, that I began to realize the scope of this compelling cold war drama.

This is an account of the sinking of the Soviet missile submarine *K-219*, reconstructed from descriptions by the survivors, ships' logs, the official investigations, and participants both ashore and afloat from the Russian and the American sides.

It is the story of the only nuclear-powered missile submarine to be lost at sea. It is a story of bravery, cowardice, and for some, ultimate sacrifice. It has never before been told.

—Peter Huchthausen
April 1997

PROLOGUE

The cold war was deep into its endgame by the fall of 1986, though no one would have guessed it. Huge armies still faced one another across a divided Europe. Missile crews in Germany, Ukraine, Kansas, and North Dakota stood twenty-four-hour alerts, ready to launch Armageddon. And under the sea the two superpowers played a game of hide-and-seek that was real war in every way but for the final order to shoot.

The Soviet-American confrontation was dangerous, but it was also balanced. For three decades the world had depended on this balance. It came close to collapsing in the mid-1980s when the Soviets deployed the SS-20, a mobile missile aimed at the heart of western Europe. The United States responded with Pershing and Tomahawk missiles based in Britain and Germany. The ante was suddenly raised, the balance disturbed.

Basing short-range attack missiles in Europe was the nightmare scenario for Soviet war planners: for the first time, nuclear weapons targeted on the Kremlin would arrive before Soviet leaders could be warned of their launch.

To counter this threat the Soviet Navy sent its missile-armed submarines patrolling provocatively close to the American coastline. The nuclear warheads carried by their ballistic missiles could strike Washington as fast, if not quite as accurately, as American Pershings targeted against Moscow. With both capitals at equal risk, the Soviets believed the balance was restored.

They were mistaken, for nowhere was the cold war less equal than under the sea.

Special U.S. intelligence submarines kept watch outside Soviet harbors, "fingerprinting" each departing Soviet sub. Miles of supersensitive acoustic arrays monitored their passage across the Atlantic. American patrol aircraft hounded Russian subs with passive and active sonobuoys. And when they arrived off the American coast, the Soviets faced U.S. attack submarines that materialized like ghosts, silent, stealthy, able to trail—and target—the Russians without their knowing it.

Russians, like Americans, are a patriotic people. Out of duty and out of pride, knowing full well the risks, they drove their clanking, obsolete vessels under the noses of a superior enemy. But the stepped-up tempo of operations quickly took a toll. By late 1986, the Soviet Northern Fleet was scrambling to maintain the politically mandated schedule of submarine patrols. Inevitably, shortcuts in safety were taken.

One such warship was *K-219,* an outdated submarine of a class the NATO powers called YANKEE. Her twin nuclear reactors were of an old and dangerous design. Her original battery of sixteen missiles had been reduced to fifteen by a near-catastrophic explosion in the mid-1970s.

Now, in September of 1986, her 119-man crew was crammed into a creaky steel hull, surrounded by atomic and chemical poisons, hunted by American forces they could not even detect. They sailed from their Arctic base with the sure knowledge that should war break out their life expectancies would be short. Not that war was their greatest fear. Like all sailors, no matter which flag they fly, they were too busy fighting the greatest enemy of them all: the sea.

CHAPTER 1

Gadzhievo had two faces; the one you were
happy to leave, and after three months on patrol
the one you couldn't wait to see again.

—*Gennady Kapitulsky,*
Propulsion Engineer, K-219

3 SEPTEMBER, GADZHIEVO, DAY 1

Soap, hot water, fresh vegetables, and toilet paper were unreliable commodities at the Soviet Northern Fleet base at Gadzhievo, but snow was almost always abundant. The calendar said it was the first week of September, but here at the head of a twisting fjord above the Arctic Circle, exposed skin knew that winter had already arrived.

The fjord's rocky hills were covered with snow. Flurries fell from a sky the color of wet cement. It accumulated on the concrete docks, the rust-painted loading cranes, the gravel roads, and on the slick black missile decks of nuclear submarines.

"Engines astern, slow," said Captain Igor Britanov, the commanding officer of the ballistic missile submarine *K-219.*

His order was acknowledged by Vladmirov, the new *starpom,* or executive officer, stationed in the central command post below the sub's open bridge. The *K-219*'s twin screws began to turn.

A young captain of thirty-six, Britanov was a handsome man with a fringe of dark hair that contrasted with brilliant blue eyes. His bushy black mustache and nearly bald head gave him the look of a pirate. But up here on the exposed bridge atop the conning tower, what American submariners call the sail, he was just a pair of frosted lashes peering out from beneath a fur officer's hat. With each breath, the cold passed through five layers of wool and oilskin to lodge directly in his ribs.

Britanov leaned close to the sprayscreen for shelter against the wind. The *K-219*'s flag snapped. The surface navy had to put up with weather, but Britanov knew that a warm, dry submarine had its advantages, even a submarine like *K-219*.

Launched in 1971 at the nuclear submarine yard in Severodvinsk, she was an elderly example of the NAVAGA class known to the west as a YANKEE-1. Nearly four hundred feet long, her twin VM-4 reactors provided light, heat, water, and fresh air to her 119-man crew. New, she could make twenty-six knots submerged. These days Britanov would be satisfied with twenty.

"Right full rudder."

The screws churned the icy black water to froth. The stern began to slip away from her berth.

"Captain!" came a shout from the pier.

It was Igor Kurdin, Britanov's former executive officer. Kurdin waved, cupped his hands to his mouth, and shouted, "After this cruise they'll have to give you a pass to the rest center!"

Britanov waved back, wishing Kurdin, and not the inexperienced Vladmirov, was with him as his *starpom*. He huddled back behind the sprayscreen.

The lookouts to either side of him on the open bridge were completely exposed, their unhappy faces red with cold, wet with melted snow, their shoulders dusted in huge white flakes.

"Rudder amidships," Britanov ordered.

The intercom squawked acknowledgment.

The warship shuddered as her screws beat water already clotted with a greasy skim of ice crystals. Leaving port was no easy matter. The boat looked and handled like a wallowing log and the channel leading out to the open sea was treacherous. Britanov knew the whole base, from the conscript with a mop right up to the Flotilla commander, would be watching and evaluating his performance.

The ten-thousand-ton sub backed away from her berth, her bow drifting out to give the attending tugs a place to push.

Britanov looked aft across the broad expanse of her missile deck. A section of his own crew stood in ranks there, at attention. Their bright orange life vests were the only spot of color in the drab vista of white snow, black sea, and gray sky. The sixteen muzzle hatches were down and locked.

The RSM-25 missiles were her reason for being as well as her most dangerous weakness. American submarines carried missiles filled with solid propellant. Russian rockets were fueled by nitrogen tetroxide and hydrazine: two volatile liquids stored under tremendous pressure. There was no complicated firing system: hydrazine and nitrogen tetroxide were hypergolic. They exploded on contact with each other. But nitrogen tetroxide was also highly reactive with common seawater. And where better to find leaking seawater than on an elderly submarine?

It had happened before on this very boat. Just a few years from her commissioning, silo sixteen had sprung a leak. Not a large one, but it didn't take very much. A misaligned gasket. A cut in the thick rubber seal. A pinhole in the membrane that covered the silo's mouth.

Whatever the cause, water mixed with a tiny pool of leaked nitrogen tetroxide and formed powerful nitric acid. The acid ate into a welded hydrazine line and the pressurized tube gave way. The two fuels mixed, and what happened next was an unstoppable chemical reaction. Fuel and oxidizer exploded not in the combustion chamber of a rocket, but inside the submarine's missile silo. The resulting blast killed a sailor. Water flooded the missile room. The captain managed to drive the boat to the surface and vent the tube before the submarine sank. Now silo sixteen's muzzle hatch was permanently welded shut.

It had nearly happened again just this past January. On a live-fire exercise in the Barents Sea, they'd struggled for hours trying to launch one missile into the test range near Novaya Zemlya. Poor Petrachkov, the weapons officer, had worked like a demon. The rocket finally fired, but then the damned hatch refused to close.

They'd been forced to steam home on the surface into a Force 8 winter gale. The air was so cold the seaspray froze on contact with the submarine, with flesh, with anything. Britanov had stood watch right here on the open bridge for five hours. When they finally came up to relieve him, his arms were frozen into a position that made him look like Christ in oilskins. They'd poured hot water over him to thaw his clothes enough to get him inside the main trunk hatch.

Those missile hatches were a NAVAGA's weakest point, even more than her two cranky nuclear reactors. Weld all those hatches shut and *K-219* would be noticeably safer. But her mission was to carry her remaining fifteen missiles and their thirty warheads to the very shores of the enemy, and that was precisely what Britanov was going to do.

White steam plumed from the base power plant. He heard the sound of a truck growling its way down the guarded road leading to the docks, loud voices from the deckhands aboard the nearby tugs. No bands played. No flags dipped in honor of their departure. It was officially forbidden for family or base personnel to even stand and watch.

The flurries intensified, bringing a curtain down across Gadzhievo, concealing the shoreline where the crew's families would be watching despite the official ban. The departure of a NAVAGA was a closely guarded secret, but not to the families. All Gadzhievo knew the precise details to the minute.

His wife, Natalia, would be there, silent, holding both children. The youngest, barely four, hardly knew him. It was Britanov's fourth three-month cruise; it added up to a full year away from her, mostly under the sea. A year away from the light, the sun, the sky, the air. It was amazing when you thought about it, which Britanov found himself doing more often these days. It was good Natalia had so many friends.

Irina Kapitulsky, the chief propulsion engineer's wife, would be standing with her. Britanov was lucky to have Gennady Kapitulsky in his crew. He was one of the best nuclear engineers in all the Northern Fleet. Kapitulsky could have had his pick of any one of the newer submarines. But the *K-219*'s old reactors, and Britanov, needed him more.

To Natalia's other side would be Olga Aznabaev, his navigator's wife, even more worried-looking than usual. Navigator Zhenya Aznabaev had spoken to Britanov about the condition of the submarine two days back. His round, jovial face was frozen in a rare frown. The crews had worked around the clock making *K-219* ready for her scheduled departure. Or at least as ready as possible. Everyone knew there would be problems. It was just that Aznabaev had found too many for his liking. The normally talkative navigator had retreated into a brooding, silent shell, immersing himself in the details of the patrol.

Britanov believed Aznabaev about the flaws, but it didn't make a difference. What would you expect of an old NAVAGA? Wait for perfection and you'd never leave the pier. There were always problems. They would have three months of sailing to keep busy and the captain planned to use the time to correct the many minor squawks the base crews could not, or would not, fix. If they were lucky, they would bring the boat back in better condition, plus the crew would know a few things about a NAVAGA. If Kapitulsky said his reactors and his engines were ready, it was enough.

The snow flurries lightened. The shoreline emerged.

Britanov saw the knot of figures against the gray rocks. Wives, families, friends. One wife who would not be there was Lyudmilla Petrachkov, his missile officer's spouse. She'd thrown him out and was living with another officer. Three months away might heal some of Petrachkov's wounds. What a mess. *He's probably the happiest man aboard,* thought the captain. He waved, hoping they would be able to see him, hoping they would realize that everything would be all right. In isolated Gadzhievo where nothing was known and everything rumored, worry spread like flu.

"Engines all stop."

Steam generated by the twin VM-4 nuclear reactors was diverted away from the turbines. Her big bronze screws slowed, then splashed to a stop. The tugs moved in eagerly.

A thump, a thudding jar, and *K-219* began to turn under their push until her bow faced north. The fjord swung into view. Ahead was the first channel buoy. Two chuffs of black diesel smoke and the tugs backed away, taking position to either flank. Off in the distance the open ocean, the Barents Sea, was the color of slate.

Here we go.

Britanov touched the intercom mike to his lip. It didn't freeze. When they came back in three months, it would. So a captain of the Northern Fleet marks the passage of the seasons, not in kilometers sailed, not in children growing up in his absence, not in more gray strands mixed with Natalia's black hair, but in the speed with which flesh freezes to metal. Submerged, there would be no time but Moscow time, no seasons except for those dictated by the submarine's cranky environmental systems—usually sweltering summer.

Not that a little heat would be so bad right now.

"Helm," he said, "engines ahead, slow."

"Ahead slow," said *Starpom* Vladmirov.

The screws began to turn, sluggishly at first, then faster. The beat of bronze blades against the sea became a continuous cataract rumble. The steel hull vibrated with it, *with life*, thought Britanov.

He'd risen to his command from the ranks of radio-electronics specialists, an unusual route for a submarine commander. Britanov's cool, calculating exterior came from his exposure to puzzling schematics and complex circuitry. His approach to command was very much the same.

Among his peers, Britanov had the reputation of an inspired tactician, a chess master who played with ten-thousand-ton pieces on a gameboard that stretched from horizon to horizon. Hobbled by a dangerous, obsolete ship, he had no choice but to play a deeper, more unpredictable game against the technically superior Americans.

Once a daring Soviet captain had run the whole east coast of the United States, inside territorial waters, in a NAVAGA just like this one. Trying to find him had driven the Americans crazy. Much as he would have liked to repeat that foray, Britanov knew it was no longer possible. The game, and the advantages, had shifted in the West's favor. Now it was enough to carry out his orders: patrol the American coast and threaten the enemy with the same, near-instant destruction their forces held over the fatherland. American missiles in Europe were on a hair trigger; it was not such a bad idea to remind them that there were other hair triggers in the world. Britanov thought it was crazy, sure. But also necessary.

Although there was little sensation of motion, Gadzhievo was far behind them now. A sheet of fast-moving water flowed over *K-219*'s spherical bow. It washed away the accumulated snow in a pattern that left an arrow-shaped ridge of white along the foredeck. What did the damned political officers call the submarine service? The tip of the fatherland's spear?

It could almost be true.

Looking down from the exposed bridge was nearly like flying over the waves; the two diving planes sprouted from the sail like wings. Speed gave him control. It transformed the bobbing log into a sleek, black man-of-war. It thrilled Britanov in a way he would have found difficult to describe. It was like being free.

The second channel buoy slid by. The next loomed from the mists.

"Vladmirov?" he said into the intercom. "Come to three five five degrees."

The bow moved to port. The channel was tight, but it was a matter of pride for Britanov to navigate it without the constant nagging of the tugs. He knew that Navigator Aznabaev would be plotting their track on his chart; it was good for a worried man to keep busy, especially now that their first dive was coming. The first dive after being tied up at pierside was always a little thrilling. Even for veteran officers, never mind the young sailors whose underwater experience had been gained for the most part in bathtubs. Three months from now when they surfaced again at the mouth of this same fjord, they too would be veterans. Britanov would see to that.

The fourth channel buoy loomed ahead.

"Right rudder, Helm. Make your course three five eight."

One of the tugboat captains was leaning out of his high wheelhouse, his hand held up. Was it all right to leave?

Britanov waved back, then saluted.

The tug skipper quickly shut the hatch against the icy wind. Done. The tugs pulled away and allowed the submarine to go her way alone.

The snow on the foredeck was nearly gone now. Washed clean by the sweep of the bow wave. The fjord was wide here. The open ocean near. Britanov put the microphone to his lips. "All ahead one-third. Surface section belowdecks."

Aft of the conning tower, the orange-vested surface detail made their way to the hatch and disappeared, leaving only the two lookouts remaining topside. They would not see natural light nor breathe clean air for another ninety days.

The fifth buoy. The sixth.

The snow closed in around him again. Britanov could no longer see land.

A sheet of frigid water flowed completely over the bow. The conning tower sliced it cleanly in two. Freedom. Who else in all the Soviet Union was as free as the captain of a nuclear submarine? Who else lived and worked so far from the eyes and ears of the state?

True, there was Sergiyenko, the boat's political officer, the *zampolit*. He had no special training other than that needed to maintain political reliability. He was about as useful as a teat on a boar, yet as the Party's official representative aboard the sub, Sergiyenko wore one of the three nuclear release keys around his neck. Not that he knew anything about the missiles, the engines, the submarine. Sergiyenko was more interested in Party discipline and in reporting his fellow crewmen for minor infractions. In any kind of emergency he would only get in the way. Britanov did his best to ignore him though he had to be careful. Sergiyenko reported back to the Flotilla Political Directorate, and they had an inordinate say over matters of promotion and assignment.

Maybe not for long, Britanov thought with a smile. Romanov had gotten his snout in a crack for seducing the wives of submariners out on patrol. The women all wanted passes to other cities for shopping, for visiting relatives, for seeing a new face after being isolated at Gadzhievo for months on end. Romanov had offered them a quid pro quo: one night for one pass. It was a real scandal that might blow the whole political section apart. With any luck it would.

And poor Petrachkov, his missile officer. When they'd come back from a complete foul-up of a live-fire exercise, he found that his wife had left him for a petty officer. Britanov counted himself lucky *that* man wasn't on his crew. Imagine being sealed up for three months with the man who stole your wife!

A definite pitch and roll now. Wave action sent spray against his windscreen.

There was a subtle difference between the deep waters of the fjord and the open ocean. It didn't take the first sea buoy for Captain Britanov to sense it. It was a certain majesty, a certain power, in the rise and fall of the waves. There was no chop, no halfway measures. The sea simply became more serious. So did the game.

Specially equipped American submarines were lurking on the bottom, listening for his sounds, cataloging them, sending warning that *K-219* was under way. Britanov knew from here on he would have a bell around his neck, one that would summon American attack submarines. There was nothing he could do about it now. But later? He might just surprise them. The ocean was a very large place, even for the smug Americans.

He spoke into the microphone. "Retract the masts."

Behind Britanov the big radar mast began to slide down. The cone-shaped transceiver at the top would fit flush into the steel plating atop the sail. The slimmer radio whip followed, though when it was half gone it stopped and automatically began to fold aft, down into a special groove that would protect it.

The snow dribbled to a sputter, then stopped. A shaft of sunlight appeared. The break gave Britanov a last view back to his homeland. He waved one last time, knowing there was no one to see the black shape as it drove its bow into the north wind. Then, as snow drew itself across the mouth of the fjord, the land vanished.

"Ice to starboard!" came the shout from a lookout.

"Depth under the keel?" Britanov called down to the CCP.

"Seventy meters, Comrade Captain."

A steeper wave. The bow plunged straight into it, swiping the black hull clean of all traces of snow. *K-219* was charging into long, low rollers. There was sheet ice everywhere, but here and there were taller chunks that could present difficulties. Britanov's face was soaked. It was time to go where his warship was meant to go, away from the dangers of the surface, the waves, the ice. Britanov took a deep lungful of air, cold, sharp, but so fresh, so sweet. He turned his back on Natalia, on Gadzhievo, on the Soviet Union itself, and gave the orders.

"All ahead two-thirds," he said into the intercom. "Clear the bridge! Lookouts below!" Another deep breath, then, "Prepare to dive."

The blue and white flag with its prominent red star came down. The sprayscreen was carefully stowed. Britanov checked back to be sure the weather deck was empty, the lookouts below, the open bridge set for the dive. Only then did he go to the main trunk hatch, step down to the ladder, and grasp the chain attached to the heavy steel cover.

USS *STURGEON*-CLASS SUBMARINE, BARENTS SEA STATION

The sonar operator listened to the noisy boomer churn overhead. Her twin five-bladed screws made a lot of racket. The American intelligence-gathering boat was sitting on the shallow sandy bottom, absolutely silent, on station off the fjord leading to the Soviet base at Gadzhievo. Her job was to keep tabs on all Soviet submarine traffic coming and going, to record coastal radars, and above all to remain undetected.

"Bedcheck" duty was close, dangerous work. By international standards they were eight miles inside Soviet territorial waters. By the limits claimed by the USSR they were hundreds. That made being here an act of war, but only if she got caught.

Chugga-chugga-chugga-chugga.

He fed the soundprint into the digital analyzer and in a few seconds knew all he needed to know about the old cow steaming by overhead.

YANKEE-1, *K-219/220*?

A YANKEE-1 was a real old-timer. The acoustic analyzer wasn't sure which boat the sounds most closely matched. The sonar specialist could almost hear her clunk by without the headphones.

Chugga-chugga-chugga-chugga-clang!

He sat up. "Conn, Sonar."

"Conn, aye," came the immediate answer from the INTEL boat's captain, a very careful young commander. Careful was how a commander got to be a captain in the intelligence game.

"Transient on the contact. Evaluate he's preparing to dive."

"Speed and course?"

"Blade count for thirteen knots, course three three eight."

"We have his ID yet?"

"Yes, sir." He checked his display. The acoustic analyzer had resolved its indecision. "She's a YANKEE-1," the sonar operator said. "The *K-219*."

K-219

Britanov inspected the main hatch seal and checked to be sure the automatic locking mechanism was engaged. He dropped down into the pressure hull, waited while a *michman* warrant officer spun the second hatch shut, then walked into the enclosed bridge. The inner bridge portholes were awash. The waves made the deck pitch uncomfortably. He could hear them strike the steel plates of the sail. Below him was the central command post.

He descended into the small, familiar space. The *K-219* was a hot, noisy boat and the central command post was a hot, noisy place. The low-ceilinged compartment was located immediately under the submarine's conning tower. It was a bedlam of whining machinery, clanks, buzzes, and the hivelike hum of equipment cooling fans.

Large as a modest American living room, about fifteen feet long by ten across, the CCP managed to contain twenty men seated at their consoles. Two smaller alcoves opened off it: the navigator's space and the radio room. Hatches led up the sail, aft to compartment four, the missile room, and forward to compartment two, the main engine control area where Gennady Kapitulsky sat like a spider in the middle of a nuclear web.

Vladmirov, the young executive officer who had taken Igor Kurdin's slot, stood in the center of the CCP, the white armband denoting his position as officer of the deck a bright contrast to the dark blue coveralls all the crewmen wore. It was his first patrol on *K-219*. Indeed, he'd never before sailed in a submarine quite as old as this one. He looked properly terrified.

The helmsman had both hands on a knurled wheel the size of a dinner plate. The wheel controlled the sub's aft stabilizers. Next to him the planesman sat with his hands on the twin joysticks that operated the diving planes. They faced a wall of depth, speed, and course instruments; old, round-faced "steam gauges" mounted on a beige metal console. Next to them, the sonar officer watched a screen that showed two white waterfalls of sound; they alternated left and right as two high-frequency transducers in the bow blasted the sea ahead with sonic energy. The sonar operator wasn't worried about enemy vessels; he was keeping a close watch on the display for ice.

Continuing around the compartment's perimeter were consoles for radar, electronics countermeasures, weapons, and damage control officers. They all were arrayed in a semicircle around Captain Britanov's raised, ceremonial chair.

Dozens of black intercom wires dangled from overhead like party streamers. At the end of each hung a *kashtan* microphone, named for the chestnut it vaguely resembled. The *kashtan* was an absolute requirement. The noise level in the command post was so great Britanov would shout himself hoarse trying to make himself heard without it.

The *K-219*'s CCP sounded more like a locomotive factory than the nerve center of a ship whose very survival depended upon stealth.

Britanov was beginning to sweat. He shouldered his way out of his foul-weather gear and hung the oilskin up on a hook on the bulkhead. Next to it was a plaque he had ordered framed and installed:

SUBMARINE LIFE IS NOT A SERVICE, BUT A RELIGION.

Sergiyenko, the *K-219*'s political officer, had objected to the plaque, saying that putting service to the fatherland and religion on an equal footing was hardly appropriate, even in these days of *perestroika*. Britanov told him to mind his own business.

"Ready to dive, Captain," said Chief Engineer Krasilnikov. A real old-timer at thirty-nine, he was known to the *K-219*'s crew as Grandfather. Two years older than Britanov, Krasilnikov was responsible for the submarine's delicate mechanical systems. Divorced, the large, gruff officer virtually lived aboard the sub; he spent most of his time in port on *K-219* with disassembled parts spread before him on a worktable. His age gave everyone added confidence. If he could survive so long, he must know a few things about a NAVAGA.

Propulsion Engineer Kapitulsky had a similar reputation. In charge of her atomic power plants and engines, Kapitulsky spent all his time in main engine control up in compartment two. The space was located forward of the CCP, and was even more crowded with dials and levers. It was decorated with photographs of Western women barely dressed in lacy underwear. All the controls needed to run both nuclear reactors were routed forward to his compartment. Some sailors said it was a measure of how unsafe the reactors were that the man responsible for them worked so far away. Kapitulsky took his health very seriously; he was almost the only man aboard who did not smoke.

It was Kapitulsky's wife, Irina, who had denounced the Flotilla political officer, *Zampolit* Romanov.

A dangerous thing to do, thought Britanov. An act like that could reflect badly on a husband's career. But Kapitulsky had a lot of *blat,* or pull. He hoped he had enough.

Between them, Grandfather Krasilnikov and Propulsion Engineer Kapitulsky knew every inch of the old NAVAGA, every last nut, bolt, and wire. If they said *K-219* was ready, Britanov could count on it.

The captain glanced at the status board, then at Vladmirov. This would be his first operational dive on *K-219.* It was time to get him wet behind the ears. "Status?"

"All hull openings green. All systems aligned," said Vladmirov. His voice broke, rising an octave. He cleared his throat. "We are rigged for dive, Captain."

Britanov examined the lights on the dive board himself. It was the one almost modern-looking display in the CCP, and, he knew, a direct copy of the video screens the Americans used. On it every hull opening, each door, each hatch, was shown red for open or green for shut. From the stern escape trunk to the sixteen missile hatches, the conning tower hatch, torpedo tubes, and forward escape trunk, everything showed a straight-across green. Next to it the high-pressure air console kept tabs on each of the submarine's ten main ballast tanks. All green. But the first dive after laying up at the pier was always something to watch very closely.

"Very well." He turned to the young *starpom.* "Set depth for forty meters. Flood the main ballast tanks. Ten degrees down on the planes. Dive."

Vladmirov pulled the dive alarm. It was possible to hear the buzzer over the noise, but just.

The hull was filled with the long, sad sigh of air venting from the ballast tanks. Seawater flooded into the bottoms as the air whooshed from the tops.

USS *STURGEON*-CLASS SUBMARINE,
BARENTS SEA STATION

Chugga-chugga-chugga-whoooosh!

"Conn, Sonar. There she goes. The YANKEE's flooding tanks."

"We heard," the commander of the superquiet sub answered dryly.

The sonar operator listened to the gurgle and hiss as the Soviet boomer vented air and took on seawater ballast. *What do they pay them?* he wondered. *Not enough.* Reactors without adequate shielding. Steam pipes welded by drunks. You didn't sail a boat like that. You gambled with it.

K-219

The deck tilted down. The whoosh of air subsided to a whisper as the sub took on tons of dead water weight. It seemed to instantly grow warmer in the already sweltering CCP, but Britanov knew that was an illusion that came with driving ten thousand tons of steel underwater. The pitch and roll of the waves was already gone. Even he could feel the tension in the air as *K-219* was swallowed up by the black waters of the Barents Sea.

The deck leveled. The hull popped and creaked under the pressure. A few of the younger men in the CCP stopped what they were doing and looked up, their faces pale.

Vladmirov especially. He was looking up when a sharp snap made him jump and turn his head. Grandfather Krasilnikov threw the broken pencil aside and laughed.

The planesman sat with his two joysticks, flying the submarine through the sea. He pulled back as he kept a close eye on the depth gauge. "Level at forty meters, Comrade Captain."

"Initial course three one zero, Captain," said Navigator Aznabaev.

"Helm, make our course three one zero. All of you, well done," said Britanov. "Damage Control, have all compartment commanders report."

The damage control console was manned by Lieutenant Sergei Voroblev. The twenty-eight-year-old lieutenant was a brilliant officer and the only man in all the Northern Fleet "triple qualified" to serve as weapons specialist, damage control head, and chemical officer.

"Compartment one?" asked Voroblev.

"Torpedo room manned and ready," came the immediate reply from the K-219's most forward compartment. "Escape hatch is dry."

Britanov nodded. That was good news. In addition to the main trunk hatch in the conning tower, there were just two escape hatches leading out from the sub: one in the bow, the other all the way back in compartment ten in the stern. More than one Soviet submarine had nearly sunk when, on their first dive, a panicked seaman had tried to claw his way out.

"Compartment two?"

"Manned and ready," came the quick, confident reply of Gennady Kapitulsky. "Both engines connected. Both reactors are normal."

Compartment three was the CCP. Voroblev spoke once more into the kashtan. "Compartment four?"

Aft of the central command post, Voroblev's voice came over the speaker mounted in the large, vaulted missile room located under the submarine's "hunchback" deck.

Weapons Officer Alexei Petrachkov swore as he hurried along a catwalk suspended midway across the vaulted compartment. Although fourteen men worked here, it was big enough to seem almost empty. The officers had a smoking lounge down at the lower level. Even the cooks came forward to compartment four to rest their eyes. It was almost like going outdoors.

He made a quick survey of each fat missile tube. There were sixteen of them, each five feet in diameter and thirty feet tall. They went from the bottom plates all the way up to where they pierced the pressure hull. The Americans called this place Sherwood Forest because they painted their silos green. The *K-219*'s silos were painted a bright acid yellow.

Only fifteen of them contained missiles; the last was permanently sealed after an accident, an explosion caused by seawater leaking into the silo.

Now, one of those tubes, silo six, was leaking again.

"Compartment four?"

Petrachkov reached for the intercom, but then he stopped his hand. He eyed the water gauge on silo six. It had risen in the first few moments submerged, but now as pressures changed, it seemed to slow, maybe even stop. It was well under the safety limit of four liters. Still, a leak was a leak, and a submarine was not a good place to have one.

Petrachkov sweated heavily, and it wasn't just the close, humid air. Use the word *leak* and they'd have to return to Gadzhievo. Their cruise would be delayed, who the hell knew how long? Those bastards at the base were drunk half the time anyway. Try to fix one leak and they'd end up creating two more . . .

"Missile Room! Report!"

Britanov would get a black mark if they turned around and broke their patrol schedule. They all would. Petrachkov had been criticized twice this year alone for not having his missiles ready for a test firing. Britanov had stood behind him one hundred percent. That was the way things worked in a submarine. It was an elite organization, better paid, better fed, a softer life for the families. Not that he had one to worry about anymore. That bastard. A petty officer! If he ever saw him again he'd squeeze him like a boil! Not that his wife was innocent. She'd made her own bed. The final separation papers were waiting back at the base. Turn around and he'd have to deal with that, too. No. He was glad to leave all of them behind, to be alone inside *K-219* for a while, to think out his future and to let his wife sweat it out for three months more. He eyed the gauge. It seemed steady now at four liters. The maximum safe level. He could assign a seaman to pump it a little more regularly, and the world would go on as before.

He took the intercom. "Compartment four, manned and ready."

"Thank you," said Voroblev, relieved. "Compartment five?"

Petrachkov listened as Lieutenant Igor Kochergin, the *K-219*'s doctor, reported from his sick bay.

Petrachkov tapped the gauge. The needle quivered, then went down. Sometimes a little leak solved itself. Like the *K-219*'s crew, the seals had to adjust themselves to life underwater. Anyway, nothing in this life was perfect, was it? He smiled at having made one of those difficult decisions of command, and making it well. He turned. "You!" he said to one of his men, a missile control technician on his first undersea patrol. "I want you to keep an eye on this silo. There may be a slight weeping but most probably it's just the muzzle gasket settling into place. If it goes above four liters, strip it out at once. Understood?"

"Yes!" The young seaman eyed the silo warily. He knew what could happen if one of those big bastards sprang a leak. But if Petrachkov said it was just weeping, it couldn't be much of a problem, could it?

FLEET OCEAN SURVEILLANCE INFORMATION CENTER, NORFOLK, VIRGINIA

Lieutenant Commander Gail Robinson was INTEL watch chief at FOSIC this morning, not that anything much was going on. With a major summit between Gorbachev and Reagan due in the next few weeks, ship movements of the two great superpowers had definitely declined. The Reykjavík summit might not amount to much in the push and pull of grand nuclear strategy, but it sure was saving everyone a lot of fuel in the meantime.

It was a slow day at FOSIC. For such a large room, there were few people in evidence. Robinson counted just the mid-watch staff updating ship positions based on the most recent intelligence; satellite imagery, ELINT intercepts of electronic, radar, and radio emissions, physical tracking by U.S. forces, and the most sensitive, the reports sent in by U.S. submarines lying doggo on the bottom outside, and sometimes inside, Soviet harbors.

An enormous chart of the Atlantic basin covered one of the walls. It encompassed the whole of the ocean from Antarctica down near the floor to North Cape up by the ceiling.

On the left side, blue silhouettes of U.S. ships were clustered around Chesapeake Bay from Cape Charles to Newport News. Out in mid-ocean, an American carrier battle group was en route to the Mediterranean.

On the right, the ship symbols changed colors to red: elements of the Soviet fleet operating in waters close to their bases, plus Warsaw Pact merchantmen and fishing trawlers. They often were used as naval auxiliaries, shadowing American fleet movements, sometimes deploying acoustical gear and sensitive antennae to eavesdrop on coded naval traffic.

Trawler, freighter, or missile cruiser, there was no such thing as a friendly Red ship. Least of all the stacks of red submarine symbols arrayed by the Soviet Union's Northern Fleet bases on the Kola Peninsula.

But not all those submarines were so distant.

Three were very close to American shores, each within a defined patrol box off the east coast of the United States. Each box contained a Soviet ballistic missile boat tasked with launching nuclear-tipped rockets against major American cities. They were there to give the Russians what was known as a "depressed trajectory shot"; the ability to fire a missile and have it arrive over its target almost before NORAD could send out the warning.

An old YANKEE boat held the northern box while more modern DELTAs patrolled the middle and southern zones. A new YANKEE was due out to allow the old YANKEE on station to go home. The timing of this intricate shuffle was known only to the Soviet fleet command, but it never took FOSIC very long to catch on.

As Gail Robinson watched, the mural plot on the big chart was getting updated. She watched as one red submarine was plucked from the stack by Gadzhievo and placed offshore the Kola Peninsula in the Barents Sea. She knew they were already stretched thin putting YANKEE boats out on the front line. They were more of a danger to their crews than a threat to the United States. If the Reykjavík summit did anything positive at all, it would send those old boats back home for good. Where was this one headed?

Bingo, she thought when the symbol for the boomer patrolling the northern box of the east coast was moved to the east, heading home. One YANKEE in, one out. Shuffle the box and cross your fingers they stay in one piece long enough to sink in deep, distant waters.

USS *AUGUSTA*, SSN-710, OFF MARTHA'S VINEYARD, MASSACHUSETTS

"Conn, Sonar. Range one thousand yards."

Commander James Von Suskil had been tracking a surface ship now for the better part of an hour. The target, a United States Navy frigate, had no idea she was walking into the nuclear boat's sights. And he'd done it despite the fact that the frigate had been warned she would be playing tag with a nuke.

Augusta had made like a hole in the water, utterly silent, as she maneuvered into optimum attack position. They'd detected the frigate from an unheard-of distance of nearly fifty miles; testimony to the new acoustic gear's worth. The approach was being made on passive sonar only.

Augusta was one of the newest, most capable fast-attack subs in the fleet. Attached to Submarine Development Squadron Twelve, the improved *Los Angeles*–class boat was fresh from an electronic refit during which a new suite of acoustic sensors and processors had been installed. So far they'd worked perfectly.

"Okay, people, we're going in. Close quarter procedures."

"Close quarter procedures, aye," said Lieutenant Commander David Samples. He was *Augusta*'s executive officer. He knew that "close quarters" meant one thing to the Navy and another to Von Suskil. The captain liked to get close enough to a target to, in his words, "see the whites of their eyes." It made for some nerve-wracking moments, though everyone said no one was better at it than Von Suskil. Or, as it was also said, luckier.

"Conn. Range now five hundred yards. Target bearing one four two, speed eighteen knots, course two six one."

"Up scope!" Von Suskil ordered.

The attack periscope slid up from its well on the starboard side of the center pedestal. A quartermaster's mate dropped the handles into place and trained the scope to the correct bearing. Von Suskil put his eye to it and swiveled it slightly, centering the crosshairs on the frigate's clipper bow.

"Bearing, mark!"

The quartermaster squeezed the button on the scope's "pickle," transmitting the attack data automatically to the Mark 117 fire control computer.

"Angle on the bow, starboard twenty. Range three hundred yards."

The fire control tech punched the new data into the computer.

They were on a collision course if Von Suskil didn't do something about it and fast.

"Solution set," the fire control tech reported. "Tubes three and four ready, sir."

The U.S. Navy frigate was marked for destruction.

"Range two hundred yards, Captain . . ."

"Flood three and four."

"Sir?" The XO said, puzzled. The frigate's sensors would certainly pick up the sound of water rushing into *Augusta*'s torpedo tubes. It was like rubbing the frigate's nose in the fact that she'd been meat on *Augusta*'s table.

"Clean your ears out, Mister Samples. I said flood three and four."

"Sir!" The XO nodded. The rumbling sound of water filled the attack center. It was an unmistakable gesture of contempt for the frigate.

"Conn, Sonar. Target changing speed and course!"

"You see that? He heard," Von Suskil said with a grin. "He had no idea we were here."

"Yes, sir," Samples agreed. They'd sailed damned close to that frigate. A wrong turn, a mistake, a hesitation, and they'd have gotten themselves run over for their troubles.

"Close three and four," Von Suskil said with a chuckle. "We sure rattled his cage, didn't we?"

"Range opening to four hundred yards."

"Yes, sir," the XO agreed.

"Mister Samples, make a mental note. That's the way to break a man," said Von Suskil. "Break his nerve that way. Makes 'em too jumpy to think straight. He can't think, we kill him faster. You see what I mean?"

"Yes, sir." It made a lot of people jumpy, thought the XO.

"Right," said Von Suskil. "Now let's go do it to some Russians."

K-219

It was 0759 Moscow time when Captain Britanov entered the CCP armed with a fistful of index cards. The forenoon watch was set and the galley was busy turning out a meal for the watch-standers coming off duty. Britanov took one of the hanging *kashtans* and sat down at his central, ceremonial chair. At precisely 0800, he began.

"Comrades. Men of the *K-219*. We have passed the first test of this patrol. Our initial dive was flawless. Our ship is in optimum condition to meet the tests that lie ahead and, I am proud to say, so is our crew."

Weapons Officer Petrachkov stopped in the mess line, a tray in his hand, and gazed up at the loudspeaker. His plate held bread, cheese, and a fried lamb cutlet. A glass brimmed with hot tea. Today was his turn to eat with the crew, to provide an officer's presence in the mess, and presumably an officer's discipline if needed. He was nudged to keep moving to where the kasha was being spooned out.

"You all know where we are going," the captain continued. "It's no secret to you, and to be frank, it's no secret to our enemies, either. They will be waiting, comrades, waiting to pounce on us if we give them the smallest chance. Well, I don't know about you, but I don't intend to give them that opportunity. Compartment one!" he called out as he glanced at the note card showing the names of the torpe-domen. "Sergei, Alexei, Pyotr. Some would say that torpedoes are good only for the alcohol they contain in their engines. But let me remind you, every man of the *K-219* is depending upon you to keep them ready. Our lives may depend on them, and so our lives depend on you." He shuffled the cards again. "And Gennady Kapitulsky, every-one knows we can trust you to keep the atoms where they belong. My wife, who is a close friend of your wife, has been informed that al-though you smoke after sex, you do not yet glow."

A snicker went through the mess line. They all knew Kapitulsky hated cigarettes. Petrachkov hardly noticed the buzz of conversation as he mechanically moved along the serving line.

"And while we all know that the aged must get their rest, let me say that I hope Grandfather Krasilnikov does not sleep too deeply. Keep one eye open for us, will you?"

More chuckles in the mess.

"And men of compartment four. You are the reason we sail to the front line. All of you in missile control, fire control, and chemical stations. Igor, Stepan, and Ivan. Listen to Petrachkov. Follow his lead and remember, your missiles are the necessary force that keeps the world from going any crazier than it is. Your total watchfulness is demanded by your crewmates, your Navy, and your fatherland. I know you will not disappoint any of us."

"Kasha?" asked the server. His mouth glittered with gold teeth.

Petrachkov looked down. "What?"

The messman scowled at him. "Kasha? You want some or not?"

He held out his plate. A steaming white pile of groats was placed next to the fried lamb. He moved off and found an empty table as Britanov's voice marked off each compartment and each crewman for individual attention.

"Men of compartments six, seven, and eight!" called Britanov. "Without your engines we aren't going anywhere. Sergei Preminin! This is your first cruise as an engineer-seaman. Pay close attention to Lieutenant Belikov. Never pass up an opportunity to learn. When we return to Gadzhievo, you will be the veteran that others will rely on."

Lieutenant Voroblev pushed a chair next to Petrachkov. He wasn't scheduled to be in the crew's mess, but on a NAVAGA, it paid for the damage control officer to become friendly with the man in charge of the dangerous missiles. "Something wrong?" he asked when he saw Petrachkov's expression.

"Why do you ask?" the weapons officer answered. He outranked Voroblev, but the head of damage control had the authority to make anyone's life miserable.

"Comrades!" Britanov was finishing now. "Men of the *K-219*! Everyone, from the commanding officers to the young comrades new to the sea, must work together as one team. The stakes are very high.

The Americans think they own the ocean. Well, we will prove that they do not! With your help, your skill, your eternal vigilance, we will make our ninety-day patrol a memorable one for all!"

I hope not too memorable, thought Petrachkov as he chewed.

"How's your compartment shaping up?" Voroblev gently probed. "Anything to worry about?"

"Nichevo," Petrachkov replied. Nothing.

CHAPTER 2

The Soviet subs patrolling off our coasts?
We weren't that concerned about them.
We had them pegged twenty-four hours a day.

—*Rear Admiral Ted Sheafer,*
Atlantic Fleet Intelligence Officer

K-219, 5 SEPTEMBER,
THE GREENLAND-ICELAND-U.K. GAP, DAY 2

K-219 glided straight and level, submerged at a depth of two hundred meters. They were off the southernmost spur of the Jan Mayen Ridge, a vast undersea plateau halfway between the Faeroe Islands and Iceland. South of the ridge, the sea bottom fell away to the Katja Drift and the north Atlantic abyssal plain.

"Anything?" asked Britanov.

"Still no target, Captain," said Sonar. He was listening closely, the big black headphones pressed to his ears.

Things had been going exceptionally well until now. Britanov had operated *K-219* the way a submarine was meant to operate: independent, alone, lost in the vastness of the sea. Now this. Leave it to the Soviet surface fleet to really screw things up.

A door leading off to the tiny navigator's alcove opened. "SOSUS line in twenty kilometers," Aznabaev reminded them. He still had a worried look on his face. His short black hair was slick with sweat. It looked almost painted on. "We'll enter detection range in eighteen minutes."

Britanov fumed. They were approaching the SOSUS line, an acoustic fence made up of thousands of sensitive hydrophones strung along the sea bottom. There were just so many routes between the Barents Sea and their patrol box off Bermuda, and the Americans had them all wired for sound. There was no way they could evade that fence. But there was a way to confuse it: a tactic known as "buggering the whale."

Britanov would rendezvous with a naval auxiliary, an especially noisy freighter, then maneuver *K-219* very close to its thrashing screws. In theory, the hydrophones would record the freighter and miss the subtler sounds of the nuclear sub. Once safely through the SOSUS line, *K-219* would disconnect from its whale and run submerged at high speed to its patrol station off the American coast.

It was a trick that was as hated as it was necessary. Forget the real risks of collision. Submariners prefer to operate alone, lost in the open sea, not cruising in the oily, garbage-strewn wake of a freighter. It fouled the water intakes. It took uninterrupted concentration for the entire time the two vessels were paired. But more, a submarine, like an airplane, affords three dimensions of motion. For a swift nuclear boat to remain tied to a slow, unstealthy surface ship was nearly unbearable. If there was another way to beat the SOSUS line, Britanov would have jumped at it. But there wasn't.

Their escorting "whale" today was the Soviet freighter *Yaroslavl*. A Soviet Navy officer on board would take charge during the delicate underwater ballet with *K-219*. Of course, taking charge meant he had to stay awake.

Britanov thought, *Can you imagine how badly you would have to fuck up to be assigned to* that *job?* And *this* was the man he would rely on to get them through the SOSUS line.

Once through, *Yaroslavl* would set course for Cuba with a cargo of machinery and *K-219* would sprint for its missile patrol station off Bermuda. So far there was no sign of *Yaroslavl* on passive sonar. That meant Britanov would have to hunt for him by radar. Radar meant sending energy out that his enemies were no doubt already looking for. The only thing riskier would be rising near the surface and putting his eye to the periscope. If a patrol plane happened by they'd be detected. He knew they were getting close to the SOSUS line. A patrol plane was an unknown.

He got up from his chair and paced. "Helm, make your depth twenty meters."

"Twenty meters."

The submarine began to rise, driven by her engines and the hydrodynamic action of her diving planes.

"Engine turns for fifteen knots."

The tooth-drill whine of turbomachinery eased. As the sub began to slow, the controls became looser and less precise. The helmsman had to make larger movements of the wheel to keep *K-219* on course. Once they were hooked up with their whale, the job became even harder, and more vital; allow the submarine to be drawn upward into the low-pressure zone created by the freighter's hull and you had a glancing collision at best, a hull breach at worst.

"Eighteen knots," Helm reported.

Slowing reduced the amount of noise the *K-219* generated. It also improved the efficiency of her own sound-detection equipment. "Sonar?" asked Britanov.

"Still nothing."

If their whale didn't show, they'd have to make the run across the SOSUS line unescorted. That meant disobeying his sailing orders which, unfortunately, the boat's political officer also knew. He could deal with *Zampolit* Sergiyenko. Britanov was more worried about the Americans.

Trigger the SOSUS alarm and they would be on him like hungry mosquitoes for the next nine weeks. He drummed his fingers on the armrest. Sprint across the SOSUS line unescorted? Wait? He couldn't send a radio signal. There were very strict rules about maintaining silence. . . .

"Depth fifty meters," the planesman called.

"Captain," said Sonar as he ran a big black volume knob up full. "Possible contact bearing one zero three. It comes and goes but the blade count is steady at ninety-eight rpm."

The agreed-upon propeller speed Britanov had read in his sailing orders. It had to be *Yaroslavl.*

"Speed fifteen knots," said the helmsman. "Depth is steady at twenty meters."

The sonar operator stiffened. "Contact verified! A single three-blade screw turning at ninety-eight RPM. Range sixteen kilometers, course two two zero, speed eight knots. It's our whale, Captain. I'm sure of it."

"Plot it," Britanov told Aznabaev. Sixteen kilometers, thought Britanov. The Americans could hear such a ship from five times that distance. His acoustic gear was so bad the whale was creeping up on him. If it had been an American warship, a destroyer, it would have been able to fire before Britanov even knew what was coming. The first clue would be the *scree* of the torpedo. And what was true for a noisy destroyer was doubly true for one of their stealthy attack subs. "Helm, come to zero one zero. Make your depth fifty meters. All ahead two-thirds. We'll circle around to the north and let him catch up."

The engines began to whine again as more steam was directed to the turbines. The deck tilted slightly as the ten-thousand-ton sub banked into the turn. It thrilled Britanov to feel the ship heel under his command. *K-219* might be an old submarine, even an obsolete one, but with both reactors and both engines on line she could really make speed underwater.

"Losing the contact."

"Very well, Sonar." He'd expected that. The hiss of water streaming by her hull at high speed degraded her acoustic gear tremendously. A sort of whiteout, a blizzard of noise. "When we pass abeam his last plotted position, we'll turn and slide in behind him. Understood?"

"Understood," the helmsman replied.

Britanov took the *kashtan*. "Special maneuvering watch to central command!" he ordered, then let the intercom dangle. The special watch was made up of his most experienced officers. He winked at Executive Officer Vladmirov. "First we'll sneak up and bugger this whale," said Britanov to the young *starpom,* "then we'll do the same to the Americans. I'll be back in a moment. You have the conn."

He went through the CCP's forward hatch to compartment two. Gennady Kapitulsky was "tending the stove" in main engine control; tweaking the reactor controls, issuing commands to alter the ferocious nuclear fires back in compartment seven.

Britanov sank into a chair beside his chief propulsion engineer. "We're making our final approach. So?"

"Everything is fine." Kapitulsky was watching a needle twitch. He had a broad face, prominent ears, and jet-black hair.

"We're about to spend forty-eight hours thrashing around in the wake of a freighter commanded by a drunk and steered by an imbecile and you think everything is fine?"

"Not everything," Kapitulsky admitted. He adjusted the position of a valve in the secondary steam loop and watched as a needle that measured flow and vibration responded. "Just everything I can do something about."

"How's Irina?"

At hearing his wife's name, Gennady turned away from his wall of dials and gauges. "She's going to neuter a pig while we're gone."

"She's keeping animals now?"

"One. His name is Romanov."

"I see." Lev Romanov was the political officer back at base who traded travel passes for sex. "She may have to stand in line for the operation," said Britanov.

"In Russia everyone has to stand in line. She's going to cut his balls off and send them to Moscow."

"Well," said Britanov, "it's efficient."

The engineer cocked his head. "Efficient?"

"Romanov can sign their travel passes."

Kapitulsky roared. Everyone hated the *zampolits*. Seducing officers' wives while they were out on patrol just gave them all another reason. "Fucking *zampolits*. Who needs them anyway?"

Britanov stood and clapped him on the shoulder. "If I see Sergi-yenko," he said, meaning the *K-219*'s own political officer, "I'll be sure to ask."

"By the way. Keep an eye on Petrachkov."

The missile officer. "Why do you say that?" asked Britanov.

"His wife," said the propulsion engineer. "You know what happened?"

"I heard rumors."

"All true. Some bastard off a DELTA moved in while Petrachkov was on patrol. He's even living in their flat. Some nerve. Petrachkov couldn't go in and collect his things. Can you imagine? The divorce papers are waiting on the pier. I wouldn't be surprised if he wasn't so anxious to go back."

"After ninety days, I promise you he'll be anxious."

"I don't know. He looks worried. You know?"

"*Ya panimayu,*" said Britanov. He understood. "I'll keep it in mind."

SOSUS CONTROL, NAVAL OCEAN SYSTEMS ATLANTIC, NORFOLK

The Cray supercomputers in the basement of Naval Ocean Systems were the biggest, fastest machines of their day. The enormous task of SOSUS, the Sonar Surveillance System, demanded it. The machines sat in a guarded room bathed in arctic chill by powerful air conditioners. Nevertheless, so much energy went through their tightly packed circuits that the cylindrical main processing units would catch fire without constant water cooling.

The Crays gathered sounds from thousands of hydrophones arrayed across strategic bottlenecks in the Atlantic. Undersea soundtraps were strung across the Greenland-Iceland-U.K. gap, the Mid-Atlantic Ridge, the approaches to the American coast, even inside the Russians' own backyard Barents Sea.

They heard everything, even things they weren't supposed to be able to hear: the love songs of whales, the crunch and snap made by the jaws of millions of tiny shrimp, the low seismic rumble of magma shifting below the earth's crust. And of course, submarines. The computers recorded everything, but it took the duty crew upstairs to make sense of it, to distinguish a great white from a different sort of undersea predator.

The operators' room was a very quiet place; here, oceanographic technicians wearing heavy, sophisticated headphones were jacked into their workstations, their eyes unfocussed, their ears spring-loaded to hear the sloshes, whispers, and sighs of nuclear submarines. Though each man was responsible for a particular sector, their sectors overlapped, creating a seamless acoustic fence not even the superquiet American attack submarines could sneak by. They tried to all the same.

Behind the operators was a master tactical display board showing the current status of all SOSUS contacts. On the opposite wall was the glassed-in control room, ruled by the presiding duty officer. It was elevated a few feet to permit him to see all his operators as well as the main display board.

A chief petty officer was on watch over a particular sector of the Greenland-Iceland-U.K. gap. He'd been listening to a surface contact for the last half hour as it struggled to make eight knots. The tag said she was *Yaroslavl*, a merchie headed for Havana, but she was in ideal position to act as an escort to a boomer trying to beat his fence. Not that he would let them. Soviet boats were getting better, getting quieter, but that just made the game more interesting.

He suddenly sat up, cocked his head, then typed in a series of commands on the desktop keyboard.

The Crays down in the basement began to manipulate the sounds coming from four particular listening posts, washing out some noises, amplifying others. He could mask the sounds of breaking waves, of a billion whitecaps, of nearly anything, once the program learned to recognize it. Erasing the cluttered slate left room for the sounds he was interested in.

The slosh and surge of the surface contact faded. He ordered it to vanish. Now he could hear the steady heartbeat of underwater screws.

"Gotcha." He picked up the telephone and dialed the duty officer up in the glass cage.

"Control."

"We've got the Barents Sea YANKEE again, sir. He's maneuvering east of the line to make rendezvous with a merchie."

"Too bad she's just a YANKEE," the duty officer replied. "They won't bother sending out a P-3." There was no need to go to extraordinary measures to keep tabs on a boat as noisy as a YANKEE. "You have a track on her yet?"

"Heading two two six, fat, dumb, and happy."

"She'll enter the Brits' sector. Maybe they'll send a Nimrod out to take a look." The Nimrod was the British equivalent of the American P-3. "Mark it and store it. Keep an eye on him, chief. Let me know if anything exciting happens."

"Aye aye." He'd listened in as another Soviet boomer drove right into the surface escort she was trying to follow. He could still remember the crunch and scream of ripping metal. Why did they bother trying to sneak through SOSUS anyway? It was useless. In calm sea states, SOSUS could hear airplanes flying *over* the water. Ivan would be smarter to just drive on through at high speed. Hiding in the baffles of some banana boat didn't make any difference. Zero.

Of course, if they were smart they'd stay home in bed rather than seal themselves up in a an old tub of a YANKEE. It gave him the shivers just to think of it.

The oceanographic technician typed another set of commands, and a light illuminated on the master display board: YANKEE-1: *K-219.*

K-219

"Target two kilometers, still making eight knots."

"Prepare for close approach," said Britanov.

They were already beyond the point where the freighter was supposed to accelerate to twelve knots. Even at that speed it would take a full forty-eight hours of close, dangerous steaming to clear the hydrophone-infested SOSUS barrier. Britanov had a lot of confidence in the men of the special maneuvering watch. Flying his boat in close formation to *Yaroslavl* demanded his best planesman, his best helmsman, his best sonar operator. But two days of this and they'd all be exhausted.

"Range one kilometer."

"Make your depth twenty meters. Turns for fifteen knots." Britanov was mentally calculating the approach, picturing the movement of the two ships. He had to slide in from behind, slightly faster than *Yaroslavl,* then gently, carefully, move into position.

Once they were close the stakes became even higher. "ESM sweep."

The mast bearing a thin, whiplike antenna rose to cut the surface of the sea. Its purpose was to listen for the telltale emissions of enemy radars.

"ESM clear, Comrade Captain."

"Very well. Up periscope." Britanov made his way up to the periscope platform directly above the central command post. He got there as the metal cylinder slid to eye level. He grasped both handles and pushed. The periscope jerkily ground its way around in a full sweep.

"Depth steady at twenty meters, Captain."

He pushed on the handles and the periscope turned. Dark on dark. The faintest hint of the coming dawn to the east. The view was very low to the water. The sea was mercifully flat, though that cut both ways; it made it easier to keep station with their whale, but it also made it easier for their periscope to be detected.

He swung the handles. The motor jerked the periscope another few degrees. *Where was that son of a . . .* He stopped. *There!*

The white stern light appeared bright as Venus above the eerie glow of the freighter's wake. It seemed dangerously close, but that's where he had to be if he wanted to beat SOSUS. "Range to target?"

"One hundred meters, Captain."

They had to get closer, but very, very gently. "Helm, turns for twelve knots."

The boat lurched as it passed through a knot of turbulence left by the *Yaroslavl.*

"Range now seventy meters."

The boat pitched and yawed in response to the freighter's wake. He put his eye to the periscope again. Now he could see the two dim red lights flanking the white stern beacon. It was the coded signal that proved he was following *Yaroslavl* and not some random ship.

"Fifty meters, Captain."

Now if they could just hold this position. "Gennady?"

"Propulsion," answered Kapitulsky from compartment two.

"Take number one reactor off line. Secure the port engine and trail the port screw. We need to walk quiet as a cat."

"Understood."

Securing one reactor and one of the turbine engines, allowing its propeller to "windmill" in the watery slipstream, would reduce *K-219*'s sound signature to an absolute minimum. It also would make maneuvering more difficult, more chancy.

"Entering SOSUS detection zone in five minutes," said Aznabaev.

They bobbed and swerved through another eddy of turbulence. *Two days of this,* he thought as he took the *kashtan* intercom and pressed the transmit button. "This is the captain," Britanov said. "All compartments, rig the boat for quiet running."

"Target holding steady at fifty meters. Bearing zero one zero. Speed twelve knots now."

Finally they were speeding up. Britanov would have liked twenty knots even more. How fast could—

Suddenly there were two sharp explosions. Britanov's heart jumped as the blasts reverberated through *K-219*. He took hold of the periscope and looked out again.

Two white fans of water were slowly subsiding from either side of the *Yaroslavl*'s stern. The twin blasts were concussion grenades meant to signal the approach of an enemy sub-hunting aircraft.

"Down periscope! Retract all masts! Set depth for fifty meters!"

The submarine angled down as the steel periscope slid into its housing.

How did they know to arrive right here, right now? Spies at Gadzhievo? Some acoustic trap they knew nothing about? *How?* It was infuriating! With ASW planes overhead they'd have to steam blind using their sonar and passive arrays to keep them from tangling with *Yaroslavl*. It was a tight fit: in calm seas there was a scant fifteen meters of water between the freighter's keel and the top of the submarine's conning tower.

He descended the ladder to the central command post. "Range?"

"Still fifty meters, Captain."

"All right. This isn't going to be as easy as we hoped."

"Then it will make better practice, Comrade Captain," said Vladmirov, the new executive officer with just the right degree of enthusiasm. He'd decided that even if this submarine were old enough to draw a pension, between Kapitulsky, Krasilnikov, and the captain, he was safe enough.

Britanov was proud of his crew, even if he hadn't developed the close relationship with Vladmirov he'd built up over so many long patrols with Igor Kurdin, the boat's regular exec. He looked around the CCP. Some of his men were new, yet they were handling it like professionals.

The clank and thud of *K-219*'s own screws subsided. The boat rose, then fell, echoing the waves. It became noticeably quieter in the CCP. Normal conversation was almost possible.

Britanov looked up as though he could stare through the hull at the churning bubbles left by the freighter's screws. He placed a finger onto a steel frame and felt a new vibration, not one from *K-219*—he knew all of those—but the beat of another ship's engines.

"Helm?" asked Britanov. He felt the deck begin to rise under his feet.

"Depth..." He pushed sharply forward on the joystick that controlled the diving planes, then back level again. He was sweating profusely. "Depth steady at fifty meters."

The thump was stronger now, you could hear it right through the steel hull of the submarine. There was a definite metallic rasp and rattle to it as well when the screws came free of the sea. Britanov smiled. The freighter's propeller shafts sounded as if they were made from links of loose anchor chain.

"Her main bearings are shot," said the sonar officer as he listened to the sounds.

Britanov shrugged. "Will they last forty-eight hours?"

Grandfather Krasilnikov laughed and said, "They've probably sounded that bad for forty-eight years. What's another two days?"

Two days. It would leave them all stumbling with fatigue. Britanov thought, Let this whale make all the noise she can. It would shield them from the confident Americans and their vaunted technology. The ocean was a big place, and K-219, with a little help, could get lost in it. Let the Americans be surprised for a change.

"Range to target is steady."

Target. It was another proof that to a submariner all surface ships, even your own, were the enemy. "Good," said Britanov. "Navigator?"

Aznabaev appeared from his little alcove off the CCP. Like Vladmirov, his worried look had mostly evaporated. The navigator's broad, chubby face was almost back to its impish normal.

"Let me know the minute we're beyond the SOSUS line." He looked at the CCP crew, taking care to catch each one's eye. "Comrades? The join-up was very, very good. Congratulations to every one of you."

The sea bottom plunged beneath the two ships as they chugged slowly southwest. It took forty-eight hours to steam through the SOSUS fence. Abeam the drowned seamount known as Outer Bailey,

Britanov ordered the special maneuvering watch off duty, a new course and speed set, and when all of this was done he went down to his cabin and fell into his own bunk and collapsed, exhausted.

SOSUS CONTROL, NAVAL OCEAN SYSTEMS ATLANTIC, NORFOLK

It was amazing. Did the Soviets really believe that hiding in the baffles of a noisy freighter could beat SOSUS? The oceanographic technician jacked into a small part of the Greenland-Iceland-U.K. barrier listened as two targets, *Yaroslavl* and that noisy old YANKEE boomer, separated and went their own ways, one heading for Cuba, the other making a beeline for the American coast. Their tracks were reflected instantly on the Big Board, the map of the Atlantic.

The chief smirked. Beat SOSUS with an old trick like that? It was almost insulting, though he had an idea it wasn't very pleasant duty for a sub to keep constant station with a merchie. He hoped they sweated it, but then the petty officer hated submarines and submariners. They were all sneaky. He came from the surface navy, and to him, all submarines, no matter whose, were the enemy.

The light on his telephone blinked. He picked it up.

"Chief?" It was the duty officer up in the glassed-in control booth. "Would you mind coming back up here for a minute?"

"On my way." The SOSUS technician took off his heavy headphones, rubbed his sore ears, and made his way back to the control room.

"New London's sending out a modified boat," the duty officer explained. "They hung some new ears on her and they're looking for something good. Got anything we can throw their way for a test?"

New London was home to Submarine Development Squadron Twelve, the place where exotic acoustic gear, computers, sensors, and processors came from. They'd try out a new box on one boat, then, if it worked, they'd send it out to the fleet. Or not. There was no pre-dicting the submarine community. They lived inside a wall of secrecy so high it even excluded most of the U.S. Navy.

"We've got two DELTAs on station," he explained. "They're send-ing one YANKEE home and relieving her with another. She just went through my sector."

"She running solo yet?"

"Just separated," the chief said. "What boat's New London sending out?"

"Augusta."

"Caesar Augustus?" the chief snorted. "Be fun to nail him on the net." All attack sub captains were cowboys, but the captain of the *Augusta*, a nuclear submarine of the advanced *Los Angeles* class, was the Lone Ranger; a commander with a very high opinion of himself and his boat. "Can we take him down a notch, sir? Maybe have LANTFLEET order a P-3 out and drop on him? Bet that would rattle his cage good."

"We're not supposed to be able to track *Augusta*. He thinks he can beat SOSUS."

"So do the Russians."

The duty officer smiled. "I'll let New London know about the two DELTAs and the YANKEE. Which YANKEE did they sortie?"

"The *K-219* sir. She's a YANKEE-1."

"A dash one?" said the duty officer. "They must be getting des-perate."

K-219, 15 SEPTEMBER, MID-ATLANTIC, DAY 12

The submarine cruised over the vast undersea mountain range of the Mid-Atlantic Ridge. If the mountains had been on dry land, the ridge would be the greatest range on earth. But here, drowned beneath three thousand meters of water, they were just another part of Britanov's hidden world. For a man sealed inside *K-219*, there might be no other world.

The crew had settled into the habits of steady cruising. The neo-phyte's fear of the first dive was lulled by the routine of standing watch, eating, sleeping, and standing watch again. Vladimir, the new executive officer, had begun to relax under Engineer Krasilnikov's endless teasing. Even Navigator Aznabaev seemed more at ease. He had started telling jokes again, and though everyone knew them, it was a good sign.

The galley turned out excellent meals. The steam *banya* was a re-laxing place to let the sweat of the day flow from your pores. Nothing vital had broken, not even the VCR they had on board to watch Western movies and rock videos.

So far they'd encountered no enemy other than boredom. No sign of American submarines or surface ships. No weather, no wave reached down to remind them of where they were.

With both engines and both reactors back on line, they were driving southwest at just over twenty knots. Britanov didn't need to look over Aznabaev's shoulder, he didn't need a line on the navigator's chart to know that soon, perhaps very soon, he and his crew would have to be sharp, indeed.

The mid-Atlantic was too big for the Americans to wire for sound. There were too many canyons, too many undersea mountain ranges to hide in. But as they neared the American coast, everything would change. They would be in the enemy's own backyard, far from home, from support, more dependent on their own skills than ever.

It was time to shake things up a little bit.

Britanov got up and stood next to his chair in the center of the CCP. He had an awkward emergency breathing-apparatus canister hitched to his belt. Big as a coffee can, it contained a rubber mask and hose that could be plugged into the boat's oxygen supply, or in more dire circumstances, into a self-contained canister known as an OBA.

The self-contained OBA allowed a man to walk around and breathe, though it was good for only ten minutes; as long as it would take for an orderly evacuation of a stricken submarine. Of course, an evacuation from a burning, poison-filled sub was usually anything but orderly. Perhaps if the ship were on the surface, in good weather, with plenty of light to see by. In other words, useless except in the sort of textbook drills they might dream up in sub school.

The *K-219* had a central oxygen system piped in to each compartment. It worked like those found on airliners: each man would plug his own black hose into the overhead oxygen port and breathe clean air.

In theory. Britanov believed it was one thing to sit in an airliner seat and breathe, another to walk around and fix whatever catastrophe had struck, in darkness, with the ocean rushing in and the sounds of breakup in your ears.

Why couldn't the designers make useful assumptions about emergency gear? Why couldn't their portable canisters be smaller, lighter, and more efficient? If you made them really well you could do away with the overhead oxygen manifold entirely. Why couldn't they see that?

Because, thought Britanov, the designers aren't submariners. He reached into the pocket of his dark blue overalls and pulled out a stopwatch. Then Britanov caught Lieutenant Voroblev's eye.

The damage control officer stiffened. He knew they were overdue for a casualty drill, and the stopwatch in Captain Britanov's hands erased any further doubt.

The captain lunged for the intercom microphone. "Toxic fumes in compartment five! Toxic fumes in sick bay!" Then after a moment of stunned silence and ashen, frightened faces he added, "This is a drill!"

Lieutenant Voroblev grabbed his own microphone. "All compartments! Don individual life support systems!"

In a frenzy of activity that was part ballet, part riot, each of the twenty men in the central command post yanked a length of black hose from his waist pouch and slammed it into the overhead oxygen ports. Next from the same pouch came a rubber mask. Soon the CCP was a cacophony of seal-men barking through their heavy masks. Eye contact was barely possible through the tiny lenses; making yourself heard, much less understood, was not.

Why, wondered Britanov, could the designers not understand that as well?

The damage control officer flipped open a greaseboard outline of *K-219*. The outline was divided, like the sub, into ten compartments. In a real emergency, there was no way to make your way through the boat once the hatches closed. In a real emergency, each compartment lived or died by the efforts and skills of those sealed inside its steel walls.

Voroblev glanced at Britanov. He was holding the stopwatch up to his mask, watching the sweep of the second hand mark off the divisions between death and survival. "All compartment commanders report!"

Elapsed time, one minute.

Voroblev checked off each compartment as the reports came back that they were manned and ready and protected from toxic fumes.

Britanov walked over to Voroblev, took a grease pencil and marked a big black *X* over the outline of compartment six, the equipment space immediately aft of sick bay. He leaned close to the damage control officer and shouted, "Fumes reported spreading! Life support lost from frame 236!"

Voroblev blinked from behind his fogged-up mask, then reached for the microphone. "Damage control party four go to five now! Provide! Boundaries are compartments four and six! Move out now!"

Provide meant that full-body protective gear was now demanded. The heavy suits did for efficiency what the masks did for communication.

The chief engineer appeared in CCP in his mask. Britanov motioned him over. They put their heads together, then Grandfather Krasilnikov nodded and went to a power distribution board.

Elapsed time, two minutes.

Suddenly the lights aft of compartment five failed. The battle lanterns were supposed to come on in the event of a power loss. Instead they flickered white, went yellow, then blinked out in seconds. Frightened men were engulfed in pitch-darkness as they struggled into their full-body suits. A siren began to wail.

"Power alarm, compartments five, six, and seven!" Voroblev yelled. "This is not a drill!" Five was sick bay, six an equipment space, but compartment seven was the reactor room and it was no place for games.

Britanov pointed at Grandfather Krasilnikov and snapped his finger. The chief engineer dashed out of the CCP to find out what had happened.

Three minutes.

Britanov could see from the sweat, from the jerky movements of the CCP staff, that events were pushing them over the edge. One more problem and they'd lose the ability to function as a team. Two more and they'd lose the ability to function, period. Not good.

"Secure from drill!" he barked into the intercom. "Exercise aborted! Propulsion engineer to the CCP!"

Gennady Kapitulsky staggered into the CCP looking crestfallen. His face was smudged with black grease. He was breathing hard, covered with sweat. The reactor compartment was his responsibility.

"What happened to your lights?" Britanov asked him.

But before he could answer, Grandfather Krasilnikov came in, his face also covered with a sheen of sweat and machine oil.

"It's my fault," he said, tossing his rubber mask to the chart table. "We lost all power in five, six, and seven when I shifted over to the emergency circuit. The breaker on my main panel tripped and I couldn't get it back on line."

"What about the battle lamps? They have their own batteries."

"There must be a short in the charging mechanism. I'll—"

"An emergency circuit that breaks in an emergency isn't much good," said Britanov.

The two engineers stood silently.

Britanov saw the effect of his words on them. He put his hand on Grandfather Krasilnikov's shoulder. "We'll run the same drill later today. I want all compartments manned and ready in two minutes, not three. Come on," he said to them, "let's go down to my cabin. We'll figure this electrical problem out."

Missile Officer Petrachkov yanked the foul-smelling mask from his face and threw it down. The fourteen men under his command stood on the mid-deck level, staring at one another. He'd just ordered them to begin pumping out silo six when the captain ordered that damned drill.

Why did they run drills when he was trying to get important work done? Didn't they know that if he didn't keep a close eye on things, the next alarm would be for real? He went back to the gauge that measured water levels inside the silo.

The dial showed just less than the four-liter maximum. At first the leak seemed to heal itself, but it was definitely coming in faster now. One pumping per day was no longer enough. "All right," he called down. "Stop standing with your hands in your pockets. Get six emptied now!"

The men below went to their normal workstations, shedding masks and rubber hoods.

Petrachkov tapped the water gauge again, hoping the needle would fall. A certain amount of seepage was dangerous, but accepted as normal. The fumes that formed when seawater and missile oxidizer mixed dissipated into a special venting system; in fact, the same vents that choked on the steady clouds of smoke rising from the officers' smoking cubicle below.

But let too much seawater in and you had a different, more dangerous problem on your hands. Allow water and oxidizer to mix in sufficient quantity and you had a powerful, poisonous acid that could eat through nearly anything. Wires, seals, even the aluminum body of the missile itself. That's when a problem could turn into a catastrophe.

It was the private nightmare of every submariner to serve on board a NAVAGA: a seawater leak started a chemical chain reaction that would eat through the rocket body, breach the highly stressed fuel tanks, and mix the two poisons inside the silo. The explosion would rupture the silo, smash the nearby missiles, mix more fuel, more seawater. The explosive chain reaction could quickly doom the boat and its crew. Even if they were on the surface.

Petrachkov eyed the gauge, then made a mental note to have it pumped dry twice a day. They were well into their patrol, though still not halfway home. Not that he was anxious to go home. He wasn't even sure there was a home waiting for him. He didn't even have his own flat, his own kitchen table, anymore. That bastard. He'd moved in while Petrachkov had been on patrol. Now she wanted a divorce. Well, the worthless bitch would have to wait until he was good and ready. Even a leaky NAVAGA was better than going back with your tail between your legs. It was better to be far away and in control of your fate, not crawling on hands and knees.

He saw the needle on the silo six guage move. Besides, it was too late to go back now. There would be too many questions leveled at him for not reporting the leak sooner.

He would live by his decision, and so would everyone else.

CHAPTER 3

Soviet boomers were no match for
our fast-attack boats. That's not to
say a real skillful Soviet skipper
couldn't occasionally surprise us.

—Captain James Bush,
Retired Submarine Commanding Officer

K-219, 17 SEPTEMBER 1986, WESTERN ATLANTIC, DAY 14

"Depth steady at eighty meters, Captain," said the helm. "Course is
two three eight. Turns for fifteen knots."

"Very well. Hold course and depth. Trail the probe," ordered Britanov.

At the stern of the ballistic missile submarine, a thin wire began to
unreel from its fairing; the wire, known as the "rectal probe," was
spun from a special biconductive blend of metals; the differing reactions of those metals to an electric pulse would tell Britanov the temperature of the sea. It was not a minor concern.

They were just two days' sail from their patrol zone off the American coast. Two days closer to the array of antisubmarine forces the

Americans were certain to throw at him: aerial surveillance, under-water hydrophone lines, and most feared of all, American hunter-killer submarines. They could hear Britanov and remain invisible. They could hide in acoustic thickets the more primitive Russian gear could never penetrate.

Underwater sound was profoundly affected by underwater temper-ature. That meant temperature was something Britanov could use, if he were very lucky, to turn the tables on the smug enemy. For a warship utterly dependent upon stealth, the ability of the sea to trans-mit sound was as vital as air, as light.

Captain Britanov glanced at the paper chart posted by Aznabaev's navigation cubicle. On it, drawn in a careful hand, were isobars show-ing zones of constant temperature and depth.

The ocean was separated into distinct layers of temperature and salinity. Each layer had its own properties, and a submarine in one layer would be harder to detect from another, acoustically separate layer. It was like looking into a mirror that becomes more or less reflective with changes in temperature. Pick your place and your depth well, and it would be possible to dive through the mirror and become, to all intents, invisible to the rest of the world. The division between layers, the surface of the mirror, was called the thermocline.

Invisibility had its obvious benefits for a noisy sub like *K-219*. But it also gave Britanov an opportunity to be the hunter, and not merely the hunted. American subs often stayed in the upper, warmer zones where their own minimal sounds became lost in the difficult acoustic conditions. They knew, correctly, that Russian sonar could never see them there. Their own sonar equipment was good enough to turn the murky, warmer waters transparent. They had no difficulty tracking Russian subs.

What was true for the shallows was also true for the deeps: in the cold, acoustically clear depths, American sonar could pick up deep-swimming Russian submarines from a great distance. It was only when the Americans were above the layer, and the Russians below, that the situation became more difficult, more equal. It put the antagonists on opposite sides of the "mirror." A clever, careful Soviet captain could use this to his advantage.

It was a devilishly difficult proposition. Indeed, most Soviet captains didn't bother with it, resigning themselves to the invisible presence of an American attack boat somewhere nearby.

Not Britanov.

"The layer's down to eighty meters, Captain," said Lieutenant Cherkasov, the assistant navigator who had the job of operating the temperature-sensitive wire. Inevitably, he was known as Comrade Rectal Probe.

Eighty, thought Britanov. Not enough. The warm waters of the Gulf Stream were thickening; below eighty meters the sea was dark and icy cold; sound would travel a long, long way. Above it the water was more temperate. Eighty meters represented the surface of the mirror. But it was still too shallow to dive through. "Start logging it on the half hour," said Britanov. "We're getting close to hostile waters. Someone could be waiting for us ahead."

"They're all hostile waters, Captain," quipped the chief engineer, Grandfather Krasilnikov. "Any body of water too deep to drink is hostile."

Britanov smiled, then turned to Cherkasov. "Let me know when the layer goes down to one hundred meters."

"I will if you don't chew up my wire." Fouling the propellers with the rectal probe was a common occurrence. The bronze screws chopped it to pieces when the helm maneuvered without warning the temperature logger.

"Comrade Rectal Probe thinks we're driving this submarine to carry his damned wire," said Krasilnikov.

"For the next few hours we are," said Britanov.

For three hours Cherkasov busily filled in the chart with his colored pens, plotting the depth of the thermocline as it dipped deeper and deeper. Heading southwest, they were fast approaching the main core of the warm, northward current.

"Ninety meters thick, now," said Cherkasov.

It was time. "Helm," said Britanov. "Take us down to ninety."

"Ninety meters, aye aye."

The deck tilted downward almost imperceptibly.

"Not too fast." If they burst through the layer and into the cold, clear zone below, their own noise would travel from here to New York harbor.

"You think they're out here?" asked Vladmirov, the young executive officer.

"I think we're going to find out," Britanov answered.

The planesman was sweating at the controls. To keep a submarine at a precise depth required almost paranormal concentration. The deck shifted down, corrected up, too much, then slid down again. The depth gauge twitched, then stopped. "Steady at ninety meters, Captain."

"All right," said Britanov. "This is what we're going to do. We're going to skim the layer until it goes down to one hundred meters. Then we're going to go through, cut our engines and drift. Sonar, I want your ears sharp. When we go below the layer you'll have your best chance of picking up something. Understood?"

"Understood, Comrade Captain."

"Helm, as soon as we're through, we'll turn south and cut engines to dead slow. I want only enough power to hover in the current. All right?"

"Aye aye, Captain."

It was, thought Britanov, a lot like fishing. Move suddenly and the fish are gone. Move slowly, lull them into believing something that isn't so, that the feathery, improbable lure is breakfast, and you might have a chance to hook a fat one.

"Layer is dipping, Captain," said Cherkasov. "It's down to one hundred meters and holding."

"All right," said Britanov. "Be very gradual. Very easy. We don't want to spook our fish. Helm? Down planes. Make your depth one hundred meters."

USS *AUGUSTA*, SSN-710, WESTERN ATLANTIC

"Conn, Sonar. Red Two is changing depth again."

Captain Von Suskil nodded, then said, "Bearing?"

"Unchanged. She's staying pretty close to the layer." Forward and starboard of the boat's attack center, the sonar room was crammed with new acoustic receivers and signal processors that recognized the distinctive sound signatures of each and every Soviet boat. "She's got one screw turning. Blade count still shows fifteen knots. Range fifteen miles. She's coming in straight and dumb."

"Don't they all." Von Suskil smiled. Why couldn't those weenies on the pier find him a worthwhile target for once? It was almost beneath his dignity to trail a slow, old YANKEE, although he understood very well why it was important.

The sub might be slow but her sixteen missiles could fly pretty damned fast. From here they could be over Washington before the president would even know about it. That was why Von Suskil had a freer hand than usual to take whatever measures seemed appropriate if his target started acting oddly; odd as in looking as if she were getting ready to launch. From now until *Augusta* was relieved, a brace of Mark 48 torpedoes and some SUBROCs would have Red Two's name written into their electronic brains. Red Two was a zombie; the walking dead.

"Conn, Sonar. Range ten miles. She's right on the edge of the layer now. I'm starting to get some reflections."

Could Red Two know that *Augusta* was out here, waiting to slide into optimum firing position after she chugged by? No.

The improved 688-class submarine couldn't be detected by *American* sensors, much less Russian. And her own sophisticated gear could listen in on the clanky Russian machinery from a long way off. He had to give credit where credit was due. The new acoustic processor installed up at Groton was pretty good. *Augusta* had been able to track a Soviet DELTA boat to the south as well as this old YANKEE. She was a noisy devil, but *Augusta* had been able to detect her from extreme range; over thirty miles. Not that her captain would stay so far away. That wasn't how this game was played.

He wondered who was commanding Red Two, what sort of man he was. *Probably a second-stringer,* he thought. Who else would be driving an old boat like that? These waters belonged to the United States. Red Two was up against the varsity team, the best attack skipper in the whole Atlantic fleet, commanding the best-equipped boat with a new set of ears.

"Conn, Sonar. Range is now six miles. She's starting to fuzz up in the layer."

Von Suskil had used the heavy maritime traffic off the east coast to drill his crew and refine his technique against live targets: warships, crude oil carriers and even passenger liners when the opportunity presented itself. The new acoustic gear had allowed him to position the boat athwart his victim's path, to remain absolutely silent, while the target barged into his sights and killed itself.

He'd maneuvered so close to a departing American aircraft carrier off Norfolk that her captain had lodged a complaint, not that it would go anywhere. Submariners looked out for one another, and embarrassing a carrier, a ship protected by the very best antisubmarine warfare technology in the world, was considered a badge, not a problem.

Von Suskil was going to do it again, this time for real; his target was a Soviet missile boat. At least one, and more likely two, of the SS-N-6 rockets it carried was targeted on Groton, Connecticut; his homeport. Each one carried a pair of five-hundred-kiloton warheads. The birds had a flight time of under ten minutes. Thinking of the game in this way made it more than just a professional challenge. It made breaking the enemy's will a personal matter.

"What's he up to, Sonar?"

"Red Two's depth is now three hundred feet. He's merging with the layer. Ghosting. Kind of comes and goes."

"He can run but he can't hide," said Von Suskil. "What's the range?"

"Four miles. Heading and speed unchanged."

"All right, people. Anyone makes a noise is swimming home," said Von Suskil. He didn't say it with a smile. "Helm, be extra smooth. I don't want any knuckles in the water."

Knuckles were knots of swirling, turbulent water created by sudden maneuvering. Knuckles made noise.

"We're going to let him clank on by, then fall in behind. Meat on the table."

Augusta was hanging in the sea, all but silent, astride Red Two's predicted, and predictable, course.

"He's starting to fade," said Sonar. "Range three miles. He might be diving under the layer. If he is, he's doing it real slow and sneaky, Captain."

"He can't know we're here. He's just trying to play cute," said Von Suskil.

"Conn, Sonar. Red Two's passing now. The signal's strong but it's spread out. He's below the layer for sure. Course is two five five."

Von Suskil said, "Helm, ahead one-third, come to two five five. Make your depth three hundred feet." He turned to his executive officer and said, "Let's go down and get this bastard, Mister Samples. Order close quarters procedures."

"Engines all slow," said Britanov as the submarine slipped through the layer and cruised in the deeper, colder waters. "Course one eight zero."

He was pointing the bow of the submarine into the strong north-flowing current of the Gulf Stream. By a careful balance of power, he could "hover" the boat in place like a kite in a steady breeze and ride the current backward with his bow pointed south. The bow held his sensitive acoustic gear. He'd be in optimum position to hear anything coming by.

"One eight zero. Speed is now three knots, Captain."

"Sonar?"

"Nothing yet." The sonar operator was peering at his green display, or at least he seemed to. His eyes were actually closed. He was concentrating on the signals being picked up by K-219's bow hydrophones. He shook his head. "There's nothing . . . wait. Wait."

Britanov shot him a quick look. He could see a fuzzy spike of green light on the circular display before the sonar man. It faded, ghostly, in and out.

"Possible contact . . . It's . . . I mean—"

"What is it?" Britanov had to force himself not to shout.

"It's close!" said the sonar man with a look of wonderment. He'd never before heard an American submarine in earnest. Never once. It was like a visitation by angels, rare, improbable, even beautiful. "Evaluate as a possible submarine. Bearing zero nine five!" His voice had gone up an octave. "He's diving!"

"Calm down," said Britanov. The whole watch team was staring at the green display. Picking up an American sub was a real honor, something that almost never happened. "Everyone. Back to your posts! Sonar, put this on tape."

The green spike grew brighter. "Captain," the sonar man whispered. "He's coming straight in! *He doesn't see us.*"

"What do you mean contact is lost!" Von Suskil bellowed. They'd just dived through the thermocline. He expected Red Two out ahead, directly off the bow. But when she'd burst through the surface of the layer, the Russian boomer was gone.

"Possible contact bearing zero one zero, but if it's Red Two she's stopped. The signature is way, way down."

Then he saw it. Red Two had gone cagey on him. She'd stopped and drifted north in the current. Perhaps Von Suskil had been overconfident, too sure his opponent was just another dumb target and not a skilled enemy. "All stop. Rig the boat for ultraquiet," he said between tight lips. "Sonar, I want a resolution of that contact. I want it now."

"Nichevo!" said the sonar operator. The green spike on his display paled, then disappeared. His fingers flew over the big black dials that tuned the acoustic array. "I . . . I lost him! No contact."

Britanov looked unhappy but he wasn't. Even a fleeting contact with a ghostly American killer sub was worthwhile. "Last position?"

"South of us, heading south by west," said Vladmirov, the executive officer. His eyes were wide. He wasn't exactly sure how Britanov had done it. How did he know the Americans would behave that way?

"Sonar, I want one ping on the active set. Half power. On my signal."

"Sir?" The sonar man looked as if Britanov had issued the order in Urdu.

An active ping was not by the book. Sending a blast of sound out into the water was reserved for extreme situations, for times of war. But Britanov was tired of being a slow, stupid target for the clever Americans. He wanted whoever was out there to know that the tables just might be turned. It didn't happen often. To know that it was possible, that was enough.

Then Britanov raised his hand. "Hold course," he said quietly to the helmsman. "Up angle on the planes, rudder amidships." Britanov felt the deck begin to rise. He lowered his hand. "Sonar! Transmit one ping. Half power. *Now.*"

Ping!

A sharp, high-frequency tone echoed through the boat as the bow transducers sent a wave of acoustic energy into the sea.

Seven seconds later came a faint, but satisfying, *Pong!*

"Contact!" cried the sonar man. "Target reacquired!"

USS *AUGUSTA*

"Jesus H. Christ," Von Suskil said. The ping died away. He winced as though he'd been slapped on the face. "Sonar! How strong was that ping?"

"Low edge of detection. We're way too close. He could definitely have us."

A full-power ping and that ballsy bastard would definitely have a firing solution. *How the hell did he know we're here?* "XO, take us back out east. I want to gain some distance from this joker."

"Zero nine zero, aye," came the response.

"Range opening," said Sonar.

"We'll loop around to seaward, then reacquire," said Von Suskil. He cleared his throat. "Well, people. That was different."

K-219

The bright green spike on the sonar operator's display faded away. "He's gone!"

"We chased him away!" crowed Krasilnikov. "That will teach him!"

"Maybe," said Britanov. He was grinning. The tension in the central command post snapped. He winked at Krasilnikov and gave him a thumbs-up. To the executive officer he said, "Resume course and speed to station."

"Aye aye, Captain!" Voroblev replied with even more enthusiasm than usual.

"Sonar," said Britanov, "make me a copy of that trace. Log the contact as a possible hostile submarine, *Los Angeles* class."

"Yes, sir!"

"You see? Not every patrol is boring," said Britanov. "Now when we get back we'll really have something to talk about."

CHAPTER 4

When Moscow said to be aware of
an American submarine, I thought,
What will they warn us about next?
That the sea is wet?

—*Captain Igor Britanov, Commander,* K-219

K-219, 3 OCTOBER 1986, WESTERN ATLANTIC, DAY 31

Captain Britanov sipped tea in the CCP. Drinking hot tea made less sense here in the warm waters of the Gulf Stream than on patrol in the icy Barents Sea, but habits were hard to break.

A bead of sweat trickled into Britanov's collar. The command post smelled of machine oil, hot electronics, stale air, unwashed uniforms, and sweat. Their blue coveralls were not regularly cleaned. There wasn't enough fresh water. The first month was always the worst; after thirty days your nose simply stopped working. He glanced at the navigator's chart plot.

Cruising at a depth of one hundred meters, thirteen hundred kilometers southeast of New York City, *K-219* would shortly take up a southerly course to their second patrol area near Bermuda. Two weeks of plying the northern patrol box was nearly complete. Soon they would rise to periscope depth to permit their new orders from Moscow to be received. It was known in the Soviet Navy as a "séance," with Moscow's ghostly low-frequency whispers snatched from the air and decoded, a ritual conducted by the boat's communications officer, Markov.

As soon as they received those orders, *K-219* would proceed south to relieve Boris Apanasenko's DELTA-class missile boat already on station. The DELTA would head for home, and a new submarine would take *K-219*'s place in the northern area. If, thought Britanov, they could find a submarine fit to sail.

Britanov knew they'd been very lucky so far. Catching that American attack sub was almost unheard of. And other than a crewman coming down with a bad appendix, it had been a textbook patrol. The ship's doctor, Igor Kochergin, had cured the appendicitis with a massive dose of antibiotics rather than by meeting up with a freighter someplace and transferring the sick man over the side.

Even luckier, there had been no further encounters with American forces. Although, he knew, they would now be more circumspect. *Good. Let them learn the lessons for a change.*

He took another sip of tea and listened to the sounds of his ship. After a month at sea he had all but stopped hearing the racket, the whoosh of steam, the thud and clank of her two engines. But he knew that here off the east coast of America, *K-219*'s noise was tantamount to a giant set of crosshairs centered on his back. The Americans could hear him. They'd been very lucky to catch that American sub napping. But luck was never something to rely upon.

He scanned the instruments arrayed on the beige control panels around him. He peered at the round "steam gauge" dials as though they were tiny windows, as though he could see through them into the warm Atlantic waters streaming by his submerged hull. What would it look like? Would sunlight penetrate one hundred meters of ocean? No. Not even the gloriously clear waters of Bermuda. Outside it would be pitch-black. Below the keel was the Hatteras Abyssal Plain. A place, he thought, suitable only for monsters.

A small electric samovar sent steam into the already humid air.

They were running on one reactor, one screw. It was standard operating practice aimed at reducing the *K-219*'s "noiseprint." The second propeller turned in the watery slipstream like a child's pinwheel. Another trick to make the sub quieter and harder to detect. He swiped at the beaded sweat on his neck, then turned to the chief engineer. "Can't you lower the temperature in the boat any more?" he asked Grandfather Krasilnikov.

Krasilnikov didn't even look up. "We're at maximum cooling already, Captain. As you already know."

As he knew? Krasilnikov was becoming irritable. Britanov couldn't blame him. The command center was like a *banya,* a traditional Russian steam bath. Located just beneath the submarine's conning tower, the heat of the entire ship accumulated up here. Only the reactor room was worse. The *K-219* had been designed for the cold waters of the Arctic; here off Bermuda the ship's environmental controls could not meet the demand.

Britanov gazed up at the steel overhead, wishing they were running beneath the ice of their home waters, preparing to surface off Gadzhievo, to see the knot of color against the rocky cliffs of home and know that Natalia was there, safe. His eye stopped at the small framed placard he'd ordered displayed.

SUBMARINE LIFE IS NOT A SERVICE, BUT A RELIGION.

Markov, the boat's communications officer, opened the door to the radio alcove. "Séance in five minutes, Captain."

Britanov's expression betrayed nothing. In five minutes a coded signal would be transmitted from Moscow ordering them south to their next patrol zone. Britanov would have to rise near enough to the surface to extend his antennae above the waves.

He assumed that the enemy knew Moscow's broadcast schedule at least as well as he did. They would be waiting up there, looking for the telltale streak of his antennae breaking the waves. The Americans didn't have to surface to receive their special low-frequency signals. He wondered sometimes just how meaningful any of this was. He swallowed the rest of his tea and slapped the glass down onto the chart table loud enough to make the planesman jump.

He glanced at the sonar display. Fed by arrays of sensitive hydrophones spaced across the *K-219*'s bow, the screen was empty. Nothing. He snorted. Under way, there was too much flow noise to really listen carefully. Even if an American attack boat, a *Los Angeles,* was sitting directly off his bow, they were so damned quiet he might not know it until he hit it broadside.

But they wouldn't be off his bow. They would be watching him, tracking him from a long distance now that they'd learned to be more cautious. They'd slide into the blind spot behind his thundering screws to practice the complicated art of undersea murder. He thought back to his rendezvous with the *Yaroslavl.* To an American skipper, his nuclear boat was like that old freighter; a plodding, noisy whale fit only for buggering by the swift, silent Americans. But sometimes the whale won. Not often, but it could happen. He smiled.

He glanced at the ship's chronometer. Three minutes. It was time. He turned to his executive officer, Vladmirov.

"Let's get this over with. Sound battle stations. Come to periscope depth."

"Understood, Comrade Captain." Vladmirov picked up the kashtan microphone. "Battle stations! Battle stations! Make depth for twenty meters!"

It was a measure of Britanov's ability as a commander that the crew responded so quickly, so efficiently, in the soggy heat. Two minutes after his order, the *K-219* was rising smartly as her diving planes drove her up toward the moonlit waves. Pressures changed, ballast was shifted. The dials registered the diminishing stresses on the aging hull.

Everything seemed perfectly normal, if being locked inside a steel pipe beneath the ocean, carrying enough firepower to end the world, could be considered normal.

Britanov watched as the planesman pushed his joystick over to stop their ascent. The submarine wallowed level at a depth of twenty meters. It took a watchmaker's touch to operate the *K-219* safely. You had to anticipate some things, wait patiently for others. And that was when things worked as they should.

What was remarkable, thought Britanov, was that for thirty-one days they had.

"Radar, power up the ESM mast."

Atop the sail, a special antenna shaped like an old-fashioned stop-light began to reach for the surface. Designed to sniff out electronic signals from the Americans, it would warn Britanov that someone was up there waiting and possibly watching for him.

"My display is clear, Captain. No signals."

No signals, or no enemy? One did not directly translate to the other. There would be no telltale signals if the Americans already knew he was here. "Very well. Extend the radio whip. Comm?"

"Sir?" Markov replied.

"Prepare to receive orders."

Aft of the central command post, in compartment four, the missile room, the gauge showing the water level in missile tube six had Petrachkov's total attention once again.

The vaulted compartment was divided into three levels. The lowest, the bilge, held a bank of toilets plus the tiny smoking cubicle used by the officers. Someone was down there now. He could smell the smoke despite the special scrubbers installed. The mid-deck contained all the missile firing controls as well as the pumps used to "strip" any seawater that might leak into the silos. Fourteen of his men were stationed there as well as a few cooks who had wandered in from the overheated mess area. Petrachkov stood at the forward end of the upper level, a kind of catwalk pierced by the fat yellow missile tubes.

As Petrachkov watched, the needle in a gauge mounted on the side of silo six moved upward.

He sucked on his lower lip. They were planing up into shallow waters. He could feel it, sense it. A normal leak should diminish as hull pressure dropped. They'd been stripping the silo twice a day per his orders. Twice a day was no longer enough. That meant the leak was growing worse. Could he make it last until the end of their patrol?

He leaned over the railing and called down to one of the missilemen on the mid-deck below. "You! When was tube six last stripped?"

"We've been pumping it twice a day," the young seaman replied defensively and not entirely forthrightly. "You ordered us to—"

"I *know* what I ordered. I asked *when* it was last pumped!"

The missileman looked at his mates for support. No one had an answer to offer. "I don't know, Comrade Lieutenant."

"Then do it *now*. Line up the stripper pumps. From here on it's *your* job to keep tube six at four liters or less. If that means twice a day, if it means fifty times a day. *Is that understood?*"

"Understood, Comrade Lieutenant."

Petrachkov pulled at his clammy overalls. After a month at sea even he could smell himself. He thought of his wife. He thought of the petty officer who'd stolen her away. How did he smell? Of some fancy cologne? *Bastard.*

He watched the jiggling needle. Could it be a gauge malfunction? Perhaps there was not so much water in there. How could a leak get worse as they neared the surface? The pressures should be less up here. The heat made it hard to think. He wiped away a salty bead of sweat from his eye. Maybe he should have a talk with the damage control officer. Let Voroblev make up his mind and take some responsibility for a change. He picked up the intercom microphone.

"Lieutenant Voroblev to compartment four," he said, then hung it up. He'd kept the leak quiet for over a month. It was time to let someone else know.

Captain Britanov turned to the planesman. "Depth?"

"Steady at twenty meters."

"Radar?"

"Still no emissions, Captain. It's night up there. Maybe they're all asleep."

"Give me two sweeps at low power. We don't want to wake anyone."

A feather of ghostly green wake plumed as the radar mast cut water.

The *K 219* rolled slightly as the waves reached down and pushed her one way, then the other.

The white radial line swept the green radar display. Once, then again. "No surface targets, Captain."

Not that there would be. Britanov was more concerned with other submarines. "All right. We can't wait forever. I'm going up to take a look. Up periscope and satellite antennae. Navigator?"

"Sir?" said Aznabaev.

"You'll have exactly two minutes to update your inertial computers, Zhenya. Two minutes. Not three."

Here was a real irony, thought Britanov as he climbed up into the enclosed bridge within the submarine's conning tower. *We use American navigation satellites to target their own cities with our missiles.* Could the world be as insane as it seemed?

He grasped the handles of the rising periscope. He put his eye to the lens and pushed on the handles. A grinding motor slowly pulled them around in a full sweep.

Weather clear, seas calm. The low silvery hills of waves glittering in moonlight. He could almost smell the fresh air. When last had he smelled good, clean air? The weather as they left Gadzhievo was cold, misty with snow showers. It was warm, tropical up above. Flowers? No, they were too far from land. But still. A little new air. Wouldn't that taste sweet?

As he looked, Aznabaev took a satellite fix, refining their position and feeding the results into the missile-guidance computers. As Americans slept, Aznabaev used the whispers of American satellites to put their cities into the electronic crosshairs of his fifteen RSM-25 missiles. *Jacksonville, Kings Bay, Norfolk, Washington, New York, Groton.*

A new voice broke into the hothouse that was the CCP. "Message received and decoded, Captain." Lieutenant Markov, the sub's communications officer, held a piece of paper torn from his teletype. "Sir, I'd like to go aft and check on my section."

"Down periscope." Britanov took the paper. Some of Markov's men were sitting through the political lecture. "You'd better go back and wake them up," he said. Markov left and Britanov scanned the message.

The Soviet Navy, like its American counterpart, used low-frequency radio to communicate with submarines on patrol. A farm of tall antennae sprouted from the grasslands southeast of Moscow for this purpose.

PROCEED TO AREA TWO. WARNING: ALL SOURCE INTELLI-GENCE INDICATES THE PROBABILITY IS HIGH THAT AN AMERICAN *LOS ANGELES* ATTACK SUBMARINE IS OPERATING IN YOUR PATROL AREA. ASSUME HIGHEST, REPEAT, HIGHEST STATE OF ASW READINESS.

Britanov chuckled as he crumpled the message. Only someone in Moscow would think that such a warning would be useful. American submarines were in every ocean of the world. Sometimes they were even inside Soviet waters. They'd be lucky if they weren't inside the harbor at Gadzhievo. *K-219* was patrolling right off the enemy's coast. What did Moscow think this game was all about?

But seeing the warning in black and white excited Britanov. It had been long enough since their encounter with the enemy. It was time to stir the pot again, if for no other reason than to keep his crew's edge intact. The game they played was very much a mental exercise where spirits, and skills, could be broken by an aggressive opponent.

Britanov wasn't going to sit idly by and let that happen. *K-219* was a warship, not some tugboat bobbing down the Neva. "Helm, prepare for evasive maneuvers. Sonar, get ready. I have a feeling we might catch the Americans asleep again."

The sonar officer grinned. Tracking an American submarine once, even briefly, was considered quite an achievement. But twice? He would be the one everybody back at Gadzhievo would want to speak to, to buy drinks for. Catching the enemy twice was worth anything, even if your own submarine had to squirm, dive, and twist like a hooked eel to do it.

The Americans called it a Crazy Ivan. With no warning at all, a Soviet sub would execute a tight, spiraling turn. This allowed the sensitive acoustic receivers on her bow to listen for a trailing submarine.

But when a submarine turns, she throws her stern away from the direction of travel, directly into the path of a following sub, forcing her to stop, to make an emergency turn herself, or best of all, to dig great holes in the ocean with her screws as she tries to maneuver away from a collision. When those holes collapse under the tremendous water pressure they make noise, and noise was just what Britanov needed to find the superquiet American *Los Angeles* his gut, not Moscow's message, told him was still nearby.

Voroblev and Petrachkov stood together on the upper level of the missile room. "How long has it been doing this?" Voroblev asked as he tapped the water gauge mounted on silo six.

"A while," Petrachkov answered uneasily. One of his missilemen looked at them from the mid-deck. He looked worried. What brought the ship's damage control officer here? Nothing good.

"How long a while?" Voroblev persisted.

Petrachkov shrugged. "It seemed to stabilize so there was no need to bring it up."

"How long? One day? A week? The whole cruise? *Exactly how long?*"

Petrachkov swallowed. "There was some seepage on our first dive."

"*Our first dive?* And you didn't think to tell me?"

Petrachkov didn't answer.

Both young officers stood at the forward end of the compartment. The fourteen men on the mid-deck level tried to look busy, but they kept eyeing the two officers above. Two lounging cooks paid no attention at all.

"How often does it need pumping now?" Voroblev asked finally.

"Twice per day. Sometimes a little more."

"From the beginning?"

"No. At first it was just once a day."

"The seal must be deteriorating." He leaned close to Petrachkov so the missilemen wouldn't hear. "Don't you understand what that means? Are you crazy?"

The weapons officer stiffened. "I understand it would send us back to the pier. Our sacred duty to the—"

"Don't lecture me about sacred duties!"

The missilemen below all were looking up at them now. Even the cooks sensed something. They were watching like spectators at a cockfight.

Petrachkov didn't need some golden boy of a junior officer making trouble in his compartment. "Maybe you don't know, but we'd all get a black mark on our records if we missed our sailing date. Even brilliant young lieutenants. Think about it."

"What kind of a mark do you think we'll get if that thing lets go?"

As they both watched, the needle jiggled upward.

"Captain Britanov must be told," Voroblev said.

As though he'd been listening in, Britanov spoke over the intercom speaker. "Set readiness condition two on deck level two." It announced that the second section was to assume the steaming watch, allowing the first section to leave their posts and grab something to eat.

"Fine," said Petrachkov. "You're the damage control officer. You tell him."

The off-duty men wearily made their way to the mess deck for a quick breakfast of cottage cheese, black bread, and tea. They moved like rundown automatons as they weaved their way down the serving line, groggy with the heat and fatigue, before collapsing into chairs set at fifteen small tables. They ate slowly, making each bite last, knowing that there was no reason to hurry, for they would not be allowed to leave the mess area until the boat's *zampolit,* Political Officer Sergiyenko, finished with his damned lecture on *perestroika* in the Navy, whatever that meant. Where was he, anyway? The sooner Sergiyenko began, the sooner he would be finished and they all could stumble off to their bunks for some much-needed sleep.

The mess sweltered from the convection ovens, the warm Gulf Stream waters beyond the hull, and the rank heat rising from the tired men. It was tough enough trying to stay awake when you were at work, on watch. But to sit here waiting for the tangled nuances of perestroika, well, that was unrealistic.

One head after another dropped, mouths gaped open, soft snores buzzing over untouched plates of cookies. The *K-219* was near enough to the surface for the waves to impart a gentle, soporific rocking. The rich, greasy aroma of lamb spread through the room as the cooks prepared for the main meal of the day scheduled for 1100 hours.

It was 0520 Moscow time.

Political Officer Sergiyenko sat in the officers' smoking cubicle in the bilges of the missile room. From his chair he could reach out and touch the curving yellow wall of silo six. It was cold, so cold that it sweated with condensed moisture like a glass of iced tea. He was both crowded, and very much alone.

Lieutenant Markov, the communications officer, and Volodiya Vladmirov, the new *starpom,* were sharing a cigarette in the cubicle. As far as they seemed to know, Sergiyenko was invisible.

"When I first saw my orders to *K-219* I was scared to death," Vladmirov admitted.

"If it wasn't for Britanov, I'd be the same way. He knows his business. Kapitulsky, too."

A cult of personality in the making, thought Sergiyenko.

"You don't agree, Comrade *Zampolit?*" Markov asked in a way that made it clear he couldn't care less what the political officer said.

"Measured by results, Britanov is very effective."

"What else is there besides results?"

"Methods."

Markov asked, "So what is this *perestroika* all about?"

"Actually," said Sergiyenko, "it's a complicated topic."

"Actually," said Vladmirov, "he doesn't know, either."

The two officers laughed. Sergiyenko didn't. He was the fifth wheel here in every sense of the word. He knew Britanov had no use for him. His fellow officers treated him with contempt. Even Valery Pshenichny, the boat's security officer, ignored him, and he was KGB. State Security and the Party used to be on the same side. Now everything was upside down.

Vladmirov and Markov began talking about portable stereos, ignoring the boat's political officer again.

In accordance with directives of the Main Political Administration, Sergiyenko tried to look confident. He wore his white dress uniform jacket open at the neck to show the silver key that, along with the ones worn by Britanov and that smug bastard Pshenichny, would unleash atomic destruction on the land of the enemy. Wasn't that power?

But Sergiyenko didn't look confident. He wore the expression of a man asked to tell a joke he doesn't quite understand. Is this funny? Do you understand the punch line? He smashed a cigarette out in the ashtray. Someone flushed the commode and emerged. The door slammed shut. A fresh stench rolled out and across the smoking cubicle.

Sergiyenko was not looking forward to his talk. Two years junior to Captain Britanov, Sergiyenko was not really a submariner. He knew it and so did everyone else. Worse, he could no longer simply demand respect from the crew. They no longer feared him. His audience would consist of thirty tired, hot, hostile men, some older and more seasoned than he. Of course the captain was just as bad. He treated Sergiyenko like some piece of cargo he'd been ordered to haul, a piece of useless cargo at that.

Sergiyenko expected the men to be unruly as he tried to hold their attention for the hour and a half he was required to speak. *Perestroika in the armed services,* as though he had any idea what the devil that was supposed to be. All he knew was that officers didn't take politics seriously anymore. They tolerated questioning, challenges, even outright disrespect for the Party. *Submarine Life Is Not a Service, But a Religion.* Just try to get away with *that* a few years ago. Britanov would have found himself the captain of a prison barge heading for Siberia. If the officers committed such offenses, what could you expect from the men?

Not that political officers were immune from making mistakes. Look at Lev Romanov back at Gadzhievo. Taking sailors' wives to bed in exchange for issuing them travel permits or bottles of cognac or even simple nylons. He'd made a bad choice in trying to lure Irina Kapitulsky into his bed. Her slightly Asian eyes gave her an exotic beauty. But Irina had the fiery temperament of a northerner, plus a husband who was one of the best propulsion engineers in all the Northern Fleet. That meant he had at least as much clout as Romanov.

In the old days she would have gone quietly into his room and that would be that. Who would risk angering a political officer? Now anything could happen.

It was Gorbachev's fault. Everything was going down the drain.

"So?" said Markov pointedly. "Are you giving your little talk or not?"

"Duty calls," he said, trying for some small sense of irony. He stubbed out the half-smoked Belomar, grabbed his notes and stood, feeling a little woozy from the heat, the gentle swaying, wondering what sort of reception he would get when he walked into the mess room.

Markov immediately moved into his place in the cubicle.

Sergiyenko could hear voices from above. He looked up and saw Petrachkov and the damage control officer with their heads together. Voroblev's neck was red. He looked ready to take a bite out of Petrachkov.

Another month of this heat and they'd all be ready to bite.

Sergiyenko walked aft to the ladder and began to climb up to the mid-deck level. He thought, if I were in Romanov's shoes, I would have been more careful. A smart political officer should know how to pick his victims better.

———

Britanov said, "Command post ready?"

Lieutenant Vladmirov picked up the *kashtan* microphone and nodded.

"No," said Britanov. "No announcements. They should expect it. This is a warship. I want them prepared for war."

Vladmirov assumed Britanov knew what he was doing. After catching that American? He'd walk through fire for the man. Still, the submarine reached some radical attitudes in a Crazy Ivan. Not everyone had a handle to grab. "Sir, the *zampolit* is giving a lecture in the crew's mess."

"So?" said Britanov. "Seeing him fall on his ass might be good for morale."

Grandfather Krasilnikov chuckled. They all shared Britanov's view of Sergiyenko.

"Very well," said Britanov. "Sonar ready? You may not have too long a look at our American friends. Maybe we'll have some more luck."

Sonar nodded excitedly. "If they're there, I'll find them."

"Helm ready?"

The planesman hooked his shoes under a safety rail beneath his console. "Ready."

"Very well." Britanov reached overhead and grabbed a steel handle set there for just this purpose. "Set depth for one hundred meters. Make turns for twenty-five knots. *Rudder hard left! Now! Now! Now!*"

The *K-219* pushed over into a steep, powered dive, driven by her planes, by gravity, and by the furious churning of her screws. Like passengers in a plummeting elevator, the watch team in CCP nearly levitated off the steel deck plates. The *K-219* tilted hard over like a jet banking into a tight spiral turn.

A Soviet warship keeps Moscow, not local meridian, time. It was 0530.

"Conn, Sonar! Crazy Ivan!" He shouted loud enough to be heard in the attack center. He was scared because they'd slipped up behind the thudding YANKEE. They were very close. "Red Two's turning to port!"

"All stop!" the captain ordered. "Rig for ultraquiet!"

They'd been creeping up on Red Two for half a day, cautious, wary now. Von Suskil didn't want to be surprised again. But the target ran straight and stupid, as though he couldn't care less about an enemy hiding in his baffles.

"Sir, if he goes active he'll get us for sure."

"I don't think he will. I have a handle on this joker," said Von Suskil.

Now *Augusta* had more than a collision to worry about, though at such close quarters it was always a possibility. She had to remain quiet, so quiet that even the enemy's passive sensors would reveal nothing of her presence. To do this the engineers cut power to her nuclear reactor to a tiny fraction of its regular output. The S6G plant was simmering, bubbling softly without the help, and noise, of its cooling pumps.

The crew took it seriously. Even conversations on the already stealthy boat were hushed.

The XO said, "Speed's coming down."

"Range one hundred forty yards."

The captain interpreted the Crazy Ivan as a personal challenge; a round two in which he, the champ, had already lost round one.

Two could play the game rough, he thought. He was going to let Red Two get real close, and then ping him, full power, on active sonar. It was known as a YANKEE-Search, and Von Suskil was relishing the chance for a little payback. "Sonar?"

"Still in the turn, sir. Range one hundred yards. No pinging." He paused. "Still turning into us. I have target spread." The display before him showed the submarine as a real object, looming bigger by the second. "He's still turning. Target will pass under us."

The exec said, "I hope so."

"Range fifty yards."

"Very well, Sonar. We'll let him reverse under us, then we'll turn after him. Power up the active set. We'll give him one ping. Maximum power. We're going to rattle his fillings and empty his bladder."

"Captain. Red Two's passing underneath. She's close. I mean, she's way too—"

"Just keep your shirt—" But he stopped. What the devil was that sound? He looked around at the other men in the attack center.

They'd heard it, too.

K-219

In compartment four, Weapons Officer Petrachkov felt the sudden onset of the Crazy Ivan and grabbed at the catwalk railing.

Voroblev said, "What's he—"

An instant later the water-level alarm shrieked. Petrachkov stood there for a moment, stunned, then looked at the gauge for silo six.

It showed forty liters. Full.

"Pump it!" Voroblev shouted.

He screamed to the missilemen below. "Pump silo six now!" Then he vaulted down the ladder to help line up the valves and pumps. He landed on his knees and frantically spun the valves on the suction line, then slammed his fist into the black rubber start button on the pump. It started to whir.

He jumped to cut off the alarm. As he did, he saw the chemical-fume detector at full deflection, redlined. A new alarm began to sound.

Seawater and missile fuel had found one another. Nitric acid was the result. Acid that even now could be eating into the pressurized vitals of the RSM-25 rocket. An explosion could happen any second.

Only venting the missile tube to the sea could save them.

Petrachkov grabbed the intercom microphone. "Control! This is Petrachkov in four! We have a major seawater leak in tube six! There's gas! I have to vent it! Give us fifty meters! I'm disengaging the hatch cover!" He threw the *kashtan* down. He threw open the panel on the missile tube control board, flipped open the red switch cover marked Six, and turned the red handle inside.

Outside on the pressure hull, high-pressure air began to turn the missile-hatch cover mechanism to the unlocked position. The chemical-fume alarm was blaring. Petrachkov listened for the rumble of air escaping the open hatch. It didn't come. "All of you!" he shouted to the stunned missilemen. "Put on your masks now! Get them on!"

At the bottom level smoking cubicle, the executive officer sprinted forward to his battle station in the central command post. Markov, the communications officer, lingered slightly too long. He didn't make it to the hatch before all watertight hatches were sealed. It clanged shut in his face. The two lounging cooks vanished back aft to compartment five. Voroblev, the damage control specialist, stood by silo six at the upper level, his hand on the cold steel.

The process of opening the silo's muzzle hatch was automatic. Once begun it could not be stopped. But it took five minutes to complete. It was 0532, Moscow time.

"General Alarm!" Britanov shouted, all thoughts of the American submarine gone now. "Make depth for fifty meters!"

The planesman pulled his joystick back, heading the submarine up as sharply as she'd dived not a few moments ago. The hull creaked, her bulkheads groaned as the crushing pressures shifted.

———

Political Officer Sergiyenko was holding on to the hatch coaming leading into the mess area for dear life as the submarine planed steeply
up. He could hear the engines laboring, the propellers speeding. He
could hear the alarm from somewhere forward.

Forward was compartment four, the missile room.

The deck slanted up alarmingly. Suddenly, on the far side of the
mess deck, the hatch to the missile room slammed open and Weapons
Officer Petrachkov appeared along with Lieutenant Markov.

"Gas! Everyone clear out of here now!" He dove back into compartment four. Markov remained in the mess area.

After a stunned second, the sleepy men bolted from the mess, heading aft, away from the missiles, nearly trampling the political officer
as they ran. Sergiyenko knew he should do something, that he should
somehow take command. He was a representative of the Party, after
all. But the words wouldn't come, nor would his feet obey him. He
was frozen, panicked.

Captain Britanov's voice exploded over the intercom. His tone was
completely different from the one he used in drills. It terrified Sergiyenko.

"Battle stations! Battle stations! Toxic gas in silo six! This is not a
drill!"

The submarine was still pointed uphill when a massive detonation
boomed through the hull. The lights blinked out at once. The battle lanterns flickered and once again went black. The deck fell away beneath
Sergiyenko's feet as the boat stopped its rise and began, instead, to dive.

As he held on to the edge of the hatch, he could hear water rushing
in someplace nearby, flooding this dark, doomed pipe plunging out of
control to the bottom of the sea.

The rolling detonation blasted the partially open missile hatch open
and reverberated like thunder through the wounded submarine. The
command post battle lamps remained lit.

Britanov had to hold on to a steel handle to keep his feet beneath him; the deck was plunging at an acute angle.

"Planes full up!" he ordered.

"Depth one hundred meters." The planesman had the joysticks full back, trying to arrest the dive. "My planes are full up. No response."

"Engines!" barked Britanov. "Turns for twenty knots! No. Make that all ahead full, both engines."

"All ahead full!"

Navigator Aznabaev heard the shouts, the alarms. He felt the steepness of the dive, the creaks and groans of steel squeezed by the increasing water pressure.

"Two hundred meters, Captain," said the planesman. "Still diving."

"Get ready to blow all tanks—"

"Depth two hundred and forty meters!"

How deep would they go before they pulled out—

"Three hundred meters, Captain!"

The navigator's hands shook as he plotted their position from the inertial navigation system: four hundred fifty miles miles northeast of Bermuda.

It was 0538 Moscow time, and *K-219*, oldest member of the NAVAGA class of ballistic-missile submarines still in operation, had just hours to live.

CHAPTER 5

I was standing right next to silo six when
it exploded. It practically went off in my face.
For the next twenty seconds I was sure
we would split up and go straight to
the bottom.

—*Senior Lieutenant Sergei Voroblev*

The chemical explosion inside silo six ejected the smashed remains of
the RSM-25 rocket and its two warheads into the sea. Some of the
high explosive surrounding the warheads' plutonium cores also deto-
nated, scattering radioactive debris both into the ocean and down the
shattered silo. The blast caused the silo's thick steel skin to split like
an overripe banana. A cataract of seawater, plutonium fragments, and
spilled missile fuel roared through the fissure. Its thunder drowned
the screams of men and the groans of the hull as *K-219* plunged out
of control. The bottom of the Hatteras Abyss lay three and a half miles
below her keel.

The battle lamps in compartment four came on automatically at the
loss of main power. But almost at once they began to dim.

81

Two missilemen from the mid-deck scrambled down the ladder to the lower level to get away from the site of the explosion and the high-pressure stream of water. But down at the bottom near the officers' smoking cubicle, the water was already to their knees. Above it swirled an acrid brown vapor. The two missilemen started to cough, then retch. Both men snatched at their waist pouches and pulled out their masks. They managed to get them on and plugged into the central oxygen manifold as the water rose around their legs. Clean oxygen began to flow, but they had breathed too much of the strange brown mist. Their lungs began to fill with mucus, the wet tissues seared by nitric acid. A green foam flecked with red blood rose up their throats. First one, then the other, fell unconscious to the deck.

USS *AUGUSTA*

The sonar chief was checking his recording of the *K-219* encounter when the explosion blanked out his receivers. The system automatically turned the hydrophone array down to protect itself.

As the reverberation of the blast died away, he heard the chilling sound of water rushing into a hollow tube.

"Conn! Sonar! Transient! Transient! Red Two just flooded a silo!"

"Silo or torpedo tube?" Von Suskil shot back. The difference was significant. A missile meant he would fire a Mark 48 at the boomer *right now*. Every bird he stopped by killing Red Two might mean a whole city saved back home. A missile meant war. A torpedo tube meant only that war was possible. Doctrine gave the enemy the first shot.

The sonar chief watched his display. There were now two objects in the sea. Two targets, where there had just been one. "Sir! Sonar. I have separation. Red Two's diving but... *Jesus!* That's a Russian missile!"

"Ready tubes three and four! Use our last firing solution!" said Von Suskil. They'd had Red Two in their sights for a long time. Long enough to take him out with a snap shot.

"Pressure's equalized. Three and four are ready!"

"Flood three! Flood four! Fire—"

"Wait!" cried the sonar chief. "It's just hanging there! I say again, there's no ignition. The missile's just *floating!*"

K-219

"Helm!" Britanov shouted. "Full speed on both engines!"

"Sir! Engines are both full! We're only making fifteen knots!"

"Depth now three hundred fifty meters!"

Fifteen knots? Why so slow? They needed speed to energize the diving planes. Something was slowing them down. Drag? A propeller problem? There were too many possibilities and no time to figure it out. "Blow the bow tanks."

"Blowing bow ballast!"

A *whoosh* came from the forward ballast tanks as high-pressure air forced out seawater. In theory, it would raise the bow and permit the engines to pull the sub out of its dive. Britanov swayed as he held on to a steel handle. The submarine was shuddering violently as engine rpm surged. Steam from one reactor was driving both screws.

The planesman had the joystick that controlled the planes full back. The depth gauge raced in reverse. "No response!"

K-219 still had its bow pointed at the bottom.

"Gennady!" Britanov shouted to the propulsion engineer. "I need the port reactor on-line!"

"I'm already working on it," said the unflappable Kapitulsky. The blast had spun the propulsion engineer in his swivel chair away from the main reactor control panel. It left him facing a depth gauge which did not contain good news. The starboard reactor was feeding maximum steam pressure to both turbines. But he could double the amount of power by bringing the port reactor on-line. It was a process that normally took five hours, but that was only if you wanted to do it safely. He was cutting corners with every switch, every button, every valve he operated.

Kapitulsky knew the port reactor's power might be needed, and very soon.

He continued the sequence, his hands flying over the panel even before his brain knew what it was he was pushing, pulling, and switching. He activated the primary and secondary coolant heaters, then before the necessary temperature rise, he punched the button that started the reactor's electric circulator pumps.

An alarm went off. The coolant was still too cold. Thermal shock had split more than one reactor and had killed more than one Soviet sailor. But that was theoretical. *K-219* had more immediate concerns.

"What's wrong, Gennady?" Britanov called.

"Don't worry about it!" It was just a reactor alarm, a sound that would have sent men running anywhere but here. He selected the first bank of reactor quench baffles, the control rods used to smother the nuclear fires, and commanded them to retract.

Glowing in the light of the battle lamps, a beautiful woman in an ad for French lingerie gazed down on him like an angel. Did angels really look like that? As he raised the second bank of quench baffles, he realized that he might just have an opportunity to find out.

Alarms were being triggered in the central command post too fast to respond to them; the port reactor was too cold, there were fumes invading compartment four. The newest one warned of radiation in the missile room. That meant the blast had destroyed at least one of the RSM-25 rockets, and its plutonium warheads were scattered in pieces inside the submarine. Plutonium was the most deadly poison known to man, though at the moment Britanov doubted they'd live long enough to die from it.

"Depth three hundred eighty meters!"

Britanov's brain was mired, the images came too fast, his reactions too slow. He sensed the first tendrils of surrender. The feeling those lost in the snow sometimes had, when the endless white is like a warm feather bed, beckoning you down to rest, to sleep, to give in. It wasn't going to work. They were sinking deeper and deeper; the flood of water he could hear from where he stood would get worse as the outside pressures on the hull increased. At some point, the sea would simply crush them.

Britanov looked up at the small framed plaque that had caused so much consternation to the boat's political officer. *Submarine Life Is Not a Service, But a Religion.* No. He could not surrender. Not yet. This was his command. These men were his responsibility. He'd vowed to bring them home alive.

The dive made Britanov light on his feet in just the same way a dropping elevator gave the illusion of no gravity. It was like floating, floating upward even as ten thousand tons of low-magnetic steel and 119 men plunged deeper into the lightless deep.

"She's still going down!"

"Captain!" called the planesman, panic in his voice.

Britanov looked up. The CCP watch all stared at him. Sonar, the planesman, Helm. Everyone. "All right," he said. "Blow the tanks."

"Which tanks do you—"

"Everything!" he ordered. *"Blow all tanks! Emergency surface!"*

Britanov didn't know how much water she had taken in through compartment four. He didn't know whether blowing all ballast would be enough to offset the damage. It might take every liter of high-pressure air they had. For all he knew the lines themselves were ruptured and all he would accomplish was pumping precious air into the sea. But he had to try. He would not surrender. He would fight.

All that was left for him, for his crew, was to wait and see if it would be enough.

In compartment four, Missile Officer Petrachkov fought his way through a torrent of cascading water to the mid-deck intercom station to report the damage from the explosion. He was soaked to the waist and breathing heavily. At some point he must have noticed the strange smell; a sharp, acid odor mixed with the sickly sweet scent of bitter almonds. In the dim light cast by the few working battle lamps, swirling brown mist hung low to the decks, curling evil tendrils up and into the main air vents.

He began to cough. Petrachkov didn't need the damage control officer to tell him what had happened. The brown mist was spilled missile fuel reacting with seawater. He was splashing through an appalling cocktail of flammable poison. And the scent of bitter almonds was nitric acid. Petrachkov pulled a rubber mask from his waist pouch and put it on. He tried to plug the end of the hose into the central manifold, but for some reason he was having trouble seeing it.

The coughing became worse. He yanked the hose out and tried to screw the fitting onto his OBA canister. He gasped, then retched. First it was dry heaves, then wet, then burning, then agony. He staggered against a bulkhead as an evil green foam rose from his lungs and filled his throat with fire. He opened his mouth and the green bubbles flowed into his mask. He was drowning, drowning, not from the sea but from the foam filling his lungs, his throat, his nostrils. He spat it out but more came. Petrachkov couldn't breathe. He sank to his knees below the intercom as the last dim battle lamp winked dark.

In compartment five, immediately aft of the flooding missile room, Dr. Igor Kochergin picked himself up off the deck. The explosion had tossed him out of his bunk and thrown him against the ceiling of sick bay. He ended up huddled against the forward bulkhead, the one separating his cabin from whatever was happening in the missile room.

For ten seconds the deck dropped from under him. He could hear the loud creaks and groans as the submarine's skin and bulkheads were squeezed by building water pressure. The lights were out, the battle lamps dead.

The twenty-eight-year-old lieutenant from Leningrad pushed away from the bulkhead. He hunted in the dark for his slippers, feeling the strange way the deck plates were now no longer flat, but buckled upward. He could still hear the roar of water flooding into compartment four as well as the clank and thud of the engines from astern.

He found his slippers and put them on, then sat back against his bunk in the darkness, his brain mired in shock at the nearness of death. Miraculously, the sick bay battle lamp switched itself on.

Although it was the doctor's first submarine cruise since graduating from Naval Medical School, he could tell from the strange sensation of falling that the submarine was diving more steeply than he had ever felt it dive before. He knew from training that the water would crush them eventually, perhaps at a depth sufficient to compress the remaining air pockets and ignite them in a flash of fire. To be incinerated at the bottom of the sea, that was surely a curious way to die. He stared dumbly, his eyes hollow. Only after a few moments did his brain register what he was looking at.

His desk drawer hung open, pulled out by the submarine's acute dive. But on top of the desk stood a small glass dish with a sprig of evergreens in it, unmoved by blast or the steep deck angle. His eight-month-old son had given him the tiny branch the day they'd sailed from Gadzhievo and he'd kept it fresh for nearly a month. He could hear his voice, see his wife, Galina, their apartment in a gray concrete complex that overlooked the harbor, and from which you could sometimes see the mouth of the fjord itself. All from this tiny piece of green. In some way he did not understand, it gave him courage.

He stood, sliding on the angled, buckled deck, and started putting sick bay back together. The cabin was the size of a dentist's operating room. He closed his desk and locked it shut, opened his medical kit, found his supply of OBA canisters and rubber fume masks, and spread all the equipment he thought he might need out on his bunk. When his assistant, a conscript with barely six months' training, came in looking pale, Dr. Igor Kochergin was ready for customers.

USS *AUGUSTA*

"Jesus!" said Sonar as he listened, his mouth open, while the submarine he thought of as Red Two, the enemy, continued its dive. He'd heard the first ballast tank blow in an explosion of bubbles, followed by the fireworks snap and crackle as the weight of the sea collapsed them. He also knew that it had done Red Two not the slightest good. "Conn, Sonar," he said. "Red Two's still diving. I have hull-flooding noise. She's still got her engines turning, but—" He stopped, listening on the big earphones. "Sir, she may be breaking up. That missile just dropped out of sight."

Captain Von Suskil thought, Serves the bastards right, coming here with an old boat like that. "Sonar, mark that missile drop. We may want to take a close look at it later. Helm, all stop."

"All stop," the helmsman repeated.

"Speed's coming down," the XO announced.

Terrible sounds came in over the astonishingly sensitive hydrophones mounted on *Augusta*'s spherical bow. The sonar operator listened, wondering whether he really wanted to hear what would come next: the groan, the straining of steel under immense pressures, the sudden crack of structural failure, the roar of implosion. They could hear dinner plates dropped onto a deck. Would sounds rise from the throats of a hundred doomed men? The new ears they'd installed at Groton were good, and maybe too good.

Captain Von Suskil stood in the attack center. It was dead quiet. They'd all heard the muffled rumble of the explosion; it had sounded close enough so that for an instant, Von Suskil feared his own boat had suffered a mechanical casualty. They'd felt the ice of the words *missile silo flooded*. They'd heard the throb of the enemy's engines as they suddenly speeded up like a hooked fish running for its life. How deep would they get before they were crushed? "Sonar? Put it over up here. I want to listen to this."

"Aye aye." The chief sonar man also switched on a tape recorder. This was one for the books.

Von Suskil put on a pair of earphones and listened to the direct sonar input. There was the clank and thud of Red Two's engines, the whine of turbomachinery, but there was something else, too. Something ominous.

Red Two was flooding. He could hear the gurgle and roar of the leak, and the popping hiss of escaping bubbles streaming up from a hull rupture. That sound meant that men were dying. Men like himself, like his crew, except that they were the enemy. Russians. *Wonder what blew?* If it was a reactor casualty, the beaches along the east coast would see some contamination, no doubt about it. The currents here all ran strongly north by northwest. It would send a radioactive plume from the Carolinas to Canada. *Hell of a flap.* Look at Three Mile Island. Von Suskil had lived not far from the plant. People went berserk, and nothing much had been released from that accident. This would dwarf it. Wonder how many people would die?

Like Chernobyl, only right in the middle of the Gulf Stream.

If it was a mechanical casualty and not the reactors, then all bets were off. So close to U.S. bases, it wouldn't take long to go down and pick through what was left. Not long at all. They'd done it in the middle of the Pacific with that old GOLF boat. The *Glomar Explorer* was still around, available for work. This was in our own backyard. Would pieces of a YANKEE be interesting? *Maybe.*

Even if Von Suskil had felt more sympathy, he was professional enough to know there was nothing at all he could do for them. Nothing.

"Conn, Sonar. He's still making fifteen knots, still—" But then he stopped. "Wait one." A new rumble came in over the hydrophones, a rumble mixed with a powerful *whoosh*. "Sir, I think Red Two just blew her tanks. Sounds like she blew everything."

The captain heard it, too. All her high-pressure air, thought Von Suskil. You didn't do that unless there was no other choice. Use up all your pressure and maybe you'd win enough buoyancy to stop your dive. You'd bob to the surface like a piece of Styrofoam and that would be the end of a nuke boat's patrol and probably the captain's career.

Surfacing off the enemy's beach, out-of-control, was, to a submariner, like a surface commander driving a destroyer onto a sand bank. For the Soviet crew that meant a voyage to Siberia, though Siberia was a lot better than the bottom of the Hatteras Abyss.

He wondered if the Soviets ran things the same way as the U.S. Navy. *Probably.* The problem was, if blowing all your tanks didn't work, if it didn't arrest your dive, you had nothing left to work with. Nothing left at all. That had happened to a couple of American boats. *Thresher,* most recently. They'd lost their reactor in a dive and had no power and not enough high-pressure air to come back up. The Navy had visited the wreck with deep-diving submersibles and Von Suskil had seen some of the pictures. They weren't the kind of thing a man who makes his living underwater wants to see.

"Still diving, still accelerating," said Sonar. He watched the big reel-to-reel tape spin round and round. The faster you went, the more power your control surfaces had to arrest the dive. But the faster you went, the more depth it took to turn the bow around. At some point the two curves met and you'd better be above crush depth when they did. In a whisper he added, "I don't think he's going to make it."

Von Suskil didn't need to hear any more. He put the headphones away. "Very well. Helm, come to antenna depth," he said. "I think it's time we phone this one in."

"Antenna depth, aye."

A tiny shift of ballast, a small deflection of the control yoke, and *Augusta* began to slowly plane up toward the moonlit waves.

The sonar chief listened as the sounds from far below grew fainter. What a nightmare. To hear the deaths of— He stopped, cocked his head, then adjusted the filters that washed the desperate noises coming in through the hydrophones. The thrum and beat of Red Two's engines were different. It was subtle, true, but recognizing the almost imperceptible differences between one sound and another was exactly what they paid him for. He kept listening, then nodded.

"Conn! Sonar."

"What is it now?" said Von Suskil. He sounded annoyed at the interruption.

"It's Red Two!"

"Is she gone?"

"No! She's—" He stopped, ran up the volume, then smiled. "She's coming back up!"

CHAPTER 6

I was suddenly aware that I was shouting
with the full force of my lungs.
I was holding the microphone so hard
it was like I wanted to kill it. My knees
felt weak, my bowels relaxed. Thank God
I didn't foul my uniform in front of the whole
watch team.

—*Captain Igor Britanov*

"Captain! Helm is answering!"

"Depth now three hundred fifty meters."

"Mother of God," someone whispered. *"We're going up!"*

A cheer went up in the central command post. But Britanov knew it was premature. New alarms were still going off. The precise nature of the explosion was not yet identified, and they were still taking on water. But it was no small victory that the bow continued to rise under the influence of the pounding screws and the fully deflected diving planes.

"Where's Voroblev?" Britanov demanded. He needed his damage control specialist at his side.

"Compartment four, Comrade Captain," said someone. "Petrachkov called for him."

Compartment four. Was Voroblev even alive? Was Petrachkov? What had happened to his submarine? The fume alarm meant a chemical explosion had taken place. The radioactivity alarm meant the blast had damaged at least one of *K-219*'s fifteen missiles. The water meant a hull breach. Fumes, plutonium, and flooding. If even one of those was true it was too soon for cheering.

With one hand holding on to the steel handle to keep his balance, Britanov grabbed the *kashtan* microphone and tried to calm his breathing and his voice before he spoke. He took a long, deep breath, then let it out.

"This is the captain. All compartments report! Set the emergency damage-control bill! Report from compartment four!" The words came automatically, without any thinking, the result of years and years of practice and drilling, all against a moment like this. But those were drills.

"Compartment one is manned and ready," came the quick reply from the forwardmost space. "No damage, no casualties."

"Two is manned and ready and very busy just now," said Propulsion Engineer Kapitulsky. "You'll have more power soon if we don't blow up or sink first."

"Helm?"

"Depth two hundred meters, Captain. Still rising. Speed eighteen knots."

The CCP watch team was beginning to function again. "Keep us heading up. All the way." Not that he could stop them. With her ballast tanks filled with air, nothing could keep them from bobbing to the surface now. It was the end of the patrol for certain. The only thing that remained to be seen was whether they could save the boat, and to see what the butcher's bill already totaled.

"Compartment four, report," he said.

There was no reply.

"Compartment four, answer."

"They must have evacuated it," said someone.

Britanov nodded, but he was thinking of the blast, the flooding. There could be twenty men inside compartment four. More if some off-duty crew were caught in there. How many of them were—

"One hundred meters depth, Captain."

The bulkheads creaked and groaned as the sea's fist slowly relaxed. Dust rose into the air, and loose gear not already knocked to the deck by the blast and the dive slid off in a clatter. The battle lamps blinked.

Chief Engineer Krasilnikov swore as his hands flew over the main power distribution panel. The lights faded, then brightened, then faded, as though trying to decide whether to fail.

Please, thought Britanov. *Not now. Don't die.*

"There!" said Krasilnikov as he lined up his switches. He threw a final one and the CCP's main lights came on strongly. The battle lamps winked out.

"Well done, Grandfather!" Britanov clapped him on the back.

"Depth fifty meters."

Almost periscope depth. Why wasn't he getting damage reports from aft? Had he lost communication with the rest of the submarine? Were they all dead? Why—

The rising submarine broached the surface like a missile fired from underwater. The bow rose, rose, then in a huge wave of white water, the ten-thousand-ton vessel stopped, and slowly slid backward.

The world seemed to tumble inside the CCP. If Britanov had let go of the handle he would have been dashed first against the overhead, then the rear bulkhead. He rode the violent rocking and rolling, feeling each motion slightly less than the one before.

"Engines all stop!"

"All stop!"

The lights flickered once again, but came back burning more brightly.

K-219 was on the surface under the stars, rolling in the low seas, her weather deck nearly awash, a black, smoking shape darker than the moonlit waves.

"I need damage reports. Someone go aft and find out what's happened," said Britanov. "And stop those damned bells!"

The alarms went off one by one. Then it was strangely quiet except for the normal hum of machinery.

It was 0540 Moscow time; just two minutes since the explosion. Two minutes for *K-219* to die, and to be reborn.

USS *AUGUSTA*

The stealthy American attack sub hung just below the surface, making only enough speed to maintain constant depth.

"Conn, Sonar. Red Two is on top. Range six hundred yards, bearing one four two. Lots of machinery noises. He's running both his plants. He'll never hear us."

I'll be damned, thought Captain Von Suskil. *The bastard made it.* "What speed? What course?"

"No bearing change, sir. He's dead in the water."

What was Red Two doing? They'd heard an explosion, seen a missile pop out of a silo, then sink. They'd listened as the Soviet boomer plummeted to almost certain destruction, then rose as fast as she had dived. She was now sitting on top. Was it something like a missile blowing up, or was it the high-explosive shell of a nuclear weapon? He wouldn't put it by the damned Reds to let a warhead blow up accidentally. They were mighty careless. Thank God it was just a low-order explosion and not the nuke; if it had been, they would have vaporized a few cubic miles of ocean, and *Augusta* would have gone along for that ride.

It could even be a mutiny. Maybe someone tried to fire one of those goddamned missiles and the range safety package went off first. Could she be getting ready to let another missile go even now? "Helm," he said, "let's get some distance. I want to open the range in case they want to fire again. All ahead two-thirds."

"Engines are answering. All ahead two-thirds."

When *Augusta* had moved off to a safer distance, Von Suskil said, "Come to heading three three five. Up the attack scope."

A quartermaster's mate got behind the rising instrument and dropped the handles into place. Von Suskil stepped up and turned until he had the low, alien shape of a Soviet conning tower in his crosshairs. The image was electronically enhanced, brightened so that by the light of the low moon, Von Suskil could make out the plume of smoke. At first it made his heart race. Smoke could be from a missile taking off. But it wasn't that dense, it wasn't that white. It looked a purple-brown in the image-intensified view. "He's burning," he said at last. "I have smoke from aft of the sail."

"The missile compartment," the XO whispered. "That's happened before."

"Looks like it happened again." He swung the crosshairs back to center the enemy's conning tower. "Bearing and . . . *mark!*"

"Sir?" said the XO, confused. What was he doing working up an attack solution on a burning—

"I said, bearing and mark!"

The quartermaster squeezed the button on his pickle, transmitting the precise bearing to the Mk 117 fire-control computer. "Angle on the bow, port fifteen," he told Von Suskil.

A fire-control technician punched in the data. "Solution set."

"Ready tubes three and four. If he looks like he's going to flip another missile, I want to be ready to take a snap shot at him."

"Didn't you say Red Two was on fire?" the XO asked Von Suskil at last.

Von Suskil watched the smoke billow from the wounded sub. He slapped the handles back down and the instrument slid down into its well. "He may be on fire. It may be a ruse. I'm not in this business to take that kind of a chance. If he so much as opens one of those muzzle hatches, I'm taking this joker down."

Von Suskil turned to the communications officer. "Comm, get ready to send a contact report to COMSUBLANT. Report reads as follows." He dictated to the comm officer.

"Got it," said the comm officer. "How do you want it signed?"

"Sign it *Caesar Augustus*." It was the name Von Suskil had taken, even to the point of having it made into a decorative plaque and mounted on the door to his cabin.

In Norfolk, a teletype began to chatter noisily in the heavily guarded headquarters of the Atlantic submarine fleet; an inner sanctum even the regular Navy could not easily visit. The message read:

FLASH/CRITIC

SECRET CRITIC

RAINFORM RED

BT

AAA//RED TWO

BBB// 30–43 N

CCC// 54–27 W

DDD// 030338Z OCT86

EEE// CONTACT SUFFERED MAJOR UNEXPLAINED

    EXPLOSION. CONTACT ON SURFACE FIGHTING

    FIRES AND FLOODING. AM STANDING CLEAR

    OF CRITICAL ZONE PENDING FURTHER

    ORDERS. UNODIR WILL MAINTAIN COVERT

    SURVEILLANCE—CAESAR

Britanov was about to go back into compartment four to see for himself what had happened when the squawk of a man speaking through a heavy rubber mask came in over the *kashtan*.

"Compartment four . . . heavy fumes. Heavy fumes in here!"

"Who's reporting?" Britanov demanded. "Petrachkov?"

"Petrachkov is . . . there's fumes. He's . . . he's unconscious."

The intercom went dead for a moment, then another voice came on.

"Compartment five manned and ready," said Dr. Kochergin. "I can go forward into four if you want, sir. I have no communication with anyone in there, though."

The first voice came back. "We're in here! It's hot! It's hot in here. Water . . . there's smoke and fumes everywhere! Request permission to evacuate compartment four!"

Smoke, heat, and fumes. A missile-fuel accident for certain, and perhaps a fire, thought Britanov. Petrachkov was unconscious, but Dr. Kochergin was ready to treat casualties. Britanov put the mike to his lips. "This is Britanov. All compartments don life-support masks. We'll vent compartment four from here. Doctor, is Voroblev with you?"

"No, sir."

"Then you'll have to do it. When I give the word, I want you to go into four and report to me at once. Make sure everyone's on their OBA. Understood?"

"Understood."

Kochergin slipped on his rubber mask, checked to make sure the air bladder was inflated, then joined Security Officer Valery Pshenichny at the sealed hatch leading into the stricken missile compartment. A gauge mounted on the bulkhead showed the pressure differential between four and five was high, but coming down slowly. Tons of air pressure locked the watertight hatch in place. The seal could not be broken until pressures inside the two compartments were roughly equal. The door would not operate.

The doctor felt the need to do something. He found the *kashtan* hanging by the hatch and dialed Kapitulsky. "This is Kochergin in five. Are there any casualties forward?"

"We're all right," said the busy propulsion engineer. "But I'm getting some strange readings from four."

"Strange?"

"Radiation. Make sure you're protected before you go in."

The doctor hung the mike back up and looked at the security officer. There were no antiradiation suits in compartment five.

"Where's Voroblev? We need him. What do we do?" the doctor asked the security officer.

"Take your pulse, Doctor, and calm down. There are procedures for this. We'll follow them." Pshenichny was the senior officer in compartment five; maybe, depending on who was still alive, the ranking officer in the entire rear half of the boat. Even though he was a KGB man, Pshenichny had completed submarine training and earned the honor of being a qualified watch officer. He'd served aboard several Gadzhievo submarines and the crew respected him in a way it did not respect *Zampolit* Sergiyenko. That he shared their disdain for him and made no attempt to hide it only left Pshenichny more popular with the crew.

"There's radiation," said Kochergin.

"We'll follow procedures, but we'll follow them fast. Agreed?"

The doctor swallowed. "Agreed."

The gauge on the bulkhead now showed zero. Britanov's calming voice boomed over the intercom. "Pressures in four and five are equalized. Open the hatch and evacuate those inside to sick bay. Look for Petrachkov."

"You're ready?" asked Pshenichny. "What's your pulse?"

"Offscale," said Kochergin. He reached for the bar that would unlock the hatch. He noticed the silver glint from the security officer's
open collar. A chain. From that chain dangled one of the three keys
necessary to launch *K-219*'s missiles. Britanov had one and so did
Sergiyenko. Nuclear missiles meant to destroy people Kochergin didn't
know, men and women he didn't have anything against, really. Those
overaged, obsolete, dangerous damned missiles. They were why they
were here. Why, the doctor was now quite sure, men on the other
side of the steel barrier were dead and dying. He swung the lock bar
down and opened the hatch.

Sergei Voroblev, the damage control officer, nearly fell through the
opening. He was staggering under the weight of a body in his arms.
He was wearing his OBA, at least. The doctor only gradually recognized the body as Markov, the sub's communications officer. Markov
was not wearing any protective gear at all. His face and uniform were
flecked with green foam. Five more men of the missile crew followed
them, all of them wearing masks.

"Take Markov to sick bay!" Kochergin shouted through his OBA
mask.

Beyond the open hatch, compartment four was dim, filled with a
thick brown mist and eerie with the sound of dripping water. There
was a sizzling hiss Kochergin could not quite identify. Like meat
frying in a cast-iron pan. He turned to Pshenichny. "I'll take the mid-
deck. You go up. Petrachkov is there someplace."

Together they gingerly stepped inside the damaged space. Kochergin was first. Not two steps in he stumbled against something soft on
the deck. He looked down, shining his explosion-proof lamp to see
what it was.

He'd stepped on a sailor lying on his back, his fingers clutched
tightly against his throat as though he were trying to rip away the
skin. His mask was partly on, but all around it oozed a flood of bright

green foam. It dripped onto the deck. Kochergin had slipped in it and his own shoe was now covered.

The sailor was drowning in green foam. "It's Kharchenko!" he said to a warrant officer who had just come in the hatch. Kharchenko was on the missile crew. "Help me get him out!"

The sailor's eyes were white, his mouth open. He gasped for breath and foam pumped from his mouth and nostrils. As Kochergin pulled him up from the deck, a huge quantity of it bubbled up and spilled down his chest. Despite his training, the doctor looked away, the bile rising in his own throat. When he looked back down, the sailor was no longer breathing.

They hauled Kharchenko out of compartment four and put him down on the deck just inside five. Kochergin attempted first aid, even injecting adrenaline straight into the heart. But without air there could be no life, and there was no forcing air down the injured man's clogged throat.

Nitric acid poisoning, the doctor knew. The acid had been strong enough to eat away the metal fuel tank of the blasted missile. What would such an acid do to mere lungs? The green foam was a mucus response from inhaling nitric oxide vapor; the vapor, when combined with wet tissue, formed acid. The brown mist. Kochergin looked back into the hatch. He could see tendrils of it snaking their way into compartment five. Even through his mask he could taste the telltale flavor of burnt almonds on his tongue. He let Kharchenko fall limp to the steel deck.

"Doctor! There are more men in here!" the security officer yelled back from the brown, murky space.

He left the dead sailor behind and began to grope his way deeper into the stricken compartment, looking for men he might still be able to save.

It was a war zone in compartment four. Acrid smoke billowed up from the bilges below. It was hot, far too hot for safety. The sizzling sound came from below. Water still dripped from above. Bodies were everywhere. Kochergin counted twelve; it was impossible to know who was dead and who was alive. When the tiny sick bay cabin could hold no more, he ordered the rest laid out like cordwood in the narrow passageway.

Missile Officer Petrachkov was not among them.

Dr. Kochergin's own breathing was becoming labored. He checked his air canister and saw the rubber bag almost deflated. He had little oxygen left, and he had ample proof that the air beyond his mask was lethal. But he couldn't stop. He knew that men might be alive somewhere in the big dark missile room. Men who would die if he didn't find them.

He reentered four and found the ladder leading down to the smoking, hot bilges. His light lanced through clouds of thick brown vapor. There he spotted two more men face down on the deck. He hoisted one to his shoulder and called out above for help. For some reason he looked at his watch. It was 0745.

Someone shouted back a name: *"I have Petrachkov!"*

The missile officer! The doctor hurried up the ladder, or at least he hurried to the extent that carrying a heavy, unconscious man permitted. Kochergin was slightly built; the men joked that his arms were too thin for an injection—the needle would come through. Yet he found the strength to accomplish things his rational mind would have scoffed at as impossible.

Kochergin slid the injured man through the open hatch to compartment five, then turned back as a warrant officer carried Petrachkov by. Like the others, his face was covered in green foam.

Behind them was Pshenichny. He was staggering as he weaved in the direction of the open hatch.

As the doctor watched, Pshenichny collapsed to the deck and began groping at his rubber mask. The bladder feeding it oxygen had collapsed, the canister empty.

Not him, too. Pshenichny had to survive. He was senior officer aft. Kochergin ripped off his own mask and strapped it over the security officer's face. "Breathe!"

Pshenichny's eyes lolled.

"Breathe!" Kochergin grabbed him under the arms and lifted him to his feet. He tried to hold his breath as he dragged him back to the hatch. He nearly made it before his lungs screamed for air, and despite what he knew, despite everything he'd seen, Kochergin opened his mouth and sucked down a gulp of pure poison.

"Port reactor is now on line, sir," said Kapitulsky.

Britanov took the *kashtan* and said, "Compartment four, I need a report!"

A warrant officer surveying the damage reported improved visibility, a large rupture in the top of silo six and poisonous fumes rising from the bilges.

"What about Petrachkov?"

"We just found him. He didn't look good."

"What about the rest?"

"There are many injured. Two dead, I think. I don't know how many. Kochergin has been moving them back to five."

"Where is Kochergin?"

A pause, then, "I don't see him."

"Keep looking. I want everyone moved out and silo six purged. Can you operate the silo flush controls?"

"I don't know . . . I've never done it. I'm not assigned to the missiles, Comrade Captain."

"You are now." The ones who did know how to flush silo six were either dead or incapacitated. He needed to get that poison out of his ship before it killed anyone else.

"I'll go back myself," said Chief Engineer Krasilnikov.

"No. I need you here." Britanov gave Krasilnikov the *kashtan*. "The engineer will talk you through the procedure. In the meantime, rig some fans to blow the fumes away from the hatch to compartment five. *Panyatno?*"

"Da, yest," the warrant officer replied. "Understood."

Britanov paused, then turned to Zhenya Aznabaev, the boat's navigator. "Markov is back there, maybe dead. I need a radio officer more than a navigator."

"I can do it, Captain."

"Good. We have to send a report to fleet headquarters. Request emergency assistance from all units. The preset codes don't cover what's happened. You'll have to send it in the clear."

The young executive officer Vladmirov piped in. "It's against regulations, sir. If we break radio silence with an uncoded message, the Americans will know everything."

"It's against regulations to sink, too," said Britanov. He looked at Aznabaev. "Send it."

CHAPTER 7

The doctor, Kochergin, gave me his mask
when I ran out of oxygen. We were
carrying the injured out of four. He's sick
as hell now, but I owe him my life.

—*Security Officer Valery Pshenichny*

As Krasilnikov talked the men in compartment four through the procedure to flush silo six, the situation aboard *K-219* seemed to stabilize. At least there were no new catastrophes demanding Britanov's attention. After four attempts to attract Moscow's attention to their plight, Navigator Aznabaev finally received a terse, noncommittal acknowledgment from Northern Fleet headquarters in Severmorsk; five minutes later a second reply came from Naval High Command in Moscow.

But fifteen minutes after the warrant officers turned the last valve and then switched on the purging pumps to clear the poisonous brew seething inside the shattered missile silo, it became clear that conditions were far from stable. Gas was once more forming in the flooded bilges below the lower deck in compartment four, awash in both seawater and oxidizer, and the temperature inside had risen to one hundred twenty degrees Fahrenheit. The fourteen other missiles, although apparently undamaged by the blast, could explode if the temperature continued to rise.

"Do you want us to purge the silo again?" asked one of the warrant officers.

"No," said Britanov. "Get out of there and make sure there's no one left behind. We'll try to vent the space to atmosphere."

"There's something burning in there," growled Engineer Krasilnikov. He wanted nothing so much as to go aft and get his hands dirty solving the problem. He knew Britanov was relying on him here in central command, but he didn't like telling others how to do things that he could do better, and faster himself. Getting back there wouldn't be so easy though. Maybe over the deck and down the hatch in ten?

"What about the other rockets?" asked Britanov.

"Who knows?" Krasilnikov answered testily. "We've lost all remote readings from them. But I can feel it. We've got a fire someplace. Most likely it's electrical."

Britanov trusted the engineer's feelings. He was about to order a thorough search of the bilge areas for any sign of flame when the *kashtan* buzzed. It was Pshenichny, the KGB officer.

"Everyone's out of four, Captain. I'm ready to seal the hatch."

"Proceed."

The security officer counted noses a third time—it was too easy to miss someone when everybody wore identical rubber masks—then slammed the heavy metal hatch shut. He spun the locking wheel, then stepped back. At least there was no way the poison could come through solid—

"Look!" said one of the warrant officers. He was pointing at the hatch.

From around the perimeter came a thin stream of brown mist.

"It didn't seal."

They opened it, then closed it more carefully, pulling the locking wheel tighter. The brown mist still seeped around the edges.

When they opened the hatch a third time, Pshenichny took a close look at the rubber seals. They were curled like old, dried meat. The nitric acid from the spilled missile fuel had attacked them. He shut the hatch a final time, then retreated with the other men aft to compartment six. There he reported.

"Fumes now in compartment five, Captain."

"Five? Is the hatch closed?"

"It's coming right through. It's the acid. The seals are damaged."

Britanov unfolded the greaseboard outline of *K-219*. He put a big black *X* across compartments four and five. His command had been cut in two, with no way to send help aft through the missile room, and no way to evacuate the injured forward. Like a train with locked doors, he thought. "What about water? Will it hold?"

"I don't know if the hatch will stop it."

Poison gas, rocket fuel, and seawater. They were eating away at the vitals of his submarine. It was then, at this very moment, that Britanov thought for the first time the problems in compartment four might not be stopped before they consumed the whole boat. If the acid was destroying hatch seals so far from the explosion, what must it be doing to all the cables and controls that pass right by it? Cables that controlled the engines, the missiles, even the reactors. "Pshenichny?"

"Sir."

"There's no way you can move men forward through all that gas. Move everyone back into compartment eight. When you get everyone there, report in. Is Voroblev there?"

"I'm still in compartment six, Captain," said the damage control specialist. "I was in four when it went off."

"What's your best guess of the damage?"

"It was a leaking muzzle hatch. The explosion ripped the silo apart. There's flooding, fire, gas. It's spreading through the hatches, all right. I'm surveying now for gas."

"You heard about the seals?"

"I heard."

"Make your survey and head to eight with Pshenichny." Britanov hung the *kashtan* back up and saw the other men in central command looking at him. "Helm. Make your course zero four five degrees. Gennady!" he shouted at the propulsion engineer. "How much speed can you give me?"

"No more than fourteen knots. If we go any faster we'll take waves over the missile deck. The water will start pouring in again and those seals might—"

"Turns for fourteen knots." He looked at Grandfather Krasilnikov. "We have to isolate four somehow."

"I can repressurize the boat and vent four out to the atmosphere. It might slow the fumes down."

"Do it." Then, into the *kashtan* again, he said, "This is Britanov. Seal all intercompartment hatches now. We're going to pressurize the boat to isolate compartment four."

Krasilnikov set the air controls and looked at Britanov for a signal to activate them.

"Wait," said the captain, "I want to see for myself what we're fighting." He grabbed his oilskins from the hook beside the small framed plaque with the saying that had so upset *Zampolit* Sergiyenko. He went to the ladder leading up to the main hatch. "I'm going to have a look. Interested?"

Krasilnikov was on his feet in an instant. Together they ascended the ladder into the closed bridge, climbed a second ladder, then undogged the main escape trunk hatch.

The sound of the sea echoed down through the open hatch. For the first time since diving off Gadzhievo, Britanov breathed the sweet, salty smell of fresh ocean air. The sky was filled with the first gray light of the new day.

Single file, the two climbed out into the exposed bridge, turned aft, and switched on their portable lamps.

Water sloshed over the missile deck. As each wave cleared, it parted like a curtain around the place where silo six's hatch should be.

"Mother of God."

The hatch was gone and a shiny streak of gouged metal ran aft from it. Something heavy and sharp had cut the rubber coating that plated the missile deck, ripping away the hatch and exposing the underlying metal.

"Captain," said the chief engineer. "It doesn't look so much like a simple explosion."

"What are you saying?"

"It looks like we hit something. Or perhaps something hit us. I've seen damage like this before, but only after a collision."

Britanov swept the dark sea with his lamp. There was nothing out here to hit. Nothing, he thought, except for another submarine.

"Captain!" called up Aznabaev. "New message from Fleet."

"Let's go below," he said to Krasilnikov. "We'll have Pshenichny photograph this when it gets lighter."

Back in the close confines of central command, Britanov read the newly decoded message from Northern Fleet headquarters. Three merchant ships were changing course to render assistance to *K-219*.

Help from a freighter. He was about to comment on how quickly the situation had changed when the damage control officer called in on the intercom.

"I've just completed the damage survey, Captain," said Voroblev. "I started in four and worked all the way aft to ten. There are traces of gas as far as seven."

"Gas is in *seven*? You're sure?"

"Yes, sir. It's bad in four and five, but it's spreading through the boat. There's an electrical problem in four as well. We may have lost some wire bundles in the explosion."

"Which bundles, Voroblev?"

"It's too hot to go down and see. But the reactor control cables run right through the worst area."

"All right. We're going to close everything up and pump some air into four."

"Understood, Captain."

Britanov was about to tell him to check again when the planesman shouted. Everyone in central command stopped and looked at him as he pointed at the overhead ventilator grill.

A thin wisp of brown mist emerged from it, carrying the sweet smell of almonds, of fuming nitrogen tetroxide, of death.

FLEET OCEAN SURVEILLANCE INFORMATION CENTER, NORFOLK, VIRGINIA

The submariners run the show. They know
everything and get everything on a platter.
If you're not in the club, you don't
get anything from them. Nothing.

—*Lieutenant Commander Gail Robinson, USN*

The morning intelligence brief with Admiral Ted Sheafer was half an hour away. Lieutenant Commander Gail Robinson was staring up at the wall-sized chart of the Atlantic Ocean, putting together the overall picture to give the deputy chief of staff for intelligence. She focused on the three Redfleet missile patrol boxes right off the U.S. shore; the so-called depressed trajectory zones from which a missile could put a warhead over Washington in a matter of minutes. A Soviet preemptive strike designed to kill American leaders in one swift stroke would come from one, or all three, of those boxes.

The Russians had been shuffling boats around from one zone to the next. Sometimes there would be one boomer to a box, other days two missile boats would share one zone, leaving the third momentarily empty. Whatever the reason, it made for a fair amount of update activity on the part of the INTEL staff.

There were two distinct FOSIC watch teams: Red for Soviet and Warsaw Pact vessels, Blue for friendly ships. While there were stacks of Red submarines displayed all across the Atlantic, there were no Blue subs shown anywhere. Operations by American missile and attack boats was strictly compartmentalized information distributed on a "need-to-know" basis. The submarine community, or as it was better known, the submarine mafia, made sure that very few people outside the dolphin priesthood had that kind of a need.

Ship positions were plotted by any of several means: direct observation by U.S. forces, satellite imagery, and electronic signal interception. Each time a ship, friendly or enemy, transmitted an electromagnetic pulse, a radar sweep, a radiotelephone message, anything, special "ferret" stations located around the world would record the origin and the direction. The stations themselves resembled giant, circular Stonehenge constructions, though instead of stone the listening stations used antenna arrays. They were sometimes called Elephant Cages. By combining reports from several of these sites, a ship's location could be closely triangulated.

This morning a YANKEE-1 was cruising the northern patrol track five hundred miles off the American coast; a more modern DELTA boat patrolled the middle, with a second DELTA to the far south. Any one of them could launch a missile that would incinerate

Washington, or Norfolk, before a raid warning could be sent. It was why American attack submarines were sure to be in those three zones, too.

She watched as one of the INTEL watch staff walked to the big chart and moved a red symbol from just offshore Havana. The petty officer adjusted the projected track from northeast to something closer to due north. She looked up the vessel in her master log.

The book said she was the freighter *Krasnogvardyesk,* bound for Odessa by way of Gibraltar. She was certainly taking the long way around to the Med.

Why? she wondered. She was going to ask the petty officer what he knew about the freighter's new course—it would take her far from the regular sea lanes—when he began shifting a second red symbol. This one was the container ship *Anatoly Vasiliyev,* southbound from Halifax, Nova Scotia, and bound for Havana.

This vessel's track veered *east.*

Odd. There were no storms, no ships in distress. There was no obvious reason for two ships to suddenly change course and head for a place far from their scheduled destinations, far, indeed, from any port.

And then a third track was changed: the petty officer bent the red tape marking the projected course of the *Fyodor Bredkin,* a freighter bound for the American Gulf Coast. It veered most sharply, almost doubling back on itself, away from the Gulf of Mexico, headed instead for Bermuda.

Three ships. Three new courses. All three freighters Soviet.

"What's happening with those merchants?" she asked the petty officer when he was finished updating the plot.

"I don't know, sir. These three aren't headed where they said they were going."

She could see that. She stepped back from the wall-sized chart and mentally extended the red tapes that marked the three vessel's new courses. They would all end in the northern patrol box occupied by a YANKEE-1 boomer.

"What do we have going on in Bermuda?" she said at last.

"No surface exercises."

"What about submarines? Anything on the YANKEE?"

"No updates."

She was sure the submarine people would know very well where that YANKEE was. "Something's happening out there. I'm going to ask SUBLANT. Maybe I'll get a straight answer."

And maybe they'll pick me to be the next Chief of Naval Operations, thought the petty officer. "Good luck, sir."

"Put those three freighters on a special watch. I want their tracks updated whenever we get a new posting."

"Aye aye."

"And the same for the YANKEE. Who is she?"

"K-219."

Gail Robinson could query the techs at SOSUS over what might be happening out there, but it wasn't usually done except in times of emergency. Ask too many questions and you wore out your welcome fast. That left the submarine mafia.

She walked over to the nearest KY-3 secure phone and dialed the number for her counterpart watch officer at SUBLANT.

"This is Lieutenant Commander Robinson at FOSIC," she said when it was answered. "I've got some anomalous ship movements. Do you guys have something unusual going on northeast of Bermuda?"

"Why?" came the carefully chosen reply.

"Because I have three Redfleet merchants diverting to the northern patrol box. There's a YANKEE in it. The *K-219.* I was wondering if you might know something."

There was a moment's hesitation, then, "Nothing."

"I didn't think so. Thanks anyway." Robinson hung up. Call it situational ESP. Call it experience. Before she suspected there was something odd going on off Bermuda. Now she knew it. In half an hour she would kick it up the line to Admiral Sheafer. He was the fleet intelligence officer. The submariners were supposed to be working for *him*. Let him wrestle with the mafia.

NAVAL HIGH COMMAND HEADQUARTERS, MOSCOW

As Lieutenant Commander Robinson stared at her chart, the chief of the main navy staff, Admiral Makarov, glared at very nearly the same spot on his own wall plot. He had a clearer idea of what was going on, but not much clearer. "It's happening again," he said to Vice Admiral Novoystev, his operations chief. Makarov was muscular and moved with the nimble grace of an ex-boxer. Novoystev was short, lumbering, and portly. Both of them were staff officers with long, successful careers specializing in avoiding fatal mistakes and advancing themselves up the chain of command.

They were waiting together in Makarov's office for the Commander in Chief of the Soviet Navy, Admiral of the Fleet Vladimir Chernavin, to arrive at the emergency command center down in the sub-basement. At last report he was ten minutes out, racing downtown in his Zil limousine.

"We don't know enough to say again or not again," said the operations chief defensively. Any accusation centering on personnel or material failure would be aimed first and foremost at him.

"On the surface, an explosion, gas, a fire. No," said Makarov. "I think we know all that needs knowing. It remains to be seen, my dear Admiral, what there is to do about it. You know this captain?"

"Britanov." It came out a grunt.

"That's all?"

"To be honest, his record is not on the tip of my tongue."

"You gave him his command."

"Let me speak with Rocky before we come to any conclusions." Rocky was their name for Gadzhievo. "I'll speak to Romanov. He'll know Britanov. He's Flotilla *zampolit*."

"A Flotilla *zampolit* will know if Britanov is politically sound. He won't know a damned thing about whether Britanov knows his business in a submarine."

"One must follow the other," said Novoystev. "Of course. Only the best are chosen for command."

Makarov snorted. He resisted asking what the devil such a hero was doing commanding a leaky old tub like *K-219* if he was so good. "Well, he'd better be." He checked his watch. "Time," he said, though he said it the way a prisoner scheduled for execution might greet the rising sun.

Neither admiral was a submariner. Chernavin was and he made no attempt to hide his disdain for officers who had come from the surface navy. Somehow they would have to explain to him that one of his precious little toys was no longer working quite the way it should. Plus they would have to do it in a way that deflected any personal responsibility. They'd survived many disasters: *K-3*, the *K-8*, and *K-19*. They'd even endured the humiliation of watching, helpless, as the Americans sifted through the broken pieces of the *K-129* out in the Pacific with their *Glomar Explorer*. Somehow they would find a way to survive this one, too.

As the two admirals left Makarov's office, they bumped headfirst into Captain Gennady Antonov, a missile engineer sent from the staff Weapons Directorate to brief the brass. A former captain of a NAVAGA-class submarine, he was one of the foremost experts in all the fleet on the RSM-25 missile.

Antonov snapped to attention.

"That's enough of that," said Makarov. "What do you know, Captain?"

"*K-219* is on the surface steaming northeast with casualties, sir. It sounds very much like a fuel-water explosion. As you know, it's happened before. In fact, it happened to this same submarine ten years back. One of her silos is permanently shut from the incident."

"Yes." It was the first Makarov had heard *that,* but he couldn't let Antonov realize that. Admirals were supposed to know everything. But, he wondered, what were they doing flogging battered, explosion-prone subs to the front lines? Subs that had *exploded once already*. He would call it criminal, except that as chief of staff his head would be on the chopping block, too. "Who commands the *K-219*'s weapons section?"

"His name is Petrachkov."

"I suppose he's another perfect example of Soviet man? The best of the best?" He eyed Novoystev. The ops chief looked away.

"Well," said Antonov, "actually, there have been a few problems with Petrachkov."

"Problems?"

Captain Antonov had the missile officer's file already open. He knew every crew, every sub, of the Northern Fleet. He knew how bad the maintenance situation was up there. But rule number one in the Soviet Navy was that you never told the unvarnished truth to an admiral. You had to outline it, then let them think it up themselves. "He's a very hard worker, Admiral, but he seems to have had a string of bad luck."

"What kind of bad luck?"

"Last January during a live-fire exercise Petrachkov barely was able to fire one rocket. And after they did launch, the hatch wouldn't seal properly. They had to return to the yard for repairs."

"I remember something about that . . ." Makarov said. "They steamed to Polyarny on the surface? The captain froze his ass off?"

"Yes, sir. Apparently the captain insisted on standing surface watch alone. They had to thaw him with boiling water to get him down the main trunk hatch."

"Sounds like this Britanov is a loner," Novoystev remarked. "Perhaps the failure was in his leadership. Lev Romanov will be able to shed some light on this."

"Excuse me," said Antonov. "But Romanov is just the Flotilla political officer."

"You don't think the *zampolit* will offer anything useful?" Novoystev looked offended.

Antonov swallowed. He was dangerously close to breaking rule number one. "I'm sure Romanov has a useful view of many things, Admiral. But the inquiry you ordered came up with some specific recommendations as well as findings."

"It did?"

"Yes, sir," said Captain Antonov. "It was a material failure. You remember?"

"Of course."

Antonov breathed a bit more easily. "The Weapons Division hadn't corrected it in time. Actually, we're seeing more of this all the time. Yard work at Gadzhievo is not always the best and there's little time in patrol schedules to get the job done right."

"Responsibility rests always with the captain, young man," Novoystev intoned gravely. "Especially captains with unorthodox views."

Antonov realized he was getting drawn into a fight for which he was unprepared. "Perhaps," he agreed. "In any event, Petrachkov was blamed for being poorly prepared. Captain Britanov spoke in his favor. The Flotilla commander decided to give him another chance."

"Could the hatch have come loose?" asked Makarov. "Everyone knows the yard crews are drunk half the time. The other half they're sleeping."

"The problem in January was with silo eight. The one that blew last night is silo six. The message sent by *K-219* didn't mention the full extent of the damage. We'll know more after a full survey is done."

"This message was sent in the clear," the ops chief noted with a knowing arch of his eyebrows. "No attempt to encode it was made. Is that so?"

"Yes," Antonov admitted.

Novoystev nodded. "You see? If that's not unorthodox then I don't know what is. Britanov could hang for that alone."

"He's on fire, on the surface, Admiral," said Antonov. "American submarines are probably in the area already. Their aircraft will be overhead any minute. Remaining hidden is no longer useful. It's more important to get emergency—"

"The rules are quite specific, *Captain,*" Novoystev replied haughtily. "I find it wise to follow them. Do you?"

"There will be time enough for finding fault," said Makarov. "For now, let's find out what's happening. Perhaps the situation is stabilized. And if it isn't we have two submarines and *Kirov* heading for Bermuda."

The two subs were assigned to screen *Kirov,* but the nuclear-powered battle cruiser and her escorts were still in the Barents Sea.

"*Kirov*'s a long way off, Admiral," Antonov noted. "And the two missile boats have orders to remain hidden themselves."

"I'm aware of the disposition of our forces. Tell me, Captain Antonov." Makarov checked his watch again. "Have you ever briefed the admiral of the fleet?"

Captain Antonov's eyes widened. "Admiral Chernavin? Only once, sir."

"Excellent. Then you've met. Come," he ordered the young missile expert. "You're going to meet him again."

The three officers took the elevator down three levels to the secure sub-basement, then walked the long, carpeted corridor to the Emergency Action Center. It was known as the Sardine Can.

The room was the size of a tennis court, though with a very low ceiling. The walls were pea-green-colored concrete. In the middle was a highly polished circular table with name tags and personal telephones for the officers standing by to brief Chernavin. A red light was illu-minated by the door, indicating that matters of high security were being discussed. It was already dense with cigarette smoke.

The big chart of the western Atlantic loomed from the blue ciga-rette haze. The room fell silent when Makarov entered, then refilled with the buzz of low conversations. The officers present were mainly from Chernavin's staff. The admiral of the fleet had not yet arrived.

"The chief is five minutes out. What's the latest?" one of the staff officers asked as he plucked an open-faced salami sandwich from a tray offered by a steward.

Makarov began by explaining the search-and-rescue forces he'd dis-patched in response to the accident on board *K-219*. Then he decided it was never too soon to play politics. "But the real problem is our operations tempo," he said, pointedly looking at the portly ops chief. *Better all of his head than some of mine,* he thought. "We can barely keep boats on the line by denying rest periods and throwing overhaul schedules out the window. Yard work is deplorable. We've had acci-dents like this before. We're going to have more accidents if we don't slow down."

"Wait. Are we so sure it's an accident?" the operations chief shot back.

"What else could it—" But Makarov stopped. The door to the corridor was flung wide and in marched Admiral of the Fleet Vla-dimir Nikolaevich Chernavin.

Marched was right. Chernavin walked with an exaggerated, upright stance. He was a tall, handsome man and very pale. His iron-gray hair was cut to a bristle on his bony skull. Unlike many senior Russian officers, he carried not a single ounce of fat on him. His chest sparkled with medals. He was one of the original nuclear submariners, having served aboard *K-3* during its record-setting polar cruise. "Stop your bickering and sit down. All of you except Makarov," he commanded in a deep, clear voice. "Now," he said to Makarov. "Continue."

Makarov tensed. "Sir. Captain Britanov was just submerging from copying the broadcast from—"

"Yes, yes, I know what a séance is. I came up from submarines, unlike you. What happened?"

"His number six silo blew. He drove to the surface here," said Makarov, pointing to the chart. "They're fighting fires in compartment four and there's gas at least in four and probably five. I've directed all available forces to the area to conduct—"

"Did he send his emergency burst signal?" Chernavin cut him off.

"No, sir," Novoystev piped in. "He transmitted the message uncoded in the clear." He rolled his eyes at Makarov.

"Why?" Chernavin seemed honestly puzzled.

"Perhaps there wasn't time, Admiral," said Captain Antonov. "Or reason."

"That's against—" Novoystev began to splutter, but Chernavin waved him silent, then faced the fleet's preeminent missile expert. "Who are you?"

"Captain Antonov. I commanded a NAVAGA before coming here last month."

"All right. Then you should know something. Explain yourself."

"Captain Britanov might have believed the loss of the submarine was imminent. He might also know that American forces are already aware of his position and his situation. We believe an American *Los Angeles* is operating in his area. In that case, the welfare of his crew would naturally take precedence over communications security already compromised."

"*Nothing* takes precedence over saving my submarine. If Britanov remembers that we'll see our way through this. I'll be staying in my office until this gets sorted out. I'm supposed to brief General Secretary Gorbachev at noon. I expect to have something useful for him. What forces have been directed to render assistance?" he asked Makarov.

"*Kirov,*" said Admiral Makarov. "Two escorting attack submarines plus two DELTAs already on station."

"*Kirov* won't get there in time and my missile submarines must stay hidden," said Chernavin. "I trust you already thought of that?"

"I've also directed three surface ships to divert to the area."

"Can they accept code materials?"

The room fell silent again. Code materials were supposed to be taken from a sinking warship and kept safe by specially trained security men. Chernavin's question meant he anticipated the loss of *K-219.*

"I thought not. In that case," said Chernavin, "you'd better make sure my submarine gets everything it needs to stay afloat." With that, Admiral of the Fleet Vladimir Chernavin spun on his heel and left.

CHAPTER 8

I opened the hatch for Belikov and then sealed
it behind him. Preminin was right beside me.
After a while Belikov came back. He looked
ready to collapse. I helped him down. When he came to,
he went back into the reactor, this time
with Preminin. They took with them the last
full OBA canisters we had.

—Security Officer Valery Pshenichny

Britanov ordered the pressure increased inside central command. The
flow of poison through the ventilator grille slowed to a thin stream, a
wisp, and then finally stopped. But flushing silo six only made the
situation worse in the missile room. Britanov had no choice but to
order the space abandoned. When Security Officer Pshenichny reported fumes coming right through the dogged hatch leading to compartment five, he ordered that space evacuated, too.

Now, four hours after the initial explosion, as the sun broke the
flat, gray horizon, dense brown smoke had found its way back to the
hatch leading into compartment six, a tightly packed space filled with

reactor controls, steam pipes, and storage lockers. The fumes were briefly stopped by the steel door, but the nitric acid had lost none of its potency. Gas and smoke began to seep through the ruined hatch seals. A seaman wearing an OBA was standing watch. He tried to close the hatch tighter, but when he tightened the locking bars the seals crumbled to powder. Smoke began to pour through, filling the passageway. And something more: seawater was coming over the lower lip of the hatch, flowing unimpeded through the same faulty seals.

"Captain! Smoke . . . smoke and water now in six!" he said into the *kashtan* mounted by the hatch. He'd seen the bodies carried out covered in brown rocket-fuel slime and green foam. Before waiting for an answer, he dropped the microphone and splashed aft. As he ran, he thought for an instant that it was the first time in his young life that he'd ever run *toward* a pair of nuclear reactors in order to feel safe.

Smoke and water in six. Britanov ran his hand over his cheek, feeling the unshaved stubble. How long had he been fighting this battle? It felt like days.

Engineer Krasilnikov was watching him. "Captain? Are you all right?"

He rubbed his eyes to clear away the fatigue. To think. Britanov was trying to save his boat without knowing enough about what was happening to it. He took the greaseboard outline of *K-219* and placed another black *X* on it. That made three uninhabitable spaces: compartment four had blast damage, water, poison gas, radiation, and fire. Five had smoke so there was fire there, too. Now lethal smoke and water were spilling into six.

Three compartments, three deaths. So far. Another dozen or more of his crew were unconscious and some of them would almost certainly die without proper medical care. Kochergin, the boat's only qualified doctor, was one of the casualties. So was his communications specialist, Markov. Where would that medical care come from?

"I'm going up top," he told the chief engineer. He grabbed his oilskin coat and climbed the ladder up to the enclosed bridge. From there he climbed a second ladder, opened the main trunk, and pulled himself wearily up into the clean air.

The morning light was clear and penetrating. Purple-brown smoke billowed up in distinct puffs from the shattered missile silo like the exhaust from an old locomotive. He wondered, Why puffs? Then he saw the reason.

Low seas washed over the missing muzzle hatch in *K-219*'s missile deck. Every time water flowed down into compartment four, the column of smoke stopped. When the silo drained, smoke poured out once more.

Every wave meant more water, more water meant more reacting missile fuel, more weight, less habitable space, and less chance of saving his boat.

The clean air sharpened his thinking, blowing away the mental fog. An alteration began to take hold in Britanov, from trying to save his command at any cost to saving his men and to hell with the submarine. It was a subtle change, something like the way the waves in the fjord at Gadzhievo had become more serious out in the open Barents Sea.

Britanov had always thought of his crew's welfare. Some said he thought too much about it to be an effective commander. Well, perhaps they'd been right. His thinking now was different from what it had been when they first dived off Gadzhievo. Like the waves, it had become more serious.

He took a last breath of clean air, a last look at the light of the new day, and went back below.

"Yevgeny!" he shouted to the senior navigator, and now radio operator as well. "Find out which of those freighters is closest. I want an estimated time of arrival from all three. And let Moscow know we're still on fire with smoke and flooding now in compartment six."

"You want that sent in the clear, Captain?"

"I don't care if you use a semaphore."

His boat had been cut into two and the crew was being cornered, forced aft to escape the spreading damage radiating from the ruined missile room. At some point they would have to stop running. At some point there was nowhere else to go.

Compartment seven contained *K-219*'s reactors. Compartment eight her engines. Nine and ten housed machinery spaces as well as sonar and steering gear. At the submarine's farthest point aft in ten was another escape trunk for the crew.

The poison was herding them to it. "Damage control crews forward to six, I need a report."

A seaman in a full-body protective suit, breathing from his self-contained OBA canister, fought his way through the dim, smoky passageways and reported electrical insulation burning in five and the bulkhead to four black with charred paint and nearly glowing with heat. The deck was awash with brown missile fuel and seawater. His OBA had two cartridges each good for ten minutes of normal breathing. Under the heat and stress the rubber bladder began to collapse after only eight. Britanov ordered him aft to compartment eight to join the rest of the crew.

Britanov took stock. A fire raging unchallenged on the bottom level of the missile room. Progressive flooding spreading through acid-eaten seals. A bulkhead black with burning paint. All remote readings of the fourteen remaining RSM-25 rockets lost with temperatures surely approaching the critical point. At some point the rockets would detonate, cooking off in the heat. When they did there was no way to predict the extent of the blast. Each rocket carried two six-hundred-kiloton thermonuclear warheads.

Engineer-Seaman Sergei Preminin sat at the blinking reactor control console at the aft end of compartment six. The console duplicated the gauges and controls that Kapitulsky had in compartment two. The indicators monitored the health and status of *K-219*'s twin VM-4 reactors.

Right beyond the gray bulkhead, both ninety-megawatt power plants were putting out a sizable portion of their rated energy. A sphere of uranium nuclear fuel initiated a chain reaction, the fission generated heat, and the heat turned water into steam. This steam drove the engines as well as the generators needed to keep the submarine afloat, lit, and supplied with air.

Beside Preminin was his superior, Reactor Officer Belikov. They both wore masks plugged into the boat's central oxygen system. They were the only two nuclear-qualified men in the aft section of the sub.

The sound of pounding feet came from beyond the control space. Preminin's protective mask afforded limited forward vision and no peripheral view at all. He had to turn to see a silver-suited figure dash by, heading aft. The fleeing sailor stopped, turned back, and stuck his head into the reactor control space. "Smoke's coming through from five! There's a big fire forward! You'd better move it!" he yelled, then ran off again.

The twenty-one-year-old sat in silence, wondering why a *fireman* was running and *he* was sitting here. He wanted to run, too. But he had to wait until Belikov gave the word.

It was just his second operational cruise since graduating from engineering school. Sergei Preminin came from a tiny, landlocked village that had only recently seen the advent of electricity. He and his brother had escaped its medieval life by joining the Navy. Preminin worked hard to remain a part of the elite submarine service. He knew what kind of a life waited for him back home. He took his duty very seriously.

He watched the status board, waiting for Belikov to give the order to evacuate. All hell had broken loose inside *K-219*, and the situation was getting harder to understand. Why was gas seeping through closed hatches? Had panicky sailors fled and forgotten to shut them? All Preminin knew for certain was that compartment five was empty and that he and Belikov were now alone in compartment six. After so many days of crowded living conditions, the sudden emptiness was more than a little unnerving.

Lieutenant Belikov reached for his *kashtan*. "Captain. Lieutenant Belikov at station sixty-five. There's smoke reported now in compartment six and a fire, too."

"I heard," said Britanov wearily. "You're on ship's oxygen?"

"Yes, sir. Do you need us to remain here?"

"If it's unsafe you should evacuate to eight. The air still's good back there. Kapitulsky can control the reactors from here. It's your call, Lieutenant. Don't take any chances."

Belikov thought about it for a second, then said, "We're leaving." He hung the mike back up and nodded to Seaman Preminin. "Let's get out of here."

Together they shut down their console, leaving it on automatic status. Belikov took a last look at the gauges; coolant flow was fluctuating more than it should, but then power was being drawn from the reactors for damage control. It wasn't a matter of steady steaming.

They plugged their masks into their OBAs and made their way out into the passageway. A rivulet of seawater was already running aft along the deck. They splashed through it back to the hatch leading into compartment seven, the heart of the submarine. The reactor room.

The compartment was lit only by the dim glow of battle lamps. A minor steam line had ruptured in the initial explosion and it was still venting. Thank God it wasn't part of the primary or secondary reactor steam loops or they'd all be glowing. But it was enough of a leak to fill the air with a mist made even more eerie by the weak orange light given off by the dying lamps.

"It's hot in here," said Preminin as they passed the locked hatches leading to the reactors themselves. He could feel the sweat begin to flow almost at once. It was like stepping into a steam bath.

Belikov put his mask close to one of the remote temperature gauges. His lenses kept fogging. With poison nitric acid gas and smoke from the fires reported, he didn't dare take it off. "Preminin. Come over here. What does this say?"

Preminin came close. Why was it so hot in here? Maybe it had something to do with how the captain had pressurized the boat? It couldn't be fire, could it?

Preminin peered at the round instrument. Like the ones on Kapitulsky's console, like those back at his own station in compartment six, it looked as if it had been made for a locomotive. He read the needle, then blinked.

"Well?"

"It says—"

Before he could finish his sentence, the first reactor overheat alarm went off. Its terrifying screech echoed throughout the boat, through the burning, ruined spaces flickering with fire and through the increasingly crowded passageways where men huddled. But here, right next to the reactors themselves, it was deafening.

ATLANTIC FLEET HEADQUARTERS, NORFOLK, VIRGINIA

Admiral Ted Sheafer was early for his customary morning brief at 0600. There was no Saturday-morning traffic to contend with and he made quick time to the main gate of the huge naval complex. He already had one cup of black coffee when the FOSIC watch officer, a young lieutenant commander named Gail Robinson, arrived at his office. She knocked twice.

"Come," he told her.

"Good morning, Admiral," she said.

Robinson was a handsome woman, though it didn't mean she didn't know her business. Just the opposite. She had a way of pulling things out of a hat, seeing patterns other people missed, that Sheafer valued. Call it woman's intuition, though not out loud. Sheafer was still unsure exactly how to behave with female officers. There weren't enough of them around to establish much of a template. As an intelligence specialist, he knew that misunderstandings often started wars. They also had gotten a lot of male officers in trouble. "What have you got for me this morning?"

She described the sudden redirection of the three freighters to the regular YANKEE patrol area, then tactfully mentioned her discussion, or lack of one, with the submarine staff.

"What about SOSUS?"

"I haven't sent them a query, Admiral. But it might be a good idea."

More than you know, thought Sheafer as she continued the morning brief. He was remembering another incident with a Soviet sub that burned north of England in 1972. The *K-19,* the so-called Hiroshima Sub. Twenty-eight of her crew had burned to death, trapped in an aft compartment. It had started in just this way: freighters, all of them Soviet-bloc, suddenly heading for an empty piece of ocean that turned out to be not so empty.

"Anything else?" he asked.

"There's some preliminary indication that the *Kirov* battle group is also under way. We didn't expect that just now, either," she finished. "It might be connected with this Bermuda activity."

It might at that. "Good work," he told her as he picked up his telephone. "I'll carry the ball from here." He watched her leave, making a mental note to put a good word in her fitness report.

"SOSUS Control," came the answer on the other end of the line.

"This is Admiral Sheafer. I want an acoustic search for the following areas." He read them to the SOSUS watch officer.

In five minutes, the Cray supercomputers had sifted through millions of signals and found the one that Sheafer had asked for.

"Sir," said the SOSUS chief, "we recorded a hell of a sound spike there. We positively ID *K-219* as the source. We have her print on file. First there's an alarm, then a big boom. It sounds like she had an explosion. A big one."

"Very well. Track her," said Sheafer. "I want hourly updates."

Next he called the submarine ops desk at SUBLANT; the heart of the Atlantic submarine mafia.

"This is Admiral Sheafer. Who do we have in company with *K-219*?"

There was enough of a pause to make Sheafer angry. A two-star shout is not inconsiderable.

"The deputy chief of staff for intelligence for the commander in chief of the Atlantic Fleet just asked you a question, mister!"

"*Augusta,* Admiral. Commander Von Suskil's boat."

One of the newest attack subs in the fleet and one of the ballsiest skippers. The two naturally went together. "Very well. Have we heard anything from him in the last twenty-four hours?"

"He's under—"

"I'm aware of his communications proscriptions. I asked a question."

"I can check, Admiral."

"That would be a splendid idea." He hung up and called Operations at CinCLANTFLT. He suggested they scramble a P-3 Orion out of Naval Air Station Bermuda to take a closer look. It was an end run around the reluctant submariners. It might even work.

President Reagan was at Camp David. The secretary of defense was planning an overseas trip in conjunction with the upcoming Gorbachev summit in Iceland. If *K-219* was in as much trouble as the Hiroshima Sub back in '72, it was going to be a busy weekend in Washington.

The screech of the reactor alarm paralyzed the command post watch. For an instant, Britanov thought this could not be happening. It was one of those drills conducted by a sadistic trainer back at submarine school, one who delighted in taking you to the very edge, then giving you a good, hard shove.

He grabbed the mike and switched the intercom to Kapitulsky's station in compartment two. "Gennady! Report!"

"I've lost all remote readings to the reactors. The wires must have burned through in compartment four. I don't know what's happening, but if the overheat is real, we have to shut them down. I can't . . . there's no response from my controls. They're running away!"

Britanov heard the thin blade of panic in Kapitulsky's normally unflappable demeanor. Shutting down a reactor was normally accomplished from Kapitulsky's station. But he was no longer connected to his power plants. It was why he sounded so brittle, so near to breaking. If Kapitulsky could lose control, then anyone could. Even Britanov. "Gennady. Listen to me. Belikov is back there. Have him revert the reactors to manual control and scram them if he has to."

"I should do it—"

"No. Talk him through it. I'll stand by."

A pause, then, "Belikov?" said Kapitulsky.

The sound of the alarm doubled as the screech was fed over the intercom. "We're both still in compartment seven," said Belikov. "The readings are all going crazy back here and it's hot."

"Read me all the temperatures. Start with primary coolant."

Belikov wiped away the steam from his mask and read them off just the way he'd been taught in reactor disaster drills. "Primary temperature on number one is—" He stopped. "It's too high. It's way too high. Same with number two!"

"Coolant flow?"

"Low and dropping."

Kapitulsky thought there was a good chance the readings were inaccurate. After all, a moment before all seemed to be well with the VM-4s. What could have caused them to suddenly run away like this? On the other hand, if the readings were true, they were moments away from a real meltdown; one that would eat right through the reactor vessel, burn through the bottom of the submarine, and then, when the mass of glowing hot slag hit cold water, explode in a fireball of radioactive steam. "Captain," he said, "if we shut one down we won't be able to make fourteen knots. We may lose all power except for the diesels."

"Do it," Britanov said to the propulsion engineer. "Start the diesels. Shut both reactors down. Start with the hottest one and scram it."

As he listened to Kapitulsky tell Belikov what to do, Britanov realized the crew was not the only one getting backed into a corner.

"Unlock the gravity release for quench baffles one through four," said Kapitulsky. "Did you hear, Belikov?"

"Yes . . ."

"That should do it," Kapitulsky finished. The baffles would absorb the runaway fission reaction, dousing the nuclear fires. There was a pause. The reactor alarm was still screeching horribly. "Well?"

"Sir!" said Belikov. "I can't!"

"What do you mean you can't?"

"Something . . . something's gone wrong with the gravity release. The quench baffles won't drop. The springs . . . they aren't forcing them down. It must be the heat. The metal's binding."

Kapitulsky grew pale. The quench baffles were designed to drop automatically when reactor temperatures got too high. If they failed to drop automatically, they could be commanded to drop by a sequence of steps Belikov had just taken; if they did not drop *then,* they still could be forced down, but by hand, from *inside* the reactors, by a man wielding a specially made oversized wrench.

"Captain?" said Kapitulsky. "Scram was unsuccessful. We have to go in there and crank them down."

Grandfather Krasilnikov stepped up beside the captain. "I can go back and do it," said the chief engineer. "I can walk out topside and drop back down through the escape hatch in ten. I'm old and I have all the children I want. Let me do it, Captain."

And lose his chief engineer when he might have need for him? Britanov shook his head. "I still need you here, Igor. What about protective gear?"

"There are two antiradiation suits back in eight," said Krasilnikov, "but they're designed for steam leaks in the coolant circuit. Not for going into the reactors. It's never done."

Britanov knew why. "Gennady? Tell Belikov about the suits. Tell him they may not shield him enough to be safe."

"He knows that, Captain."

"Belikov. Can you hear me? This is Captain Britanov."

"I hear you, Captain."

"We have to scram the reactors. You'll have to go in. There are some protective suits in eight but they—"

"I know, Captain," said the young reactor officer. "I'll shut them down myself. But my OBA canister is almost empty." In fact, Belikov was beginning to feel light-headed as his portable supply gave out.

"Go back to compartment eight. Pshenichny will get you equipped."

"We're leaving seven for eight."

Security Officer Pshenichny listened to the intercom speaker as he and sixty men sat huddled in the main engine room. Fourteen of them lay unconscious on the steel deck; two missile technicians and Petrachkov were dead. It was very hot here so close to the big, steam-driven turbomachinery. The air in compartment eight smelled of oil and hydraulic fluid, but it wasn't yet lethal. Pshenichny looked back at the refugees from the abandoned compartments. "How many OBA canisters do we have?"

A quick count came up with more men than oxygen canisters; there were thirty OBAs altogether, most of them already partly used. There were just six full ones left. Pshenichny took all six and lined them up on the deck.

Belikov and Seaman Preminin showed up, their blue coveralls black with sweat. Belikov's mask was still on, the lenses were still fogged. His OBA canister was nearly empty, the sides of the rubber bladder were sticking together.

Pshenichny reached over and pulled off Belikov's mask. The reactor officer looked frightened, but then realized no one else in compartment eight was wearing a mask, either. He took a long gasp of air. The two protective suits were handed up the line. Belikov noticed the small pile of canisters. "Where are the rest?"

"Those are the last of them," said Pshenichny.

Krasilnikov still hovered by the captain. "Belikov will do the job. But when he comes out," said the chief engineer, "he'll be as sterile as a mule."

"If he doesn't get it done," said Britanov, "it won't matter."

CHAPTER 9

Preminin never hesitated. Once he saw the condition
of Lieutenant Belikov, he started suiting up to go back
inside the reactor compartment alone.

—*Security Officer Valery Pshenichny*

"I'll go with you, Lieutenant," said Preminin. He reached for the second antiradiation suit. It was made from heavy silvered rubber.

"No," said Belikov. "One of us in there is bad enough. If I can't
get all the baffles down, you'll have to finish it." He put on the OBA
mask and tested to be sure he could breathe, then stepped through the
hatch to compartment seven. It shut behind him with a solid clang.
Security Officer Pshenichny grabbed the locking bar and pulled the
dogs tight against the rubber seals.

The lights had almost completely failed inside compartment seven,
but Belikov knew every inch of the complex reactor space by feel. He
didn't need light to find his way down the ladder to the lower machinery space. When he stepped off the bottom rung he found filthy
seawater pooled on the deck. It was oily with brown fluid. A lone

battle lamp cast enough yellow light to see that when he disturbed the water with his boot it gave off wisps of smoke. He could hear a steady inrush of water from somewhere forward.

To expect a steel pipe to float had always seemed a little bit unreasonable. Of course, so was asking a man to crawl into a live nuclear reactor.

Both VM-4s were down here on the bottom level, separated from the machinery spaces by heavy shielded bulkheads and accessed through a small, low hatch ablaze with serious warnings. Belikov remembered the story of a cook aboard the *Lenin,* a nuclear-powered icebreaker. A real peasant from the *gubinka,* the deep countryside, he'd seen nothing wrong with using a high-pressure steam tap off the primary reactor coolant loop to scour a crusted pan clean. He suffered radiation burns over his whole body and died soon afterward, but he had very clean pans.

Now Belikov was the cook heading into harm's way.

The high-temperature alarm was still shrieking. He'd stopped hearing it. But then, an hour ago he wouldn't have considered walking into a hot nuclear reactor, either. It was amazing what a person could become accustomed to.

He had to bend as he made his way along the bottom level. Belikov was tall, a full six feet. He kept bumping his head against things, obstructions he couldn't quite see kept snatching at his mask, threatening to pull it off. What was the air like here, anyway? In the dim orange light he could see swirling vapor.

It was like going down to a leaky, dark basement filled with a maze of steam pipes and sparking, damaged electrical conduits. A high-pressure air line hissed where a weld had failed. The heat near the two nuclear cauldrons was intense; even outside the shielded bulkhead it was well over fifty degrees Celsius. Hotter by far than any *banya* Belikov had ever taken, though the heavy rubber suit helped a little.

The tool he needed to crank down the jammed quench baffles was stored in a locker. Water had risen to its bottom lip by the time he found it. Of course it was locked. Of course he had no key. *What do they expect us to do, steal tools and sell them to the fish?*

He felt his way around to where he knew a fire ax was mounted to the bulkhead. His gloved hand closed around the wooden handle. He hefted it and used the heavy blade to pry open the locker.

The special crank resembled an oversized meat grinder. It was heavy, made of solid steel. He dropped the ax and returned to the small hatch that led into the shielded reactor space. There was a tiny, thick window in the middle of it. Through the leaded glazing he could see the two squat shapes of the reactor domes.

He didn't bother with the warnings. No one in their right mind would come in here with the reactors running. He reached down and unlocked the hatch.

A blast-furnace gust flowed out so strongly he could feel it through the insulated suit. *Better not to waste time.* He folded himself through the small hatch, then stood up inside the reactor space.

The two reactor vessels were before him, two domed cylinders seething with nuclear fire. The heat was intense. There was an odd, ozonelike smell to the air.

A sinking submarine stuffed with nuclear poisons. They should all be paddling from *K-219* as fast as they could swim. Who cared if a reactor blew up right next to America? It wasn't as though they were bobbing off Odessa. What Russian would pay a kopeck to keep enriched uranium from dusting American beaches?

Belikov was paying a good deal more than a kopeck. He knew he was taking a huge dose of radiation by standing here. Enough to sterilize him for sure. To keep America safe. That was what he was sacrificing his manhood for.

It was really a crazy world.

He walked up to the first reactor, the starboard VM-4. Its domed top contained four hexagonal sockets. They operated a worm-gear mechanism that would force one of the quench baffles down.

Here, right next to the sizzling reactor, the temperature was eighty degrees Celsius; nearly one hundred eighty degrees Fahrenheit. Enough to cook flesh. Enough to kill. What the devil was he doing?

Belikov inserted the handle into the first socket and began to crank. He saw at once why the safety system had failed: it took all his effort to move it. The heat had warped the guides badly. And without those baffles down, the heat only became worse, the nuclear fire brighter, hotter. It was a self-sustaining reaction. Eventually, without a flow of coolant to take away the heat, the sphere of uranium fuel would melt through the bottom of the reactor vessel, through the hull of the sub, and detonate when it hit cold seawater. A hydrogen blast, not a nuclear explosion, but for anyone close by the difference would be slight. A hydrogen bubble had burst at Chernobyl just a few months back, and look at the mess *that* made.

He threw himself against the steel bar and the jammed gears began to squeal. He followed the handle around the vessel. Each time his suit touched the reactor he heard a sizzle and smelled burning rubber.

How long is this going to take? He'd performed a manual crankdown on a cold reactor as part of nuclear reactor school. Normally it took less than five minutes for all four baffles to be lowered. Sweat poured down his face as he shoved the crank with all his might. It evaporated the instant it emerged from beneath his mask. It was so hot. So very hot. And the radiation, well, it didn't pay to think about some things. He kept turning until his vision began to blur, until he was gasping. Only then did he look down at his OBA canister.

The rubber air bladder was completely collapsed. How was that possible? He'd barely lowered the first baffle. He'd only been here for . . . for how long?

Spots swam in front of his eyes. He stepped back, fighting the urge to tear off the mask and breathe. Belikov was holding the heavy crank handle. It weighed so much, it pulled his arm down to his side. He was so tired, and he'd barely lowered . . . Air. He needed air. He had to get back to eight.

Shuffling like a drunk, Belikov staggered back to the low hatch in the shielded bulkhead, got through, forgot to close it behind, remembered, stood up, and stumbled aft to the ladder leading up to compartment eight. He still had the heavy crank handle. Somehow he climbed. Somehow he made it back to the hatch. He used the crank as a hammer and pounded on the door. When it opened, he fell through and passed out on the deck at Preminin's feet.

Pshenichny propped Belikov against the bulkhead, ripped off the mask and splashed his face with water. It was warm water, but it seemed to help. "Are they shut down?" he asked Belikov.

The lieutenant's face was very pale, even though his neck was splotched red. He looked up at Pshenichny and mouthed the word *no*.

"Sergei," said the security officer to Seaman Preminin. "You'll have to—"

"I know." Preminin was already putting on the second, cumbersome radiation suit. He clipped two OBA canisters to his belt.

There were just two more unused canisters left in the whole after section of *K-219*.

WHITE HOUSE SITUATION ROOM, SATURDAY MORNING

The *whop whop whop* of the presidential helicopter came from out on the White House lawn.

"There he goes," said Navy Commander Michael Bohn to his secretary. "Maybe we can get some work done with the heavies gone."

"I've never been out to Camp David," she said as they both listened to the sound of the Marine helicopter recede. "Have you?"

"Only when they make me."

Commander Bohn didn't like to be so far away from the action, so far from the intricate web of contacts and information sources he relied upon. Bohn was the director of the White House Situation Room, the crisis center through which the world was filtered, analyzed, and presented to President Ronald Reagan. The job had been filled by an active-duty naval officer since the Carter administration. It was a coup for the service; in some ways it was even better than having a mole inside the Kremlin. The Kremlin didn't make spending decisions for the U.S. Navy. The White House did.

Not that Bohn didn't take the job seriously. Just the opposite. When Libya invaded Chad, it was Bohn who located the overhead photos Reagan had so appreciated. When Chernobyl blew in April, it was his Situation Room staff who first alerted him to the implications, and to the fact that Gorbachev wasn't coming clean to the world on the worst nuclear accident in history.

Naturally, Bohn also had the job of maintaining ties to the Navy intelligence mafia. The Navy kept Bohn in the loop in exchange for Bohn's timely warnings on anything that might blindside the Navy. Right now that meant an arms control agreement that might tilt the scales in favor of the Navy's number one enemy: the United States Air Force.

Commander Bohn had come to work early that morning, and so had much of the Sit Room staff. There was an enormous amount of work left to do in preparing the president for the superpower summit next week in Reykjavík, Iceland. "Talking points" were filed on note cards. They were amazingly detailed, even orchestrating Reagan's chit-chat with the Soviet leader's wife, Raisa.

General Secretary Gorbachev and President Reagan were both scrambling to see which parts of their respective militaries might be most profitably sacrificed on the altar of peace. Partisan politics inevitably entered into the picture: hard-liners in each camp worried that their leader was getting ready to give away the store for a handful of beans. Some were doing more than just worrying; some were actively campaigning against the summit and its goals. Chief among this last group was the Secretary of Defense, Caspar Weinberger.

"Telephone, Commander," said the secretary. "Captain Herrington over at the Pentagon INTEL Plot."

Herrington was an INTEL officer over at the Chief of Naval Operations. Theoretically, he outranked Bohn. Practically, Bohn had the ear of the president and Herrington did not. In the odd political reckoning of Washington they were unequal equals.

The call was logged in just after seven in the morning.

"Commander Bohn speaking."

"Morning, Mike. This is Dave Herrington over at CNO INTEL Plot. We may have a situation to bring you in on."

"This is the Situation Room. You called the right place," Bohn quipped.

But the captain wasn't laughing. "We've got a Redfleet boomer in distress out off Bermuda. It looks pretty hairy."

"What kind of distress?" asked Bohn.

"She had an explosion on board. Probably one of her missiles."

"Missiles? You're saying one cooked off?"

"I didn't say that. This is just a preliminary analysis, but some of the analysts say it looks a lot like an aborted launch."

A launch? "Jesus," he whispered. "Where did it come down?"

"Nowhere. There was no ignition. The bird didn't break the surface. If it had, obviously, we'd be looking at a different kind of scenario."

Not a scenario. Nuclear war, thought Bohn. "How did we find out?"

"I just got the heads-up from Ted Sheafer down at Norfolk. I did some checking with our own people and got confirmation."

Our people meant the submarine community. "How the devil did Sheafer find out before you?"

"You won't believe it. A watch officer, a *gal,* down at FOSIC put it together from raw positional data. Seems like a couple of Ivan's freighters are heading for Bermuda all of a sudden. She wondered why out loud. Sheafer took it from there."

"You say it's been confirmed?"

"A U.S. unit in trail confirmed the explosion. They're standing by."

"I presume they're not there to render assistance."

"Funny. The last word is the boomer's taking on water and burning. That shouldn't go anywhere, by the way. The last thing we need is some White House heavy gabbing about submarine ops at a news conference."

"The only heavy in this morning is Admiral Poindexter."

"Good. He's on our side. You'll be getting a call any minute from the Joint Chiefs on this. Naturally, they won't know as much as we do."

"Naturally. Who's got the duty this weekend?"

"General Burpee. He's Air Force. Don't mention this call to him when you talk. Poindexter's inside the box. Burpee isn't."

Bohn knew what Herrington meant. "I'll call Admiral Poindexter and give him the heads-up. He's in over at the West Wing. He'll ask me so I'll ask you. When do we know more?"

"Sheafer scrambled a P-3. It should be overhead in a couple of hours. We'll have a better idea what we're dealing with then. I don't suppose you have anything from the Soviets directly?"

"No FLASH messages in this morning. Nothing at all."

"Like Chernobyl."

"Chernobyl was pretty far away compared to this." Then Bohn said, "You know, a couple of hours is a long time to wait if some crazy Russian captain is trying to launch his missiles at us from off Bermuda. What if he tries again?"

"We're on top of that, Commander."

"Maybe you should get our unit out there to call in with something more detailed."

"That's being done as we speak," Herrington answered carefully. "I'll call back when I hear. Remember. Burpee stays out of the loop. We have to be careful when it comes to discussing our submarine assets."

"I understand, but the President thinks they're *his* submarine assets, too. He's going to want the whole picture."

"When I know something, you'll know it. That's the deal."

Bohn heard the finality in Herrington's voice. He knew there was just so much juice that anyone, even a fellow naval officer, could squeeze from the submarine mafia. "Jesus. It had to happen with the summit next week."

"It might not be an accident," said Herrington. "You know, it's not impossible that it could be an attempt to deep-six the summit from their end. Some hard-liner. You know what I mean?"

"There are plenty of hard-liners around this place who'd love to see that Russian captain succeed."

"The SecDef?"

"Cap Weinberger would be first on my list of suspects," said Bohn. "Except he's on a jet heading for China."

"It just means he's got plausible deniability."

Herrington might wear a blue suit, thought Bohn, but he thinks like a spook. "When will you call with an update?"

"We should be getting something from our submarine soon. Remember, except for Poindexter, nothing about that goes anywhere. Not one word. We don't want the Soviets to blame us if they lose the boat."

"Does it look like they will?"

"I hope the hell they do lose it," said Herrington. "I spent enough hours freezing my tail off on the pier at Leningrad counting silo hatches." Herrington had once been assistant naval attaché to Moscow. "We're also getting a destroyer ready to sortie out of Norfolk. You know, with some radiation specialists on board."

Radiation specialists? Were they worried about contamination of the ocean, or were they talking about *boarding* the boomer? "Thanks for the heads-up, Captain. And let me know when you hear from our unit in trail."

He hung up and dialed Poindexter. An unauthorized launch? What if it had been? What if their rocket *hadn't* blown up? From the YANKEE patrol box off Bermuda, that missile would have arrived over Michael Bohn's head in under twelve minutes. A one-megaton airburst centered on the White House would make a burnout zone that went from here to Arlington. There wouldn't be enough rubble left for a subsequent nuke to bounce. He stared up at the acoustic tile as the phone rang, then clicked.

"Poindexter."

"Admiral? This is Commander Bohn in the Situation Room. We have something for you and for the president," he said.

"He's already out at Camp David. His schedule says he's about to sit down to breakfast."

"You may want to interrupt him, sir."

"It better be worth it."

"Yes, sir, Admiral," said Bohn. "I'm afraid it is."

EMERGENCY ACTION CENTER, MOSCOW

Captain Gennady Antonov, the Northern Fleet's main expert on the RSM-25 rocket, read the latest dispatch from *K-219*. Like the others, it had been transmitted in the open. There had been no attempt to conceal the contents by using the prearranged emergency burst codes. *Even if he saves the submarine,* thought Antonov, *Britanov is finished.*

He sent the message by courier to Admiral Makarov. Makarov was due to brief the big boss, Admiral of the Fleet Chernavin, in six minutes. In turn, Chernavin would meet with General Secretary Gorbachev. What Gorbachev would do with it was anyone's guess. They'd find out in a little over an hour.

"So? What do we have, Captain?"

Antonov turned. It was Admiral Novoystev, the operations chief. The short, stocky officer sweated heavily in his wool uniform.

"Sir, *K-219* is still on the surface. The last message from Britanov reports gas now in compartments four, five, six, and seven. There's a fire in four and five and they lost remote readings from the missiles and from the reactors. They requested an emergency airdrop of OBA units. I'm trying to—"

"I'll handle that, Captain."

"They need them right away, Admiral." Antonov hoped he realized what was happening out there. Those OBA units could spell the difference between saving the boat and losing it, and her crew.

"I think that an urgent request of that nature falls within my authority."

"Of course, Admiral."

"What I want to know is, the message. How was it sent?"

Antonov couldn't hide his surprise. Novoystev was more interested in finding something to pin on Britanov than in the welfare of the submarine or her crew. "Like the others. Uncoded."

Novoystev smiled. "Worse and worse. I'll make the arrangements on the matter of OBAs, though why he needs more than we gave him I don't know. Keep me informed," he said.

Novoystev was about to leave when Captain Antonov said, "Admiral? What about the families? Shouldn't they be told?"

"Families?"

"The crew's families, Admiral."

Novoystev made a silent *oh,* then shrugged. "Do what you think best," he said, then sauntered off in the direction of a steward. The open-faced salami sandwiches were gone, but in their place had come a tray of sweet biscuits.

Captain Antonov picked up an outside phone and dialed Gadzhievo. Amazingly, the call went through.

"Flotilla. *Slushayu*. Andreev speaking."

Captain Andreev had just come from commanding a boat identical to *K-219*. Now he served on the Gadzhievo Flotilla Staff; the same position Antonov had held prior to coming to Moscow. He was a friend of Captain Britanov's.

"This is Captain Antonov in the Sardine Can in Moscow. I'm on the emergency watch team."

"Antonov! What have you heard? Are they all right?"

"No. They're on the surface, though. Have the wives been told anything?"

"It's that mouse-prick of a *zampolit*. Romanov won't allow anyone to talk to them except through him."

"He's probably afraid of what they'll say."

"Absolutely," said Andreev.

"Listen," said Antonov. "Call Britanov's wife and have her speak to me directly. Do it on my authority."

"Romanov won't like it."

"That's a good enough reason all by itself."

"What about Britanov? Is he going to be all right?"

"For your ears, they've got real problems out there. Fire, gas, and their reactor controls are burned out. If I were in his shoes, I'd start thinking about getting some of the crew off. It could go bad in a hurry."

"What about casualties?"

"Nothing official. But I'd expect them." Antonov didn't have a better answer than that.

"When will we know?"

"Makarov is briefing Admiral Chernavin now. Chernavin's going to put it in General Secretary Gorbachev's lap. Who knows what Gorbachev will do with it? Have Natalia Britanov call me," he said, then hung up.

YANKEE-1 class nuclear-powered ballistic missile submarine (SSBN), *K-219*, at pier in homeport Gadzhievo. (I. KURDIN)

K-219 in Gadzhievo. (I. KURDIN)

Commanding Officer, Captain Second Rank Igor A. Britanov on the *K-219* periscope. (I. BRITANOV)

Families of the crew visit *K-219* in homeport Gadzhievo, August 1986.
I. KURDIN)

Officers and men of *K-219* in central command post: Britanov (*bottom left*), Navigator Aznabaev (*behind Britanov*), Kurdin (*bottom right*). (I. KURDIN)

Captain Lieutenant Vladimir N. Karpachev, *K-219* Assistant to the Commanding Officer. He committed suicide six years after *K-219* sank. (I. KURDIN)

Zampolit Sergiyenko addresses the crew in the *K-219* mess decks. (I. KURDIN)

K-219 departing homeport Gadzhievo, taken from the bridge of a tug.
(I. KURDIN)

Main Propulsion Engineer, Captain Third Rank Gennady Kapitulsky (*left*) with Captain Second Rank Igor Kurdin, then *starpom*,
K-219 compartment three, August 1986. (I. Kurdin)

K-219 on the surface of
the Barents Sea, taken
from a Soviet Navy
KA-27 helicopter,
spring 1986. (Archives,
St. Petersburg Club for
Mariners and Sub-
mariners)

Captain Britanov (*bottom center*) with officers and crew in *K-219* mess decks before the final patrol, August 1986. (I. KURDIN)

Captain First Rank Igor Kurdin. (I. KURDIN)

Cartoon of a central command post on a Russian submarine, drawn by a retired Russian submarine officer.

K-219 photographed on the surface by U.S. Navy P-3C Orion, October 4, 1986.
(U.S. NAVY PHOTO)

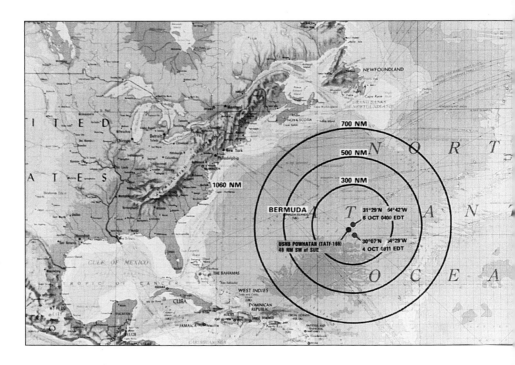

Pentagon's press briefing plot of the location where *K-219* sank on
October 6, 1986. Position of tug USNS *Powhatan* is shown to the southwest
of the last *K-219* position. (U.S. NAVY PHOTO)

Pentagon press briefing, October 7, 1986. Lt. Gen. Richard Burpee, Operations Officer, Joint Chiefs of Staff (*left*) and Adm. Powell Carter, Director, Joint Staff, answer questions about the loss of *K-219*. (U.S. NAVY PHOTO)

K-219 on the surface of the western Atlantic, struggling against fire and flooding. Taken by U.S. Navy P-3C Orion flying out of Naval Air Station Bermuda, October 5, 1986. (U.S. NAVY PHOTO)

Los Angeles–class nuclear-powered attack submarine USS *Augusta*, shortly after its commissioning in 1985. (GENERAL DYNAMICS ELECTRIC BOAT DIVISION PHOTO)

Damaged Soviet DELTA-class submarine in homeport following collision with
U.S. attack submarine. (A. Bulgakov)

Surviving *K-219* officers (*back row, from left*) Kurdin, Security Officer Valery Pshenichny, Doctor Igor Kochergin, Main Propulsion Engineer Gennady Kapitulsky; and author Peter Huchthausen (*front row, center*). Taken at the St. Petersburg Club for Mariners and Submariners, November 1994. (P. HUCHTHAUSEN)

Seaman Nikolai Smaglyuk, one of three crewmen who perished in *K-219*'s compartment four. (I. KURDIN)

Crewmen on the sail of the *K-219,* in port in Gadzhievo. (I. KURDIN)

Kurdin, Division Commander, Kontr Admiral Shabalin, Britanov. (I. KURDIN)

The crew of the *K-219* after their return to Russia, photographed on Red Square by Lenin's tomb. (I. KURDIN)

Engineer Seaman Sergei A. Preminin, who died in compartment seven after manually shutting down *K-219*'s reactors. (ARCHIVES, ST. PETERSBURG CLUB FOR MARINERS AND SUBMARINERS)

K-219

Chief Engineer Krasilnikov pulled the circuit breaker for the reactor overtemp alarm. Finally, the blood-chilling screech went silent and the command post team could speak, even think.

"Captain," said Aznabaev. The navigator held up a microphone from his ship-to-ship set. "I have direct contact with the *Fyodor Bredkin*. She's fifty kilometers out. Do you want to speak with her?"

Britanov felt both shame and relief. Shame that he might need some rustbucket of a freighter to save his command; relief that if he did need them, they would at least be here. Fumes were spreading right through sealed hatches. So was fire. So was water. The reactors would have to be shut down or else they would burn a hole right through *K-219*'s belly. Then they would all go up in a cloud of radioactive steam. Even if he did get them shut down, it left him with only battery and diesel power to control damage.

It wouldn't be enough. He knew that he would have to get some of his men off to save them. He shook his head. "I don't want to talk. I want to see him. What speed can he make?"

The sub's navigator spoke into the mike, waited a moment, then said to Britanov, "ETA is two hours forty minutes. He wants to know our condition."

"Tell him so do I."

"Captain!" came a cry from the young man sitting at the radar display. "Aerial contact inbound. He's illuminating us with search radar. It looks like an American patrol plane."

"Zhenya," Britanov said to the navigator, "tell the master of the *Fyodor Bredkin* if he wants to know how we're doing, he can ask the Americans," said Britanov. He picked up the *kashtan*. "Pshenichny! What's happening with those reactors?"

The security officer helped Preminin close the last fastener on his radiation suit. He picked up the *kashtan*. "They're going back in now,

Captain," he said as he undogged the hatch leading forward into compartment seven. "The alarm is off."

"We killed the power to it," Britanov said. "We have no readings up here at all. Kapitulsky is ready to start the diesels but you've got to get those reactors secured."

"We'll do our duty, Captain." He looked at Preminin. The young seaman had the heavy crank handle now. Belikov looked too weak to pick it up. Was it heat, the air, or radiation?

"How's Belikov?" Britanov asked.

Belikov was wobbly as he stood. Preminin took the *kashtan* and answered for them both. "We're okay, Captain. Trust us to do the job," he said, then put his mask on, checked the flow from the OBA canister, and together with Belikov, went back in.

Any idea that the alarm's silence was a good sign was instantly dispelled by the raging heat inside compartment seven. With the pumps failed, each glowing uranium sphere was dumping heat into an insufficient supply of coolant; the heat radiated through the steel reactor vessels and into the submarine.

Belikov knew it was worse than before. He followed Preminin down the ladder to the bottom.

"Comrade Lieutenant," said Preminin, "let me go in. You can stay by the gauges and relay reports to central command."

Belikov knew it was a polite way of saying that he didn't look able to help. He nodded. Preminin went through the low hatch and into the shielded reactor space.

Belikov picked up the *kashtan* by the gauges. "Comrade Captain. It's Belikov, sir. I'm at the local reactor control board now in compartment seven."

"Belikov, read me the temperatures off the panel," said Kapitulsky. "Start with the highest."

"The temperatures are all redlined. Starboard and port reactors are both starved for water. Coolant flow is almost zero in the port reactor. There's still some circulation in the starboard."

"The readings, they're accurate?" asked Kapitulsky. "What's the air temperature in there, Belikov?"

"Very hot," he said weakly. He knew that as hot as it was standing out here, inside the reactor space, right next to those two hellish vessels, it was worse.

Preminin inserted the crank and managed to force the first quench baffle, the one Belikov had started, all the way down. Even through the rubber suit it was like standing under a powerful infrared lamp; the heat was like nothing he'd ever experienced. "Number one down!" he shouted.

Belikov had cranked that one down most of the way himself. Still, it was progress. "Number one baffle down, port reactor," he reported. All four baffles were needed to surround the uranium sphere.

Preminin inserted the handle into the second socket. He pushed. It refused to move at all. He pushed harder, then with all his strength.

The handle bent, threatened to break, then, with a crack that Belikov could hear all the way outside the reactor space, it moved. Preminin cranked the second baffle down by throwing himself at it, working his way around the blazingly hot steel vessel.

"Second . . . I mean, number two baffle . . . baffle is down," he said through dry, parched lips. He picked up the handle and found it oddly difficult to insert it into the third socket. Sweat streamed down his brow and into his eyes. The intense heat evaporated it instantly, leaving a mask of salt over Preminin's face.

"Preminin!" shouted Belikov. "Check your OBA!"

"I'm . . . I'm not feeling so good, Comrade Lieutenant." He groaned the words as the steel crank fell into the third socket. He pushed. Like the others it required all his strength, all his weight, to budge. He was beyond feeling as he threw himself against the handle. It moved, stubbornly, then moved again, again, and finally stopped. He leaned against it. The steel bent. Only then did he realize the third baffle was fully down. "Number . . . number three is—" He stopped, swaying on his feet next to the steel reactor vessel.

"Preminin!" Belikov dropped the *kashtan* and rushed into the reactor space.

Preminin was on the deck. Belikov picked up the handle and inserted it into the fourth socket. Preminin had broken through the tightest place on the warped guide and it moved more easily. He cranked the last baffle down, then dragged Preminin out through the hatch to the outer reactor space.

"Captain! Belikov . . . here. Port reactor is—" He stopped and felt the heat rising up his body. The spots were back in his eyes. He looked down at his OBA canister. Once again the sides of the rubber bladder were sticking together. He was out of air! "Port reactor is secure! I'm taking Preminin . . . out."

He dropped the mike and dragged Preminin up the ladder. When they opened the hatch leading back to compartment eight, they fell through in a single heap.

"Water!" shouted Pshenichny as he pulled the mask from the lieutenant's face. Belikov's skin was dead white. His eyes bloodshot and bulging. He tried to lift his head so that he might take a sip but Belikov flopped back to the deck like a dead man. Preminin was coming around, slowly, as someone brought a cupful of tepid water. Pshenichny splashed both men, then gave the rest to Preminin to drink.

"What about the starboard reactor?" Britanov's voice boomed in over the loudspeaker.

"We're down to two OBA canisters, Captain," said Pshenichny. "We need more if they're going to both go back in." Though looking at Belikov, he didn't think the lieutenant was going to walk again any time soon, much less go back into the reactors.

"We can't get anyone back through compartment four," said Britanov. "I need that second reactor shut down now, Valery."

Pshenichny was about to tell Britanov that he would have to wait until the two men regained their feet, when a small, weak voice interrupted.

"I'll go," said Preminin. He got his legs under him and stood.

"Give him the OBA canisters," Pshenichny ordered one of the warrant officers.

"But they're our last ones," the *michman* demurred. There were no other oxygen canisters in the entire after section of the sub. If that poison gas came here they'd all suffocate before—

"Give them to Preminin." He looked at the young seaman. "You have to shut it down by yourself."

"I would have done it before, but it's hot in there," said Preminin as he adjusted the mask over his face. "Count on me."

Preminin grabbed the handle and went back to the hatch. This time when it opened, an acrid whiff of bitter almond wafted through. He stopped for an instant and turned, as though he wanted to say something, but changed his mind.

A stronger smell of poison billowed in from the dark, hot compartment beyond the bulkhead.

Preminin shuffled into the darkness, alone, the last man in compartment seven; the only one left who could shut the runaway reactor down.

"Close that hatch!" Pshenichny bellowed after Preminin disappeared. A warrant officer leaned against the steel door as two sailors dogged it down tight. With poison gas now on the other side and no OBA canisters left, they had to rely on the rubber seals around the hatch to keep them alive. "Seal it!"

The clang of the last dog was loud and final in a way that would come back to haunt Pshenichny. It would come back to haunt them all.

CHAPTER 10

Sergei Preminin was gasping, not breathing, as he went down the long, dark ladder into the bowels of compartment seven. He had to force air into his lungs through the OBA mask; he kept worrying that the canister was empty, but the real reason was the rapid buildup of pressure in the compartment. Between the broken steam line and the intense heat radiated by the reactors, compartment seven had pressurized like a hot-air balloon with the burners on full. A constant hiss of escaping steam could be heard above the gurgle of seeping water. Preminin had never felt so hot in all his life.

The sound of water cooled him. It reminded him of the stream near his home village of Skornyakovo. It was cold and crystal clear, and the fish he caught with his brother were a treat for the family; so much better than the drab tinned meat, old, moldy cheese, and hard bread from the state store. Those fishing expeditions with his brother were what made him interested in the Navy to begin with; if something so clean, so alive as a beautiful fish could be found amidst so much squalor, then a life on the water, or in it, might hold promise. It might give Sergei something, some pride, a job at the local flax mill could never supply.

The rubber suit was very heavy. It was lined with lead foil to protect against radiation. Moving was like swimming in some thick fluid, like being underwater, if the sea had turned hot enough to cook you like a crab in a pot.

At the bottom of the ladder he turned, flashed his light, then walked six meters down a short corridor. The darkness didn't frighten him. But to have it empty, filled with poison gas, to have seawater running down the passage like a stream, to be sealed in seven alone, that was something else.

Preminin turned right, then took the three steps up to the local reactor control area outside the shielded space. The hazy beam of his explosion-proof light swept the panel of gauges.

Coolant pressure was zero on both reactors. Coolant flow, almost zero. The first reactor's temperature was only now beginning to drop; the second VM-4 was pegged; the needle into the far right corner of the red zone. How far? How hot could it be in there? It had to be very close to meltdown. He thought of the men back in compartment eight. Sixty of his mates, fourteen of them unconscious, three already dead. They'd all be killed if that hot radioactive slag melted through and found the cold sea. Everyone was counting on him now. Belikov, Pshenichny, most especially Captain Britanov. No one else could do the job.

It had all come down to Engineer-Seaman Sergei Preminin.

He saw the dangling *kashtan* swinging on its cord. He picked it up and said, "Captain? This is Seaman Preminin. I'm in the local reactor control area in seven." He read the dismal numbers off the gauges, then said, "I'm going back in now."

"You can do it, Sergei," Britanov said, though his worried tone said something else.

"Yes, sir. I will." He groped his way to the small access hatch and unlocked it. The steel door blew back and slammed against the bulkhead as though someone had been trapped inside and now wanted out very badly. The high pressure hissed out through the opening, then subsided.

Beyond the hatch was an inferno. He felt the heat on his knees through the rubber, through the lead, through everything. He folded himself through the low hatch and reentered the reactor space.

He stood up. It was just three steps to the starboard reactor. He inserted the crank into the domed top and began to push.

Preminin gasped for air as he worked. The air pressure made his ears fill and crackle. He kept swallowing. His mouth, his throat, were dry as poured sand.

The first quench baffle squealed as he forced it down into position. He did the same for the second, the third. His head was light enough to float. He realized he was gasping harder now, like a fish brought up from the water. He looked down: the first OBA canister was empty. He took a deep breath.

He unscrewed the oxygen source and threw it away, holding his breath as he threaded on the second, and last canister. The fittings would not align. They jammed, cross-threaded. His ears began to tingle, his throat burned, a traitorous impulse in his lungs screamed, *Breathe!*

He had to get the second canister connected. The air beyond his mask swirled with poison. He yanked the metal cartridge off the fitting and slowly, deliberately, with all the calmness a man can muster when he is suffocating, twisted it onto the end of his air tube.

The threads lined up. He screwed it on tight, then took a small taste of air.

Something sharp etched his throat as he sucked down the air. Like breathing shards of glass. The strange feeling filled his lungs, then disappeared.

Preminin went back to the reactor. He inserted the crank into the fourth, and last, baffle. He had to push with all his strength. His home village had a communal well that still relied on the steady clopping of an old horse hitched to its handle. Round and round, the horse was always walking but it never got anyplace.

Sergei Preminin was doing the same thing, hitched instead to a ninety-megawatt nuclear reactor. He walked his way around the blazingly hot steel dome. His suit was now scorched black instead of silver. He could smell burned rubber through his mask. There were holes in the breathing tube, and through those holes he could smell bitter almond. If he took a deeper breath than normal, the sharp, glassy scratch filled his lungs. Each gasp was raw and painful, but a little poison was better than suffocating. He'd never told anyone, not the Navy recruiters, definitely not his mates on board *K-219*, but he had a fear of being trapped. He hated elevators. Let the doors shut and he'd break out in a sweat.

Well, it was too hot now to sweat, even if the steel walls curved in around him, the atmosphere heavy, hot, and lethal.

Preminin went round and round. How many more turns left? Just a few. Then he would leave this space, this oven. The doors would open. He would escape the trap.

Britanov waited with Kapitulsky in central command. There had been no word from Preminin now for too long. "Sergei?" he said into the *kashtan*. "Are they secured, Sergei?"

"They have to be," said Kapitulsky. "It doesn't take that long. It can't."

There was no answer over the intercom.

"Start the forward diesel generator," said Britanov. "We're going to need all the power we can get from it."

"Understood." The propulsion engineer went forward to crank up the emergency generator.

"Captain?" said the radar operator. "Aircraft overhead now. He's circling us."

"Sergei!" Britanov shouted into the mike. "Report!"

Still nothing.

"Captain, this is Pshenichny in eight. Have you heard from Prem-inin? We haven't seen him since he went in and our intercom won't dial into seven." Pshenichny could talk to central command, but not to Preminin. "He only had two canisters with him. Did he shut the plant down?"

"We don't know," said Britanov as the thrum and clank of the forward emergency diesel began.

"Switching the main power bus to backup," said Krasilnikov.

The lights in CCP blinked off, then grew bright.

The intercom scratched, then squealed.

A weak voice came through the loudspeaker. "Captain?"

"Pshenichny?"

"...Seaman Preminin."

"Sergei! Where are you?"

"Comrade Commander, the..." The weak voice faded.

"Sergei! What is it?"

"Captain, the reactors are secured."

Britanov realized he'd been holding his breath. It went out in a long *whoosh* as a cheer went up in the CCP.

"I'm leaving...for the exit now."

"Well done, Sergei!" said Britanov. "You're a hero. How do you feel?"

"It's very hot in here. I'm on my last OBA."

"Then get the hell out of there."

The intercom went dead.

"Zhenya!" Britanov called for the navigator. "Tell Moscow our re-actors are shut down. They're safe."

"Yes, sir!"

EMERGENCY ACTION CENTER, MOSCOW

Captain Antonov made a quiet inquiry and discovered that Admiral Novoystev had indeed ordered an airdrop of OBA units. Two long-range Illyushin jets were on the way. *At least he did that much,* he thought.

A communications specialist brought him a slip of paper. "Message from *K-219*, sir."

Antonov read the latest message and grinned. Then he saw the clock. He jumped to his feet so fast he upset a glass of hot tea. It spilled over the polished table. He didn't care. Admiral of the Fleet Chernavin was about to brief Gorbachev, and Gorbachev had to know the reactors aboard *K-219*, and America, were both safe.

THE WHITE HOUSE

"We've got a unit from VQ-2 out there." VQ-2 was a special Navy intelligence squadron based at NAS Oceana, just outside Norfolk. "He's orbiting overhead now," said Captain Herrington. He had Commander Bohn at the Situation Room on the line. Herrington was looking at a video feed beamed back from a U.S. Navy EP-3 Orion. The patrol plane was circling a smoking black cigar of a sub bobbing sideways in the rising swells. "She's lost all forward way and from the look of her fairwater planes, she's out of hydraulics, too." The two planes mounted to either side of the conning tower pointed straight up and down. "What's happening on your end?"

"Admiral Poindexter is getting set to brief the president. He's coming back in from Camp David especially for it. Weinberger is getting the word now. He's on board Air Force Two."

"Who's with him?"

"The usual zoo."

"I hope to hell he knows what not to feed the animals."

Bohn knew there was a real risk there. Caspar Weinberger was locked up with a gaggle of newsmen on the way to China. There would be a powerful temptation to tell them about the U.S. submarine watching events unfold off Bermuda, especially because it would make a bigger story, and a bigger story might just throw a monkey wrench in next week's summit in Iceland. "Tell me what else you see," he asked.

"All in all, a major inconvenience for Ivan," said Herrington. "She's smoking so there's a fire burning someplace. One of her missile silos is all busted up. That's where the smoke is coming from."

"What about the missiles?" asked Bohn.

"She still has fifteen left. You know, I bet a lot of people didn't know the Russians were running around so close to shore."

"Until one popped up like a cork. No other hatches open?"

"None. But—" He stopped as an aide handed him a slip of paper. "I have a fresh radio intercept from *K-219*."

"That's the name of the boomer?"

"Didn't I say that? Sorry. Anyway, she's broadcasting in the clear. She's begging for an airdrop of some emergency supplies. Anyway, the good news is she got her reactors shut down."

Bohn had been around Russians enough not to take anything they said at face value. "You think it's true?"

"Maybe. We're sending the Sniffer down from Patrick to take air samples just in case."

The Sniffer from Patrick Air Force base was an NC-135 transport specially modified to detect radioactive fallout from atomic tests. "We're also diverting a surface unit to stand by. *Powhatan*."

"*Powhatan*? I don't know her."

"She's an oceangoing tug. Military Sealift Command owns her, but we can use her."

What the devil . . . "You're not suggesting we pull the boomer into port?"

"Permanently? No. But I wouldn't mind borrowing her for a while. And *that,* Commander, doesn't go anywhere."

"I understand."

"Good. I'll keep you informed." The line went dead.

Bohn hung up. He knew some of the details behind the recovery of a Soviet submarine lost in the middle of the Pacific; how the CIA had built the *Glomar Explorer* out of unaccountable "black" funds, gone out and pulled up a lot of interesting things from the wreck. Not just hardware, either. But bodies. Compared to that, towing this stricken sub, the *K-219,* into an American port would be a whole lot easier. And a whole lot more dangerous. Not only for the American sailors who would board her, but to the area surrounding the docks. And what would the Russians do? One of their front-line submarines tied up in Norfolk? American INTEL types crawling through her, finding who knows what? And those fifteen rockets with their thirty warheads. Would we just hand them back, knowing they would be retargeted on us? *The Russians will go nuts!* "Christ," he said out loud. *Maybe that's the purpose!*

The Reykjavík summit was next week. There were a lot of blue-suiters dead set against any kind of arms control treaty, fearing, correctly, that expensive naval forces might be forced to bear the brunt of any cuts.

A destroyer with a special ops crew. A tugboat standing by. Commander Bohn could think of no quicker way to scuttle a summit than by engaging in something the Russians would call piracy on the high seas.

USS *AUGUSTA*

"Sonar, what's our range and bearing to the boomer?"

"Four miles, bearing is one four two constant. She's sitting on the surface broadside to the waves. I can hear hull slap."

"Speed?"

"Still dead in the water."

"Very well," said Von Suskil. "Come to periscope depth. All ahead slow," said Von Suskil. With the enemy dead in the water it didn't make any sense to keep *Augusta* hidden. If company showed up, that would be a different story. But for now they were alone in the middle of the sea under the low morning sun; an American attack submarine with a Soviet boomer square in her sights. It wasn't even good target practice.

"Periscope depth, sir," said the XO.

"Let's have an ESM sweep."

The search periscope glided out of its well. On top of it was the boat's ESM mast. It immediately detected the characteristic radar emissions of a U.S. Navy P-3 Orion patrol plane.

"Active radar, Captain. Aircraft overhead," said the radar officer. "Evaluate as a Papa Three. He'll have us if we raise the scope for sure."

To an attack skipper, especially an aggressive attack skipper, all surface ships were targets, and all aircraft, no matter what color their markings, were the enemy. It went against his inclination and his training, but the message they'd already received from SUBLANT didn't leave him any wiggle room.

"Conn, the aircraft is hailing us."

"Put him over the speaker."

"... finger Two Three, checking in overhead. How do you hear, Caesar?"

A microphone was handed to Von Suskil. "Caesar reads you five by. Lima Delta Sierra. Authenticate."

"This is Goldfinger Two Three. Golf Yankee Victor. We're an Echo Papa Three out of NAS Oceana, feet dry by the time Breezy Point happy hour starts, over."

"Roger, Goldfinger. Go ahead with your message."

"Goldfinger Two Three intends a couple of low passes on the datum. We'll orbit five downwind for sampling in case the target's hot. Will remain this push for the next four hours. My relief will be from VP-5, call sign Top Hand Four Zero, over."

"Roger," said Von Suskil. "Caesar will be standing off in the northeast quadrant. Limit Julie and Jezebel patterns to west quadrants only. Repeat, limit buoy patterns to west quadrants only, over."

"Understand west quadrants for the drops, Caesar. Be advised USNS *Powhatan* is seven zero miles northwest inbound. You've got a herd of freighters galloping this way, too."

"We know," said Von Suskil.

"Figured you would. This is Goldfinger Two Three guarding this push. Call on the slot buoy if you need anything. Out."

"Well," said Von Suskil to the executive officer. "It's getting interesting, isn't it?"

"Yes, sir." The XO knew they'd copied some sensitive orders direct from CinCLANTFLT. They were meant for Von Suskil only and so far the captain hadn't seen fit to share their contents.

"Up the search scope."

The periscope extended to full height. Von Suskil grabbed the handle and swung the eyepiece to face the surfaced boomer. He clicked in twelve power, the maximum. "Here," he said to the XO. "Have a look."

The executive officer grabbed the handles and peered into the eyepiece.

The Soviet missile boat was sitting low in the water, the waves rocking her sail back and forth vigorously. The low sun made her black hull look even darker. "She's getting pounded by the seas," said the XO.

"See the missile deck?"

He swung the handles slightly and whistled. "Smoke. She's still burning. Kind of a funny color, too."

"Purple. She's riding low, too. Note the limber holes?"

The vents that lined the submarine's flanks gushed with swallowed seawater. The occasional wave rolled right over the sloping hump of her missile deck.

"Yes, sir. She's real low considering she blew all her tanks to get there."

"Taking on water through that hatch, I bet. Joker. Serves him right."

The XO thought Von Suskil was sounding too pleased. There were men in that boat. Submariner. No doubt some were dead. To Lieutenant Commander David Samples, *K-219* had ceased to be the enemy. They were sailors in trouble.

"Conn, Sonar. I have a surface target bearing zero one zero at thirty miles. She's inbound at twelve knots. Makes noise like a freighter. I may have a second surface contact out at forty-six miles for zero three nine. Also inbound, but she's faster. Estimate eighteen knots."

"Sonar, what do we have on the DELTA down south? Red One?"

"She's inbound too, sir. But she's running a whole lot faster. Lots of plant noise. Seems like she doesn't care who knows about it."

"She won't get here in time." Von Suskil smiled. This boat, this contemptible YANKEE, was on fire, low to the water, her engines dead. Make one hell of a prize. Like the old days when you'd haul an enemy into port for stripping. He wondered how they would keep it hidden from the world. Or would they bother? Von Suskil would rather have an Alfa to play with; those titanium-hulled hot rods could cruise almost as fast as a Mark 48 torpedo could swim. Still, towing a YANKEE in was still an accomplishment. The INTEL people would have a field day, especially if she came in with the code materials intact.

His orders from CinCLANTFLT were specific:

IMMEDIATE

FROM: CINCLANT

041630Z OCT 86

TO: USS AUGUSTA

BT

SECRET EYES ONLY

PERSONAL FOR VON SUSKIL

1. ASSUME COMMAND TASK GROUP 29.1

    USS AUGUSTA TU 29.1.0

    USNS POWHATAN TU 29.1.1

    CO VQ-2 NAS NORFOLK TU 29.1.3

    CO VP-5 NAS BRUNSWICK TU 29.1.4

Jim Von Suskil was being given command of an ad hoc task force composed of an assortment of thrown-together assets. That was common enough in a world with too many missions and too few ships. What he was to do with them, however, was new and, to Von Suskil, exciting.

    2. MAKE ALL REASONABLE EFFORTS TO PREVENT

        SUCCESSFUL TOW OR SALVAGE OF RED TWO

Someone in the head office wanted that YANKEE for themselves. To tinker with, to tease out her secrets. They wanted that boat, and were giving him a wide scope of authority in just how it was to be accomplished:

    3. ALL PRUDENT MEANS SHORT OF HOSTILE ACTION ARE

       HEREBY AUTHORIZED

All prudent means short of hostile action, thought Von Suskil. He could read between *those* lines. With orders like that, the captain of the *Augusta* knew that if he failed, if he were exposed, his actions would be denied and probably condemned by the Navy, by the whole government. Not that it would slow him down.

He hadn't forgotten that moment when he'd allowed himself to be lured below the layer. The single *ping!* that still made his cheeks color.

Well, the tables were turned now. One way or the other, whether it was at the end of a tow rope from *Powhatan* or something he, Von Suskil, would do, Red Two was never going to make it back home.

K-219

Preminin slowly climbed the ladder up to the second level in compartment seven. He knew that he'd done something very important, maybe the most important thing he'd ever done in his young life. He'd saved his shipmates, his captain. He'd saved their lives and, maybe if they were all lucky, he'd saved *K-219* as well. Hand over hand he climbed, rung for rung; the heat no longer bothered him so badly but his throat burned horribly. He wondered what kind of a medal they might give him. He knew it would look good on his dress uniform. Imagine walking into the bar back at Gadzhievo with the Order of the Red Star hanging around your neck!

He came to the top, took one last look back down into the dark bilge of the reactor compartment, then turned to the hatch that would lead to compartment eight, to fresh air, the happy faces of the men he'd just saved. Someone would have a bottle, they'd open it and share it around. He was no longer the new boy. He was one of them.

He grasped the wheel that would undog the steel hatch. By turning it, the metal fingers around the perimeter of the hatch would retract and allow the door to swing inward. The wheel turned, the dogs retracted. He pulled.

The hatch refused to budge. He leaned on the wheel to be sure all the metal dogs had pulled back, then tried again. Still nothing. Had they locked him in somehow? Did they lock it from the other side to be sure he would complete the job of shutting that reactor down? He still had the metal crank. He rapped it against the hatch, then yanked back on the handle. The hatch seemed welded in place.

There was a *kashtan* station on the bulkhead. Preminin picked up the microphone. "Central? This is Preminin. I can't open the hatch into eight." His voice was curious, not panicky.

Britanov said, "Sergei, are you sure the dogs are all free?"

"It's jammed."

Security Officer Pshenichny heard the rapping of the crank on the hatch. He couldn't hear Preminin, but Britanov's end of the conversation came over the shipwide loudspeaker system.

"Captain?" he said. "Tell Preminin to open the wheel all the way. We'll push the hatch open from our side. It must be warped from the heat."

Britanov relayed the message and Pshenichny got five of the brawniest men to put their shoulders to the hatch. "Go!"

They grunted as they strained. Nothing. A sharp pounding came from the other side. Preminin was beating the steel with his crank.

"Again!"

The five literally threw themselves at it. There was not the slightest hint of movement.

"Sergei. Look very carefully," said Britanov. "Are you certain the dogs are all open?"

His chest heaved. What had taken one gasp before now took two; it was like trying to breathe through a straw that grew narrower and narrower. "Yes . . . it's . . . they're . . . open."

"Don't worry. We'll get you out. Just hold on. Sergei?"

"I'm . . . getting . . . low . . ."

"Sergei!"

". . . almost gone."

"Pshenichny," said Britanov. "You've got to get that hatch open now."

Pshenichny sent a sailor back to a damage control station for a collapsible jack. The device was a steel tube nearly two meters long with extensions on both ends that could be levered out by cranking on a handle. Designed to apply pressure to emergency shoring, it could put tremendous force on a recalcitrant hatch.

The rapping on the hatch became weaker. Pshenichny helped put the jack in place and held it while a heavily built sailor began to crank.

The door creaked as the pressure against it built.

"Keep cranking!" he yelled as the creaks became groans.

There were no more sounds from the other side of the hatch.

The handle was getting harder and harder to operate as the pressure on the jack increased. The bulkhead that backstopped it was visibly bending. Still the hatch refused to budge.

"Did you get it open?" asked Britanov.

"No, sir," said Pshenichny. "Something's jammed it good."

"Captain," said Chief Engineer Krasilnikov. "It's got to be a pressure problem. Seven is pressurized and eight is not. They're pushing against tons of differential pressure. They'll never get it open unless we equalize the two compartments. We can either pressurize eight or vent seven."

"There's gas in seven."

"Understood. I'll pressurize eight."

"Pshenichny," said Britanov, "we're going to equalize the pressure in seven and eight. Krasilnikov thinks that's the problem. Get ready to go in."

"Sir, have you heard from Preminin?"

"No. Get ready," said Britanov as the engineer threw the necessary switches on the master air panel. He nodded. The lights dimmed as the air pumps drew load from the emergency power generators.

"Stop!"

"Sergei?"

"Stop the pumps!" It was Pshenichny. "Gas! There's gas coming in!" The moment the vents began to blow in eight, acrid brown smoke began to fill the corridor where the sixty men waited.

Krasilnikov killed the pumps. He looked at Britanov.

"Captain . . ."

It was Preminin!

"Sergei! How are you doing?"

The answer came with the click of the microphone key.

"Listen. Can you operate the ventilation system on your side?"

A click.

"Good! Open the first and second valves on the starboard side of the hatch. That will vent your space to the atmosphere. They'll be in there to get you the moment you vent. Can you do it?"

Another click.

Britanov waited as long as he could, then said, "Sergei. Did you do it?"

The young seaman's voice came over the ship's loudspeaker. Everyone on board *K-219* heard him.

"They're jammed." A long sigh followed, then a sound like a sniffle, as though Preminin were crying.

"Sergei? Answer."

Nothing. Not even a click.

Preminin slumped against the bulkhead. The OBA was empty. The rubber bladder on the tube collapsed. His nostrils were wet with foam welling up from his acid-burned lungs. The mask was pinching his face. His skin tingled with the frantic electrical firing of dying cells. He dropped the heavy crank. The sound of it echoed in the empty compartment. He'd saved them. Sergei Preminin, son of a simple flax worker, had saved an atomic submarine and her crew.

His arm felt so heavy as he raised it he thought for an instant he still had the baffle crank. But his fist was empty. It floated up to his narrowing vision, just beyond the cloudy, sweat-streaked lenses of his mask. Trapped. Inside the mask. Trapped.

But there was a way out. He knew it. The trapdoor. He grabbed the rubber mask and, with all his strength, he yanked it off. He took a small breath, testing. The burning got worse. His nostrils began to gush green foam. It was almost over. There was no reason to prolong this. The air smelled strangely, of ionized gas, of bitter almonds, of hot machine oil. A roaring filled his ears. He wiped the foam from his face. He looked at the steel hatch, opened his mouth wide, sucked in a tremendous gasp of poison and let his soul go free.

"Sergei, answer."

There was no click.

"Sergei? Answer."

Kapitulsky came in from main engine control. He stood next to Britanov and Krasilnikov, trying to think of something, anything, that could be done for Preminin.

"Captain?" It was Pshenichny. "We've got problems here."

"What now?"

"The vents? Gas is still coming through them."

Krasilnikov shook his head. "Everything is off, Captain. There shouldn't be any flow at all unless the lines were damaged."

Britanov said, "We'll try to reverse the pressure. Make sure everyone has an OBA canister."

"Captain, there are no OBA canisters left."

Britanov turned to his two friends, Kapitulsky and Krasilnikov. Between them they knew every nut and bolt on K-219. Britanov could see in their eyes what they thought. He knew from their faces what he had to order.

"Captain?" said Aznabaev. "Message from the freighter *Fyodor Bredkin*. She'll arrive in a little over an hour."

He picked up the *kashtan*.

"Pshenichny? Get the men aft to ten. Prepare to evacuate through the aft escape trunk. Bring all the men and all the casualties back there and seal the hatches as you leave. You're going to have to get them out and lined up on the weather deck. Leave no one. Is that understood?"

"What about Preminin?"

The only answer Britanov had was one he found impossible to say.

CHAPTER 11

My God. Isn't there anything
we can do for those guys?

—*President Ronald Reagan*

Makeshift stretchers were lashed together from lengths of shoring lumber and sheets. Fourteen unconscious men sprawled on the deck. Among them was Belikov, the reactor officer; Markov, the sub's communications specialist; and Dr. Kochergin. Sergiyenko, the political officer, was too frightened to speak. He kept to the shadows, staring with huge, round eyes, his white uniform splotched with oil, with smudges, with green stains from the injured.

The wounded were lifted onto the improvised litters by the ablebodied and covered with another sheet. Not that it was cold; stoked by nearby electrical fires and body heat, the temperature in compartment eight was over one hundred degrees Fahrenheit and rising. How hot it might be in the missile room was anybody's guess; the remote readings were all dead. The only reliable measure would be when the fourteen remaining missiles reached their flash point and exploded.

Keeping the poisoned men's faces clean proved impossible; acid-green foam bubbled from their nostrils and through their lips as fast as it could be swiped away with a dirty rag.

The wet tissues of their lungs had been seared by nitric acid. The foam was the body's protective response to those burns. But the protection was drowning the injured sailors. Three had already died and Preminin made four. It was clear to everyone, Pshenichny especially, that if they didn't get real medical care soon there would be many more dead.

As the men made ready to move aft, a few seamen disappeared to their bunks to retrieve an important possession; a tape player, a photograph, a bottle. When they returned, Pshenichny counted them off three times to be sure no one was missing. When he was sure, a procession of sixty haggard, frightened men began their final retreat down the narrow passage through nine, to compartment ten. Seamen bearing the wounded went first, then those able to walk, warrant officers next, and finally the officers.

Ten was the last compartment. There was nothing beyond it but the sealed space between the inner and outer pressure hulls, the great bronze screws, and the sea.

Security Officer Pshenichny carried Dr. Kochergin in his arms back to compartment ten. He could have put him on a stretcher, but he felt he owed Kochergin more. After all, the doctor had given him his own OBA mask when Pshenichny was suffocating and surrounded by fumes. Kochergin was dying because he'd given Pshenichny a chance to live.

Kochergin had not regained consciousness and his ruddy skin had turned a pale gray. *At least he's breathing,* thought Pshenichny. He'd left three dead back in eight; two of the missilemen from four and Weapons Officer Petrachkov. Their bodies had bloated in the heat to the point where it was not possible to carry them through a hatch. With Preminin, they were leaving four of their shipmates behind.

Leaving them was wrong, but there was nothing at all to be done about it.

Compartment ten was a tiny space even by submarine standards. With sixty men it quickly became intolerable. The crew rarely came back here in the course of normal patrolling. The compartment was crammed with steering gear, hydraulic actuators, and the oily shafts of the submarine's twin screws. Somehow the men squeezed in, breathing, it seemed, in turns. After another count, Pshenichny ordered the hatch to compartment nine sealed.

The men clustered at the base of a tall, narrow ladder. Overhead was a wheel that would unlock the inner hatch of the emergency escape trunk. Beyond that was a last hatch to unlock, and then there would be nothing but open sky and clean air.

To the rear was a solid bulkhead through which the propeller shafts penetrated. Forward, the spaces were filling rapidly with gas. There were far too many men in here. They'd suffocate if the gas didn't get to them first. There was nowhere else to go now except out.

Pshenichny put his hand up to a ventilation grille; the flow was weak, barely detectable. He had a moment of panic when he wondered whether the escape hatch would open. If not, they'd all be dead.

It had happened before to other men in other Soviet boats; one crew rode out a terrible gale, trapped in the after compartment of a burned-out hulk of a sub that somehow refused to sink. They'd sealed themselves up and lived for three weeks until the submarine was towed into port. No light, no food other than what they'd stuffed into their pockets, no water except what they could drain from lines passing through the space. It was unimaginable. He looked up at the hatch.

He dreaded giving the order, only to find their last avenue of escape had become a trap.

One of the warrant officers produced a bottle of vodka and began passing it around, hand to mouth. When it came by Pshenichny he took a deep pull like everyone else.

The frightened, the wounded, the drunk, gathered beneath the ladder that led up to the aft escape hatch, waiting for someone to tell them what to do.

"Look!"

One of the seamen pointed at the ventilator grille. From it came a steady white mist. It might have been nothing more dangerous than condensation, but the men pushed and shoved to get away from it all the same. They were jammed together now in the far corner of the space. Jammed like atoms in a reactor nearing the point of criticality. A shout, a shove, then a punch was thrown.

"That's enough of that!" Pshenichny roared. "Sergei Preminin didn't die so that you could behave like schoolboys!"

The two combatants were pulled from one another. They glared, but they did not fight.

The security officer took the *kashtan*. "Captain? This is Pshenichny. We're all at the escape hatch now."

"Everyone?"

"Everyone still alive," said Pshenichny, and looking at Dr. Kochergin, he wasn't too sure of that, either.

"Captain?" said Aznabaev. "The master of the *Fyodor Bredkin* has us in sight. He wants to know what we need."

Britanov sucked in a long breath, then slowly let it out. He knew that his next words would stay with him forever. Had he done everything he could to save his men? *How do you lose your command?* he wondered. *Gracefully? Bravely? Or just correctly?* There were four confirmed dead. Preminin in a way was the worst. How many more of the injured would also die? He had no choice. Moscow might view things differently, but for Britanov, his men always came first. Before the submarine, before the glory of the Navy. Before his own career, whatever of that was left now. He put the *kashtan* mike to his lips and said, "Open the escape trunk. Have the men assemble on the weather deck." Then to Aznabaev he said, "Tell that freighter to send over a launch and, if they have any, some OBA canisters, too. Tell them to stand by to accept casualties."

Aznabaev saw the empty look in Britanov's eyes; it was not only fatigue. He nodded and disappeared back into the radio alcove.

"All right! You heard the captain!" Pshenichny nodded at the young seaman who had warned about the mist coming into their air. "Undog the escape hatch."

The sailor swarmed up the ladder and grabbed the wheel that un-locked the inner door.

All eyes were on him. Pshenichny was not alone in his fear of getting trapped.

The wheel spun.

Open, you bastard, thought Pshenichny.

The young sailor put his shoulder to the steel and grunted.

Open!

The heavy hatch moved up on its hinges.

Pshenichny let out a long breath.

The seaman's torso disappeared up into the escape trunk itself. It was narrow as a sewer pipe. His thighs vanished, his knees.

Come on!

There was a dull boom, a clang, and then the boy's boots kicked their way out of sight.

A cheer went up in compartment ten. Pshenichny was embarrassed to find his own mouth wide open. He was yelling at the top of his lungs.

Outside the prison of compartment ten, up on the exposed back of the wallowing sub, the air was so clean, so different from what they'd been breathing for so long. The first sailor out stopped at the top of the ladder and sniffed warily. He eased himself halfway out of the hatch.

It was a fantasy, a postcard. The sky was filled with bright morning light, the air balmy, the sea an unfamiliar blue. Low waves struck the submarine's port side and rocked her back and forth. Now and then a higher sea washed completely over the sub's backbone, sloshing up the steeper sides of the missile deck, burying it in white foam.

A loud airplane buzzed around the rolling sub; a dark shape on the horizon revealed itself to be the bow of a freighter.

Forward along the high missile deck, yellow fumes and acrid purple smoke billowed from a hole where one of the silo hatches had once been. The wind was blowing it forward, almost directly at the exposed bridge. There was someone up there wearing an OBA mask. It looked like Vladmirov, the executive officer.

An ungentle push from below popped the dawdling sailor out and onto the wet black deck. The steel plates were coated in rubber tiles. The rubber was supposed to make the sub harder to detect by the Americans. Right now he couldn't care less about Americans. All he knew was that the rubber made for better footing.

A steady stream of men began to emerge from the escape hatch. Once more it was wounded first, common seamen next, warrant officers, and finally the officers. Pshenichny was the very last. He'd passed the unconscious body of Dr. Kochergin up to the waiting hands above. Pushing him up the trunk was like loading a cannon. It would have been utterly impossible to bring Petrachkov's bloated corpse up through it.

The security officer took one final look at the empty, quiet interior of compartment ten. The deck was littered with empty OBA canisters, drained vodka bottles, filthy rags smeared a vile green. He could smell the tang of the sea cascade down from the bright white circle of sky overhead. He could also smell the sharper scent of bitter almond wafting in from the ventilation ducts in the bulkhead. And something else, something new. Pshenichny turned to look down the long, dim passage leading forward. What was it?

He took four steps to the nearest bulkhead and poked his head into a side passageway that led down a vertical ladder to the bilges.

Smoke was rising up the ladder rung by rung; the stinking brown smoke of burning hydraulic oil, of melted wires.

No wonder it was so hot; the deck beneath his boots was a griddle. Fire had crept through the bilges.

A steeper wave rolled over the submarine's tail and Pshenichny had to grab onto the bulkhead to keep from falling. It was time. There was nothing more down here. Nothing except fire, poison, and the dead. He thought about Preminin, about the young boy who had saved all of them, sealed behind a steel hatch.

"There's a ship coming!" someone called from the escape trunk.

Pshenichny went aft, put his boots on the bottom rung, and climbed to the light.

FOREIGN MINISTRY BUILDING, MOSCOW

There had been no explanation, no warning. Only a summons to the American Embassy to send someone over to receive a message meant for President Reagan from the general secretary of the Soviet Union, Mikhail Gorbachev. It brought Chargé d'Affaires Richard Combs and Political Counselor Mark Remee running. They'd driven so fast along the Garden Ring Road that they'd drawn the attention of the GAI, the Moscow traffic police, who took after them with their blue strobe light flashing. They kept a distance behind the black Chevrolet, half chasing, half escorting it.

Combs paid no attention to them. He was sure this all had something to do with the scandal rocking the embassy: the Marine guard detachment was seriously in over their heads with local Russian women, many if not all of whom worked for the KGB. To add to Combs's troubles, the United States had just expelled fifty-five Russians from their embassy in Washington. The Russians were expected to retaliate by expelling some Americans from Moscow. Was this what the urgent message was all about?

Whatever it was, a sudden demand like this was never good news.

The two Americans arrived at the Foreign Ministry building; a thirty-story pile of Stalinist masonry. They found the designated diplomatic area roped off. They pulled onto the curb and left their lights flashing as a sign to the cops. Their patrol car had pulled over to the curb down the street, the two officers watching from a distance.

Combs and Remee hurried up the stone steps, showed their diplomatic passes to the guards at the door, and were ushered into a dark hall redolent with stale tobacco, boiled cabbage, and unwashed urinals. There they met a tall, attractive Russian woman who took them up to the fourteenth-floor office of the deputy foreign minister, Yuri Vorontsov.

"Good day," Vorontsov said in Russian. He had a single piece of white paper on his desk. He put on his gold-framed glasses and picked up the paper.

Here it comes, thought Combs.

" 'From the President of the USSR and General Secretary of the Communist Party, to the President of the United States. Dear Mr. President; General Secretary Gorbachev would like you to know that one of our ballistic-missile submarines in the Atlantic has suffered a fire and several casualties. Although the submarine is still in distress approximately five hundred miles north of Bermuda, there is no danger of radioactive contamination, nuclear explosion, or accidental launch of the missiles. Soviet ships are on the scene and others are en route.' "

Vorontsov looked up over the frames of his glasses and saw Combs furiously jotting down notes. "Here, Richard," he said, offering the sheet. They were the first words in English he'd spoken. "You may have the original."

"Thank you," said Combs. "I'll get this sent right away."

"So," said Vorontsov.

It was his way of ending the audience. Combs and Remee left, retracing their steps out to the embassy car.

The traffic police had moved in and were now parked in front of the black Chevrolet. One of the cops leaned out of his window and pointed at the No Parking symbol.

"Please move your car, gentlemen," Combs said in polite Russian. "You are obstructing the conduct of diplomatic relations." He then added in less polite English, "Get out of our way, you idiots."

After a few long moments of silent standoff, the GAI cruiser inched forward and stopped, leaving barely enough room for the Chevrolet to get out. Combs considered ramming it, but figured what with the note he had in his pocket, there were enough troubles in the world this Saturday.

WHITE HOUSE SITUATION ROOM

President Reagan cut short his Saturday trip to Camp David and flew back to Washington in time for lunch. The Marine helicopter settled out on the lawn where the deputy assistant for national security affairs, John Poindexter, waited.

Commander Bohn opened the curtains of the Situation Room and watched them walk briskly off in the direction of Poindexter's East Wing office. Bohn had a packet of new photos taken by an EP-3 orbiting the stricken Soviet sub. It really did look bad; a pall of yellow smoke streamed out from a hole in her missile deck big enough to drop a Volkswagen into. The fairwater planes were straight up and down, indicating the boat had lost all power. Another photo showed a freighter racing to her aid.

He wondered whether Poindexter would brief the president about the crazy notion of bringing the Soviet boat into a U.S. port.

An aide rushed over to Bohn's desk with a sheet of paper. It was a copy of a copy, both in the original Russian and a translated version, of the note handed to Chargé d'Affaires Combs in Moscow. The note had been relayed by the Department of State duty officer who also bounced copies to the Pentagon. Just as he started to read, the telephone buzzed. "Commander Bohn speaking."

"This is Poindexter. The president wants a brief on the submarine matter. Are you ready?"

Bohn scanned the translated message. "Wow."

"Excuse me, Commander?"

"Sorry, sir. Yes. We're ready. I've got a message. It's from Mikhail Gorbachev."

"A FLASH message?"

"No, sir. It just came over from State."

"We'll be right down."

Bohn reread the message. *Why didn't Gorbachev use the Hot Line?* he wondered. To soothe us? To lull us? What was going on between the lines? It had to happen one week before the big summit. Was that chance, or strategy? The phone rang again, this time it was Captain Herrington over at the Pentagon.

He could almost feel the heat rising from the paper as he read the message to him.

Herrington said, "That note is really from Gorbachev?"

"As far as I know, Captain."

"Why didn't they use the Hot Line?"

"We're all wondering the same thing. What do you think about the text of the message?"

"It's just PR. Gorbachev doesn't know those missiles are safe," said Herrington. "There's no way he could."

"What do you mean?"

"*We* don't know they're safe," said Herrington. "So how could Gorbachev?"

Bohn sensed the arrival of the president before he saw him; there was a sudden electric charge in the air. First in was Kathy Osborne, Reagan's personal secretary. Then came John Poindexter, and finally President Reagan.

"Sir," said Bohn to the president, "this just came in from State. It's a message to you from General Secretary Gorbachev."

Reagan read it, then looked at Poindexter. "Maybe this guy is coming around. Maybe he learned something from Chernobyl after all."

"You've got the pictures?" Admiral Poindexter asked Bohn. He had a way of looking right through you.

"Yes, sir, Admiral." He opened the packet of photos and spread them out on a desk.

"On fire with all that poison around. My God. Isn't there something we can do for those guys?" asked Reagan.

"We have a rescue ship en route, Mr. President," said Poindexter, but he quickly glanced at Bohn. "She's the *Powhatan*. There's also a naval unit en route from Norfolk with radiation specialists on board."

"That's good. When will our men arrive?" asked the president.

"I'm told within the hour."

Our sub's already there! thought Bohn.

"All right. That's pretty good. I want Gorbachev to know we're doing all in our power to help."

Admiral Poindexter nodded and said nothing.

Jesus. He's not mentioning our submarine at all, thought Bohn.

"Is there any danger here, John?" Reagan asked Poindexter.

"I don't know. We've never seen this happen before, Mr. President."

"Do we know what caused it?"

"We think one of her missiles blew up. There could be radioactive contamination. We're doing some testing on that now. If we find any we'll want to keep all shipping in the vicinity very far away."

"There are three Russian freighters en route," said Bohn. "One of them should be on the scene already."

Poindexter looked at him and said, "Let them take the rads if they're so eager. It's their mess."

"What about *Powhatan?*" asked the president.

"She's equipped for towing and for fighting flooding and fires, but not nuclear materials," said Poindexter. "If the airborne Sniffer comes back positive, we may have to pull back and reevaluate. If it's bad enough, we may need to declare a quarantine zone around that submarine. As a precaution."

Quarantine? wondered Bohn. *To protect the world from radioactivity, or to let us capture* K-219 *out of sight?*

"What about Russian vessels?" asked Reagan.

"A vessel is something to hold strong drink, Mr. President," Poindexter quipped. "But just the same, you should probably express your concern to Chairman Gorbachev and urge him to keep his own people safe."

Reagan nodded. "You draft it and let me see what you have before it goes." Reagan shuffled through the photos once more. He looked at Bohn. "It sure looks like a real mess out there. Let's offer Gorbachev all the help we can on this. Tell him we've got a ship on the way and we're ready to assist those poor boys any way we can."

Admiral Poindexter smiled. "I couldn't have said it better, Mr. President."

AIR FORCE TWO OVER ANCHORAGE, ALASKA

The executive 707 leveled at thirty-two thousand feet, heading northwest for the Bering Strait and then on to Japan and South Korea. Caspar Weinberger was in the plush meeting room just behind the forward galley. The cabin was well insulated and almost dead quiet; it was far nicer here than back in steerage, the large cabin reserved for the press entourage. He read the message brought to him by his military affairs assistant, General Gordon Furnell. The text was considerably more complete than the simple note given to the president, amplified as it was by sources under Weinberger's personal command. In it was clear mention that the explosion on board *K-219* had been confirmed not only by SOSUS, but by a U.S. unit in trail; an attack submarine.

Weinberger was dead set against the upcoming superpower summit in Reykjavík. Not that lessening tensions with the Soviet Union was a bad idea. He was worried that lovable, good-hearted Ronald Reagan would give away the whole candy store. There were far too many people running around Washington who thought the cold war was over now that Gorbachev was in power, now that *perestroika* and *glasnost* seemed on the rise.

What they didn't seem to get was that Gorbachev was a pebble sitting at the top of a big, ugly pyramid. It was easier to move the pebble than the pyramid. So much easier that it didn't make much sense to agree to drastic arms cuts on nothing more substantial than Gorbachev's word.

Weinberger sat back in the leather armchair. President Reagan was a good man, but he was too eager to place his trust where trust did not belong. Too eager to see his name written on the marquee of history. Too eager to believe the best about people for Weinberger's liking. The summit would pit an old Party pro against a nice, old gentleman who didn't like working the edges, the details. Gorbachev would eat him alive.

He pressed a button and Robert Sims, the Pentagon press spokesman, appeared. "Get the press ready for a briefing," he said as he folded the message from Washington and slipped it into his suit jacket.

He waited five minutes, then went aft. "Gentlemen," he said, "I want to bring you up to speed on tragic events taking place out in the Atlantic Ocean."

At the word *tragic* the press group went dead silent and stared at the secretary of defense. They knew the code words. They were ready for something big.

"A Soviet submarine exploded off our shores yesterday evening. Preliminary evidence makes it look like one of her missiles went up in smoke. The force of the explosion was very great."

The reporters erupted.

"What about casualties?"

"Is there radiation leakage?"

"What caused the explosion?"

"How do we know it was a missile?"

"One at a time, gentlemen," said Weinberger. "We know some details thanks to a U.S. unit near the scene of the accident."

"What kind of unit?" someone shouted.

"What kind?" said Weinberger. "She's one of our submarines. You know I can't say more."

He didn't have to.

"Was it involved in the incident?"

"Trailing operations are always risky," said Weinberger. That was true. "We train our commanders to be very aggressive."

"Are you suggesting there was a collision, Mr. Secretary?"

Weinberger knew he had them now. He didn't need to say anything more. "Our sub was the one who heard the explosion and reported it. It's normal for us to trail them when they come so close to our shores. But I really can't go into that any further. You know how the submarine people are about details like that," said Weinberger with a straight face. That was also true. "Anyway, the word is it looks like Chernobyl out there. I'll keep you all advised as I hear more." He waited one beat, then two.

The reporters lunged for their assigned telephones right on cue.

Cap Weinberger didn't have a personal interest in heating up the simmering pot of the cold war, although he knew that what he had just done might be seen that way. He just thought that giving your umbrella to a smooth-talking Communist who promises it will never rain wasn't such a good idea, either.

K-219

Gennady Kapitulsky went up to the exposed bridge with an armful of blankets gathered from a locker in compartment three, and a fresh OBA canister for his mask. The propulsion engineer knew that it wasn't Gadzhievo up on top, but to an injured, perhaps unconscious man passed out on the cold steel decking, sea spray and wind could still be lethal.

The sun was intense, tropical, and not at all like the pale, weak object that hung in the winter skies of Russia.

Executive Officer Vladmirov was already up there with a pair of binoculars. He had his blue coveralls opened down to his chest. Kapitulsky stood next to him, feeling the strange heat of the sun on his own back.

"Well, this has been a hell of a first patrol for you," the propulsion engineer said. The air up here wasn't too bad as long as the wind drove the smoke away. Sometimes it didn't, and then he felt the poison's burn.

"Look." Vladmirov handed the binoculars to Kapitulsky and pointed.

Gennady took them and trained them to the east. At first the image was poor, but it sharpened as he adjusted the focus.

A mottled gray tube barely cut the surface of the sea half a kilometer distant. It appeared, then disappeared, as the waves rolled over it. "A periscope?"

"Not only that. I think the bastard hit us."

Kapitulsky turned away and looked at the gaping hole where the muzzle hatch had once been. Long silver grooves freshly cut into the steel hull scratched aft. It could be the hatch peeling back, or it could be something else, too. Kapitulsky looked once more at the periscope, then swung the glasses to the north.

The dark gray bulk of the *Fyodor Bredkin* filled the lenses. She was starting to slow, to back down to keep from running over the smoking sub.

He looked aft.

Behind, all the way at the submarine's stern, a crowd of men had gathered. Some stood, some paced nervously, some did not move at all. A few had stripped their uniforms off to bask in the bright sun.

"I'm going back to see what I can find out. You'd better tell the captain about that periscope."

Kapitulsky waited for the wind to blow the worst of the smoke away, then clambered down the ladder and stepped out onto the missile deck itself. The seas were running broadside to the immobilized sub. They were drifting north in the Gulf Stream's steady current. He couldn't see the periscope but he did spot the gray superstructure of a second freighter to the northeast; you could tell by her bow wave she was coming on fast. A four-engine plane roared back and forth, no doubt photographing him. On its next pass, he raised a fist and extended his middle finger. *Some languages,* he thought, *are universal.*

The wind shifted and the smoke surrounded him. He held his breath. He wanted to save his OBA mask for an inspection tour down below decks. He knew it was dangerous to linger here, staring, as it were, into the mouth of the volcano. He hurried around the damaged section and made his way over the intact muzzle hatches, through the crowd of anxious men, and found Pshenichny.

The security officer was on his knees over the still figure of Dr. Kochergin. A sheet was drawn up over most of the doctor's body, but his face still showed. It was a frightening shade of yellow, with green and red flecks at the corners of his mouth and beneath his nose.

Pshenichny was shaking, the effects of delayed shock now making it almost impossible to stand. He was crying as he took a filthy rag and wiped the new green bubbles away from Kochergin's face.

Kochergin must be dead, thought Kapitulsky. He took the security officer in his arms and helped him to sit. The security officer smelled of chemical smoke and bitter almonds.

Pshenichny tried to rise but, with the rolling of the sub and his own shaking, all he could do was to crawl over beside Kochergin.

"He gave me his mask," Pshenichny said between sobs. "Kochergin gave me his OBA when mine ran out. He saved my life."

"You saved all their lives," said Kapitulsky, looking at the men who stood around them. He recognized Sergiyenko, the *zampolit*. But as soon as their eyes met, the sub's political officer quickly looked away. He didn't look injured, only badly frightened. *What's his problem?* "You took charge, Valery. You kept your head and you saved your men. You did fine."

"No. Petrachkov, Preminin. Two more. All below. It's all poison and fire . . . now we're going to lose him," said Pshenichny as he stared down at Kochergin. "The man who saved me is going to die at my knee."

Kapitulsky gave him a blanket to spread over the doctor, then draped one over Pshenichny. He looked up and saw a motor launch being lowered over the side of the *Fyodor Bredkin*. "How bad is it down there?"

"Eight and nine are impossible," said Pshenichny after he stopped shaking. "Ten is starting to fill with gas. There's a fire burning down in the lower levels."

"In eight?"

"In eight, in nine, I think maybe even in ten. The missiles could blow at any time." His lips were chattering even though the sun was hot. "It's a dragon's lair down below."

"Leave the dragons to me," said Kapitulsky as the whaleboat motored up to within hailing distance.

"Is it safe?" called the coxswain, a fat, dark-skinned Tajik.

Kapitulsky stood up and shoved his way to the edge. "It's safer here than where you are."

"What?"

"Get your ass over here!" he roared. "Or I'll swim over there and kill you myself!"

The launch eased up alongside the stricken submarine. It was a sturdy wooden boat, though it had seen better days. It slapped against the rubber-tiled hull of the sub, bounced off, then banged into it again with enough violence to make the coxswain look nervously at the sideboards. The waterlogged submarine could crush it with a shrug of its black shoulder.

"The twelve on stretchers go first," said Kapitulsky.

The sailors organized a chain. Belikov, Markov, the unconscious, poisoned men were handed over the side. Kochergin was among them. The stretchers filled the small boat.

"All right," said Kapitulsky. He nodded to Pshenichny. "You go with them and see to the men. I'll stay behind to keep things organized."

He helped Pshenichny to step over and down into the pitching launch. "Go!"

As the coxswain gunned the engine, a figure jumped from the deck and landed in the middle of the whaleboat, nearly capsizing it.

Sergiyenko! The political officer. The *zampolit* huddled down among the white stretchers. Pshenichny looked at him in frank horror.

Kapitulsky stared, too. Their eyes met. Sergiyenko quickly looked away.

"Comrade Engineer?"

Kapitulsky turned.

It was a warrant officer. "If you want help going below, I'll come."

A second warrant officer joined the first. He had two explosion-proof lights with him. "So will I."

What I want, thought Kapitulsky, *is the* zampolit's *throat.* He was perfectly ready to toss the coward into the bilges and seal the hatch. "All right. Where are your OBA canisters?"

"There are no more, Comrade Engineer."

Kapitulsky had one new canister and one three-quarters full. He walked over to the escape hatch and peered down into the dark. He tossed the new canister to one of the warrants, and said to the other, "Give us the lamps and stay with your men." He put on his mask. The second warrant officer screwed in the canister and took a quick suck of air. "We're going below."

Gennady Kapitulsky and the volunteering warrant officer eased their way into the mouth of the dragon and disappeared.

CHAPTER 12

It made you feel strange. As a sailor
you were sorry for anyone needing
help at sea. But I knew that sub
carried a bunch of missiles, three of them
probably with the name of my hometown
on them. In that case, you didn't feel so bad.

—*Captain Albert Hunt, Master,*
USNS Powhatan

Gennady Kapitulsky jumped off the bottom rung to the deck of compartment ten. It was dim and stiflingly hot down here. He could actually feel the heat through the soles of his boots. For the deck to be so hot there had to be a real fire burning down below on the lower level. He thought of the missiles, still in their silos up in compartment four. If it was this hot back here, what was it like up in four? What would those twelve-meter-high missiles do when they reached their critical temperature?

A voice. "Comrade Engineer?"

The young warrant officer had joined him. The battle lamps were nearly dead. Only a weak orange glow came from them now.

"All right." Kapitulsky flashed his light around the space, then said, "Let's see how far we get. Follow me."

Together they made their way down the dark, hot passageway. As they moved in the direction of the missile room, the air got worse, the steel decking hotter. Finally, at the bulkhead to compartment eight, Kapitulsky stopped.

"They're in the next compartment," said the *michman*. He seemed frightened. "Petrachkov and two more. Their bodies, I mean, we couldn't bring them out. It was the heat, Comrade Engineer."

"The heat?"

"And the poison. The bodies swelled up like balloons. They were bloated. We couldn't carry them through the hatch."

The air was dense now with gas and smoke. Kapitulsky checked his OBA canister. Still working. He knew he'd used more air than the warrant officer who trailed behind him. He took out a thermometer from his pocket and held it up to a ventilation grill spewing dense brown smoke. The air coming in was over one hundred thirty degrees Fahrenheit.

Those rockets. He turned. "Let's get out of here."

They hurried back aft, retracing their steps until they got to the last intercom station in compartment ten. Kapitulsky picked up the *kashtan*. "Captain? This is Gennady in ten. Can you hear me?"

"I'm listening. What have you found?" Britanov answered.

"The temperature in eight and nine is way too high. There's got to be a fire down below decks. The heat seems to be coming from there. The explosion must have destroyed some bulkheads. Or maybe it's the acid eating through seals. I couldn't see to know for sure."

"Gas?"

"Spreading from eight into nine and ten. Captain? If you ask me, those other fourteen missiles could go off any minute. There won't be any warning with our remote instruments out. They'll just—"

"I understand. Get yourself out of there and seal the aft escape trunk."

"We're leaving now, Captain," said Kapitulsky. Then, for a reason he didn't understand, he said, "I'm sorry, Igor Anatolyevich. There's nothing I can do back here. I would if I could."

"I know that," Britanov replied. "I know you would."

"I'm shutting down the *kashtan,* Captain. We're leaving ten now."

Britanov knew from Vladmirov's reports that the launch was now shuttling his crew to safety aboard the *Fyodor Bredkin*. He knew a second freighter, a bulk cargo ship, was standing by ready to help. A third ship, a roll-on, roll-off vehicle carrier, was racing to the scene, too. *Those missiles,* he thought, *if they blow, we're all dead: the men standing up top on the hull, the sailors manning the launches, maybe those on board the freighters too.* Somehow he had to find out whether the missiles were really in danger of exploding, whether the fires were all burning on the lower levels. Someone had to go into compartment four again, and since it couldn't be reached from the stern, they would have to go in from compartment three, this one. He knew Krasilnikov would insist on doing it himself. But what if it blew up in his face?

Just then Aznabaev, the boat's navigator, came up and stood beside Britanov. His big, round face was covered with red lines and creases. It bled in places that were rubbed raw.

The captain peered closely at the navigator. "What happened to your face, Yevgeny?"

Aznabaev smiled one of his old, untroubled smiles. "It's nothing," he said. "I just grabbed the wrong OBA mask. It was someone else's. Two sizes too small. Under the circumstances, I made it fit." He rubbed his tender cheek.

"Your face looks like a laundry bag."

"A what?"

"A puckered laundry bag."

Aznabaev started to laugh, though it was colored by fatigue, by nerves drawn tight as piano wire.

The remaining men in central command stopped what they were doing and stared. One of them began to laugh, too. Then another.

The sound was so normal, so much at odds with everything that had happened in the last fifteen hours, that Britanov reached over and hugged him, then began laughing himself.

"We're both crazy as penguins, Zhenya," said Britanov as tears rolled down both their cheeks.

Finally, he let go and stepped back. "All right. Until I know what's happening with those missiles, we're going to get everyone off. Make the necessary signals to Moscow. Tell them I'm ordering the sub abandoned except for a damage control party. You can say the men are to be shuttled to the *Fyodor Bredkin* and—" He stopped.

"The *Krasnogvardyesk*," someone added.

"Yes. The *Krasnogvardyesk*. Say that there's an American patrol plane circling like a buzzard and one of their submarines is slinking around like a hyena. You know what they like to hear. Our radio still works?"

"Yes, Comrade Captain."

"Tell them we're securing all coded materials for transfer. Send it now." Britanov straightened himself up to full height and said, "I want nine volunteers to stay behind with me. You all heard what Kapitulsky said. The missiles could explode in the heat. I need to know what's happening in four. If it looks safe, we're going to hook up to the biggest freighter up there and make them tow us back to Gadzhievo. No one has to stay who doesn't wish to."

"You'll need a good engineer, Comrade Captain," said Krasilnikov. "Besides, this submarine is my home. I'm not ready to give it up yet.

I'll go back into four and see what's happening. If it can be fixed, I'll fix it. Then we'll both ride back to Gadzhievo together."

"I knew I could count on you," said Britanov. "Pick your own repair party. The rest of you, get ready to go. Start collecting the code materials. Everything is to be packed in the bags. I don't want anything left behind for someone to find."

The code bags were large white canvas sacks weighted with iron bars to make sure they'd sink. The CCP staff began collecting months of charts, communication records, navigation tracks, and the red-striped books with the nuclear release codes. The material quickly filled five, then six, then ten large sacks. Britanov took the silver key from around his neck that would unlock the missiles and ready them for launch.

It was such a small thing, so very light, and yet so enormous. He tossed it into the last bag.

Britanov picked up the kashtan. "Vladmirov?" he said to the executive officer up above in the open bridge.

"Captain."

"Organize a surface detail to help man the towlines. Have them open the bow locker and be ready to hook on. Which freighter looks like it has the best cook?"

There was a moment's hesitation, then, "*Krasnogvardyesk* is the biggest, Captain. She looks to be about eight thousand tons. There's a foreign ship in sight now, too."

"Foreign? What kind?"

"American. Two stacks, a big superstructure forward and nothing but towing gear aft."

"A tug." He thought, *They wouldn't dare.* But what were the rules of the sea when it came to salvage? What would the world say if the Americans found an abandoned submarine on the surface and decided to keep it for themselves? Could they be so bold as that? "How far away is she, Volodiya?"

"About three kilometers. She's standing by watching."

To see if we blow up. To Aznabaev he said, "Get the master of the *Krasnogvardyesk* on ship-to-ship. Tell him he's going to fulfill his patriotic duty and pull us home to Gadzhievo."

"What about the missiles, Captain?" asked the navigator.

"Home," said Britanov, "or into waters a little less convenient for our American friends. One or the next. Now send it and get ready to go yourself. Have the code bags taken up the open bridge."

"I can stay with you, Captain," Aznabaev objected. "You may need me to run the radios."

"I need someone to keep Moscow off my back even more."

The noon sun was intense, almost unbearably so for men used to artificial lights, to living sealed up underwater. Not even the sunlamps they had on board felt as hot.

Up on the main deck, Gennady Kapitulsky went to work overseeing the transfer of men to the shuttling motor launches. He still burned every time he remembered Sergiyenko jumping ship. *If I get off this boat, I'll strangle him.*

There was a little flotilla gathered around the smoking submarine; the freighter *Fyodor Bredkin* was a small black steamship with a dirty white smokestack. On the stack was a red and gold band that bore the hammer and sickle. It glowed in the hot, tropic light.

The *Krasnogvardyesk* was much bigger. She had a bright white superstructure and a deckful of heavy cranes for lifting bulk cargo. She too wore the red and gold insignia of the Soviet Union.

And then there was the American ship; low, gray and compact, but powerful-looking. With her boxy wheelhouse forward and sleek, flat stern she looked like a deep-chested bulldog. The red and white ensign snapping from her mast was the flag of the enemy.

The *Fyodor Bredkin*'s motor launch bumped against the low, sloping sides of the sub.

"You ten next." Kapitulsky herded another group of sailors off the stern and into the boat.

The seas had abated somewhat, at least the sick rolling was not so pronounced. It was possible to simply step off the low-riding sub and into the launch without having to time your move with the seas.

The launch motored off as a chuff of black exhaust puffed up from the freighter's rust-stained stack. As Kapitulsky watched, the *Krasnogvardyesk*'s engines rumbled to life. Her single screw began to churn the water as she swung her bow away.

Where is she running away to? He was about to go forward to ask when Krasilnikov came back, gingerly stepping over the damaged missile deck, pausing only long enough to stick a finger into the grooves cut into the submarine's plates. They went down to the first knuckle. He stood up and joined Kapitulsky at the stern.

"Where's that fat bastard going?" Kapitulsky said, pointing at the freighter.

"We're going to try to rig a tow. Some of us are staying," said Grandfather Krasilnikov.

"All right. I'll stay."

"No. The captain wants you to go over to the *Bredkin* and keep an eye on the men. He says he needs you and Aznabaev to keep Moscow off our backs. Aznabaev will work the radios, but you're an engineer. They'll believe what you tell them. Okay? Okay." Grandfather Krasilnikov wasn't in the mood for a long conversation.

"But—"

"Captain's orders." Krasilnikov turned away and picked two warrant officers from the group waiting to leave the sub. He didn't ask them. He jabbed each of them on the chest and crooked his finger. They followed meekly, if not gladly.

Tow us home? It would be one hell of an operation given that the sub had no way to steer. They'd be lucky if they could make the tow last as long as Bermuda, the nearest land. Tow us through the North Atlantic? Kapitulsky didn't think much of that idea, either.

The three engineers went back forward, leaving Kapitulsky alone with the realization that he might soon be leaving *K-219* forever. He remembered the videotape of his wedding that he'd stashed in his cabin. It was forward in compartment two. He looked around and saw a heavy tow cable being lowered from the *Krasnogvardyesk*'s high stern to a waiting boat below. He could see the sweat on the faces of the sailors as they toiled in the heat.

There was just enough time.

He ran forward, dodging the smoke billowing up from the shattered silo, and worked his way around the conning tower to the bow.

The tow locker was already open, a heavy steel loop of cable pulled out and made ready. Everyone was looking forward as the launch from *Krasnogvardyesk* slowly approached bearing a manila line. At the end of that line would be a massive hook swaged to a thick steel tow cable; the hook would latch onto a Y-shaped bridle of wire bolted to *K-219*'s bow.

No one was looking at the forward escape hatch. Kapitulsky quickly opened it and dropped back down into the sub.

It was cold as a cave out of the direct sun. Water was sloshing over the deck at the bottom of the torpedo room. The air reeked of bitter almond. Battle lamps glowed dimly in the passageway. Their weak light didn't penetrate the officers' cabins at all. He made his way aft to his own, two-man space, entered the pitch-black room, and felt his way to his locker. Where was his flashlight? He'd forgotten it. He'd been too impulsive. He had to think more slowly, more clearly. He pulled through the clothes hanging there, the cold-weather gear, the dress uniforms, pawing at them until his hand closed around a familiar object. He snatched the tape out, but before he could close the locker a sound made him stop.

He turned and saw the outline of a man silhouetted in the dim emergency lights. "Who's there?"

The shape huddled over as though trying to hide something in the folds of his jacket. There was a glassy clink.

"What are you carrying!" Gennady demanded.

The shape turned and ran.

Kapitulsky followed. He knew the spaces blind. He caught up with the phantom just as he was climbing the ladder up to the forward escape hatch. He grabbed the man's legs and held on. He wasn't letting go, and with him hanging there, those legs weren't going anywhere, either.

Kapitulsky yanked and the phantom fell onto him. They both sprawled on the deck.

"You!"

He recognized a senior warrant officer, a *michman* engineer. The man was clutching a brace of bottles to his chest. He'd obviously been going from cabin to cabin looting them from private stores.

"You've been stealing!"

"They won't do the fish any good, Comrade Engineer," he answered. He held out a bottle. "You want some?"

Kapitulsky recoiled. "How many bottles did you take, thief?" He counted them. Seven full bottles of vodka, plus a small jar of homemade brew. He looked up at the sheepish engineer. "If I find one of those bottles open, I'm volunteering you to stay on the salvage party. You'll ride the boat all the way back to Gadzhievo looking for ice. Is that understood?"

"Understood, Comrade, but—"

"Don't call me comrade. Get yourself up on deck. And remember, I've counted the bottles."

Gennady watched the chastened man disappear up the ladder. The back of his mouth tasted of almonds. He felt sick, light-headed.

He scrambled up after him and took a deep, long breath of clean sea air.

Stealing from his mates! His wife, Irina, hated these damned submarines, hated everything about them. She said it turned men into unfeeling robots.

Maybe, he thought as he watched the phantom engineer jump onto a launch, *she was right.*

Grandfather Krasilnikov shouldered his way into his old asbestos suit. It was more clumsy than the newer, rubber models, but he trusted it more. He retrieved his own private stash of OBA canisters; he knew better than to rely on the ship's supply and so he had a few hidden away for emergencies. He handed out the spare canisters to the two *michman* engineers he'd "volunteered" to help him.

Krasilnikov was not a man to be argued with in the best of circumstances. He'd been known to shove a lazy bosun down a ladder in order to shape him up. More than a few seamen wound up with broken shoulders and arms. Grandfather had never been charged with assault and the lazy individuals had been quietly removed from the crew, which was fine as far as Krasilnikov cared. Either you gave everything, or you didn't work for him.

"Let's go," he said to them.

They dropped down the ladder from central command to the next lower deck. From there they moved aft to a small space sealed with double hatches. The three of them could just fit inside. Krasilnikov pulled his mask down over his face tightly, took a quick breath to be sure there was oxygen flowing, then sealed the inner door. He glanced at the two terrified *michmani* sealed into the airlock with him. One carried a portable fire extinguisher. They all carried temperature probes. In a canvas sack were tools for opening access hatches in the silos, and a couple of spare explosion-proof lamps. One of them also had a fume detector with a meter that displayed how much poison was in the air.

Krasilnikov said, "Ready?"

Neither one said anything, or at least nothing that could be heard through their own OBA masks. Their eyes, however, showed a lot of white. What was on the other side of the hatch? A flood? A fire? A wave of poison?

"Okay. If it's bad we look around and get out. Otherwise just do what I do. You'll be all right."

With that, Krasilnikov unlocked the hatch leading aft into the damaged missile room. The instant he opened it, a dense white cloud of mist flowed in and filled the small airlock.

"Nitric acid!" said the *michman* with the chemical fume detector. "High concentration, Comrade Engineer!"

"So what? You need a bath anyway. Keep your masks on and you'll be fine," said the chief engineer as he walked into the acid mist.

Their lights penetrated only a little way into the dark space. It was like walking in some eerie, poisonous forest by yellow moonlight. The silos were all smoking, the insulation around them damaged by acid. Electrical conduits lay bare, the wires sparking and smoldering. The mist seemed to be rising from below, drawn up by the chimney of the blown-open silo hatch.

Krasilnikov went straight to silo six. He could look straight up and see light through the shattered silo plates. Deadly acid steam rose from the bilges where missile fuel and water were reacting.

"Check the silo temperature from here aft," he ordered the two warrant officers. "Anything higher than fifty degrees, yell."

With that, Krasilnikov started pulling off damaged insulation and beating out the glowing embers with his boot.

"Thirty-two degrees!" came the first shout as one of the *michmani* extended the thermometer into a well in the side of silo eight. Hot, but safe enough for now. The real danger began when the temperatures hit seventy degrees Celsius. At that point, explosion could take place at any time.

"Forty-three!" said the second warrant officer from silo eleven.

"Keep checking." The chief engineer never left the sub when she was tied up at the pier. He never went on leave. This was his home, his world. He wasn't about to see it blow up without a fight.

USNS *POWHATAN*

The master of the Military Sealift Command tug *Powhatan* stood on his bridge and watched the launches shuttle back and forth between the low black shape of the Soviet sub and a nearby freighter. What the devil was he doing caught up in *this* evolution?

The *Powhatan* was a civilian vessel, although USNS meant United States Navy Ship. She was attached to the Navy but not part of it. He was a civilian and his crew were all merchant seamen. They had no business putting their noses into this wild operation. Hell. They were sailors. Not spies.

He watched as a patrol plane, a Navy P-3 Orion, orbited overhead. Somewhere nearby an American attack sub was waiting, submerged. Somehow the skipper of the American sub was supposed to be in charge out here. Hunt had no way to talk with him directly, only by relay through the aircraft overhead. That was fine. He didn't know what he'd say to a submarine, anyway.

Captain Albert Hunt had been ordered onto a lot of salvage missions in his career. The powerful tug had towed some of the most glorious ships of the U.S. Navy at one time or another. Aircraft carriers, even the enormous *Missouri*-class battleships. Some of the operations had been a little offbeat, though there weren't any he had to stay quiet about. *Powhatan* was a tugboat, and a tugboat skipper just didn't have much call for venturing into the "black" world of secret operations. Until today.

The Navy wanted him to appear helpful while doing everything in his command to keep that half-sunk sub from going very far. He was to retrieve anything thrown over the side of the sub, collect air and water samples, take photos, and, if possible, get some of his own crew into her under the guise of helping with damage control. No American had ever seen the inside of a Soviet boomer before. Who knew when the opportunity might come again? The Navy had their own ocean rescue tugs, but none as close to the scene as *Powhatan*. The message chattering in over his secure teletype had been very clear: she was to do everything in her power to put a tow onto the damaged submarine and haul her into Norfolk, Virginia.

Captain Hunt watched as a second ship, bigger than the first, maneuvered off the sub's bow in a manner that suggested she was getting ready to rig a tow. He was innocent when it came to espionage, but Hunt knew towing operations. He didn't give the Russians a whisker of a chance.

The freighter's stern was fifty feet up and the sub was almost flat to the sea. A towing cable from that freighter would have to drop way down, dive underwater, then rise in a strained half-loop known as a *bight*. The geometry would be unfavorable. A good tow is a flat tow, straight back from the tug to the ship being pulled. *Powhatan*'s stern was built low to the sea for this very reason. How heavy was a Soviet boomer, anyway?

Hunt took a pad of paper and drafted a message for his signalman. It wasn't often you got a chance to practice sending a message using the old-fashioned light gun. He tore it off and handed it to him. It read:

To: Master of the Soviet ship *Fyodor Bredkin*
From: Master, USNS *Powhatan*, ATF-166
Greetings. I am equipped with pumps, strong searchlights, and small boats. Do you need assistance? Am authorized to provide help if you require.

The signalman climbed up to the exposed platform over the bridge and flashed the message in international code to the Soviet freighter. An answering blink quickly came from the freighter's own bridge.

"Message sent and acknowledged, Captain," said the signalman.

Hunt watched as the *Krasnogvardyesk* came to a stop directly off the submarine's bow. A heavy steel towing cable had been dragged to the bow of the sub and made fast to some sort of fitting. *Lotsa luck, pal,* he thought. He could certainly do a lot better job of towing, though he doubted the Russians would like his destination. Hauling a boomer into Norfolk. That was Tom Clancy stuff; a *Hunt for Red October* kind of story.

Only for real.

Hunt took a pair of binoculars to watch closely. He knew what would happen, just not when.

K-219

Tons of steel cable stretched down from the freighter's high stern, diving underwater only to emerge at *K-219*'s bow. There the end was made fast to a fixed loop kept stored in a special locker in the submarine's hull. Two additional cables ran in special grooves back to the conning tower; one on the port side, the other to starboard.

Britanov stood in the open bridge with Vladmirov, the executive officer. The code bags nearly filled the cramped cockpit.

"It's like summer up here," said Vladmirov.

"It's hotter down in the missile room," Britanov replied. He was sweating heavily. How did people work in such a climate? "This tow," he said. "It's not going to work."

"If he takes it easy it could."

"It's useless. We have no steering. The first wave that pushes us will make us veer off at an angle. The cable will snap and that will be that. But you know what they'll say if we don't try."

"You've done everything that's possible, Captain," said the exec.

Britanov smiled. "That, Volodiya, is probably the one thing they will *not* say."

The towing party at the bow signaled up to Britanov, then stepped back. A steel cable that big, under that much tension, could snap with enough force to cut a man in two.

Britanov had a handheld radio with him. He checked to be sure the frequency was the correct, ship-to-ship channel, then pressed the transmit bar. "Zhenya?"

"I'm listening, Captain," said Aznabaev. *K-219*'s navigator had taken over the *Fyodor Bredkin*'s radio room.

"How's Dr. Kochergin doing?"

"Still unconscious. They don't have any medical supplies on board except some alcohol. They put a soaked rag in his mouth and he's breathing through it. It's supposed to help."

Of course there would be alcohol. Forget OBA canisters. Forget using seals that actually stand up to the kind of chemicals that might attack them. Forget designing missiles that are more of a danger to the enemy than to his own crew. Forget anything that makes sense, but a Soviet ship without alcohol? Unthinkable. "Tell the master of the *Krasnogvardyesk* he can begin. All ahead dead slow, or else it will break."

"Understood, Comrade Captain."

The *Krasnogvardyesk*'s stack chuffed black soot. The cable stirred as the freighter's single screw began to churn.

The submarine's bow swung as the slack was taken up. The groan of steel under tremendous tension sounded almost human. The thick cable crackled and hummed like a plucked string. A small bow wave formed in front of *K-219*.

Britanov thought, Maybe I was wrong. Maybe he'd become so used to failure he'd forgotten how to hope. The tow was working. They were moving again. He picked up a pair of binoculars and trained them on the cable. It was a thick bastard, all right. He moved the glasses to one side.

"Captain!" said Vladmirov. "We did it!"

Britanov had caught sight of something white, something moving, out on the blue tropic sea.

"Captain?" asked the exec.

"Look." He handed the glasses to Vladmirov.

A periscope was cutting the surface of the sea at high speed, its mottled green shape rising from a boiling wake of white water. It looked hooded, like a snake rearing to strike. It was headed right for them.

USS *AUGUSTA*

"All ahead two-thirds," said Von Suskil as the fast-attack submarine accelerated.

"Conn, Sonar. Range three hundred yards. I do *not* have a good fix on that cable, sir."

"Jesus," said the sonar operator under his breath. The captain was using a billion-dollar, nuclear-powered sub as a battering ram. And worse, he was taking them all along for the ride. If something bad happened, who would be blamed?

"Range one hundred. Sir, *I still do not have the cable bracketed.* Target is at unknown depth. It could be . . ."

"Hold course and speed." Von Suskil put his eye to the scope. "Steady. Steady—"

"Sir, I *cannot* guarantee clearance to that cable." The sonar chief was sounding rattled. Striking a steel hawser thick as a man's arm at this speed would surely snap it, but what would it do to *Augusta?* Destroy her sonar dome, flood some machinery spaces for sure.

"Helm, come starboard five degrees."

"Rudder starboard five, aye," said the helmsman. He moved the yoke slightly. His knuckles were dead white.

"Range one hundred yards."

"Speed twenty-one knots."

"Down the attack scope!"

The delicate instrument slid soundlessly into its well. There was no reason to risk snagging it on that cable.

"Okay, people," said Von Suskil. "Brace for impact."

Augusta charged at a point one-third of the way between the freighter and *K-219;* it was here the steel towline would dip the deepest before beginning its rise to the following sub. Von Suskil could see it perfectly in his mind's eye. What was everyone's problem? At their speed, they would make a knot of turbulence right where the steel cable was deepest and weakest. The "knuckle" would snap the line. He had orders to keep that damned pig boat where she was. To do everything short of hostile action to make it so. Well, nobody was going to second-guess Jim Von Suskil. No one would say he was too timid, that he wasn't pulling on his oar with everything he had.

K-219

"Captain! The periscope is gone!" shouted Vladmirov.

"He's crazy," whispered Britanov.

"Maybe he's turning!"

"Not even an American submarine can turn that fast. No, Volodiya. He's going to hit."

They'd watched the alien periscope streak for the gap between them and the *Krasnogvardyesk,* sure that it would smash squarely into the cable. But it had disappeared, retracting below the waves. There was only a subtle boiling of the sea to mark the nuclear sub's swift passage.

The wake rocketed by directly in front of *K-219*'s bow. Britanov found himself gripping the rim of the exposed bridge, even though he knew the impact was not aimed at him.

There was a jerk, a loud *twang!* that reverberated right through *K-219*'s hull.

The cable slackened as the submarine's inertia caused it to keep moving ahead. The massive tow hook slipped from the wire loop and splashed over the side, sinking. The wake at their bow subsided. And then silence. Nothing more than the warm afternoon breeze snapping *K-219*'s ensign.

"He cut it! That bastard cut our towline!"

The freighter was suddenly free of more than ten thousand tons of dead weight. Her single screw cavitated, thrashing the sea to a milky froth, then dug in. The stern sledded to one side, veered back, then straightened. Men crowded at her high stern, pointing down at the dark shape barely visible beneath the surface of the sea.

K-219 was once more motionless in the water.

They were a few hundred miles from the American coast. Near some of the enemy's biggest naval bases. Home, and friendly forces, were very far away. Britanov's thinking once more began to change, to assume a different shape; how he might make certain the Americans would never get their hands on *K-219,* how he could reassure Moscow that the U.S. Navy would never be able to pick her apart, to examine her secrets, to violate her.

"Captain?" It was the handheld radio. Aznabaev aboard the *Fyodor Bredkin* was calling. "Is everything all right? We saw—"

"Signal Moscow that an unidentified submarine is interfering with tow attempts. No. Don't say *unidentified.* Say the bastard's an *American* submarine."

"We just got a message from the American tugboat. They have pumps and boats and breathing apparatus. They want to know if there's anything they can do to help."

"I'm sure they're very anxious to help," said Britanov bitterly. "Tell them to stand clear. Tell them we have everything under control. Tell them anything you want. Is there something more I should know?"

"The airdrop of emergency supplies is fifteen minutes away. Two IL-62s with OBAs and spare canisters. The first mate of the *Bredkin* is organizing boats to recover the equipment."

"All right. Good."

"Captain, Sergiyenko is here in the radio room. He wants to speak with you."

"Why not? It's a fine afternoon for political discussions."

Zampolit Sergiyenko came on the line. "Captain? I want to stress that it's against regulations to accept assistance from NATO navies."

"I'm aware of that." Britanov angrily snapped the radio off.

Fifteen minutes later, perfectly on time, two blue and white Illyushin jets roared overhead. Black smoke billowed from their tail-mounted engines, making them resemble two loud, long-necked geese.

They circled, then came back low and fast. As they passed over the submarine, a dozen boxes spilled from their cargo ramps. The jets pulled away, climbing hard, and were gone almost before the crates hit.

Twelve boxes fell in perfect ballistic arcs. There were no parachutes. There were no flotation collars. They struck the water hard, sending up huge washes of spray dangerously close to the waiting launches. When the spray subsided, the launches moved in to recover the emergency equipment.

There was little to find. The crates had split up on impact. Ten of them sank outright. Of the remaining two, only a few bits of debris still bobbed on the surface. The launches recovered six usable OBA units. The rest went straight to the bottom.

Britanov watched the whole affair not sure whether to laugh or cry. He finally picked up the handheld radio and called Aznabaev.

"Tell Moscow," he said, "that the airdrop was perfect. But there was a small problem. Tell them when you throw out heavy things over the water, according to the higher regulations of physics, they sink."

CHAPTER 13

I was in the last boat with all the code bags.
We were halfway back to the freighter when someone
yelled and pointed. The periscope was coming straight
at us again. It was coming fast enough to cut
us in two. I thought, an explosion, poison gas, fires.
I survived *K-219* only to be run over
by an American submarine.

—*Chief Engineer Igor (Grandfather) Krasilnikov*

The late afternoon sun was hot, but even in the sea off Bermuda it
was still October. Its arc across the azure sky quickly brought it lower
and lower to the sea, where the salt haze absorbed its heat, leaving
only glare. The air was noticeably cooler, though no one would mistake it for the Barents. Britanov and his chief engineer stood in the
submarine's open bridge.

"You're sure they won't blow?" said Britanov.

Krasilnikov shrugged. "The missiles are hot. There's a chemical
reaction still going on down in the bilges. It could even be fire. But
no. They aren't hot enough to explode." Krasilnikov's uniform smelled

strongly of chemical smoke, of bitter almonds, the nitric acid poison. His face was smudged. He opened his mouth wide, showing rows of gold caps. He spat over the side. "I need a cigarette to get the taste of smoke out of my mouth."

"Smoking is bad for the health," said Britanov.

Krasilnikov was about to snarl a reply when he saw the captain's expression. "Funny."

The afternoon light was fading. The dense brown smoke that billowed from the gaping silo had thinned to a stream of yellow mist. The two *michmani* who had followed Krasilnikov into the missile room were at the bow, along with the other men of the damage control party. They were watching a launch from the *Krasnogvardyesk* troll back and forth, fishing for the broken end of the towline with long boat hooks.

"You know how deep the water is here?" Britanov asked.

"Deep enough," said Krasilnikov. But then he turned. "How deep?"

"Six thousand meters."

They both glanced at the American tugboat.

As the horizon began to flare red with sunset, the American P-3 patrol plane switched on its navigation lights; three stars in close formation, one red, one green, and one white. As it swept back over the smoking submarine, a dazzling white searchlight beamed down.

"I hope he runs out of fuel and has to swim home," grumbled Krasilnikov after the plane roared overhead and banked to the west for yet another annoying pass. He had a cigarette out and lit.

"He won't have as far to swim as we will," said Britanov. "You ever wonder about driving out the taste of smoke with more smoke?"

"Never."

"That's probably best. You have another one?"

Krasilnikov looked startled. "I thought you said smoking was bad for the health."

"I'm taking a shorter-term view of things."

The white canvas code sacks were wedged in all around them. The sea was alive with ships, none of them going anyplace. It was a harbor transported to the open ocean.

The two Russian freighters had now been joined by a third, a big white container ship, the *Vasiliyev* with BSC RO-RO SERVICE painted on its side in enormous black letters. An eight-hundred-foot billboard for the Baltic Steamship Company. Her bridge was housed in an aft superstructure, and the flat expanse of deck ahead of it was crammed with containers. Her bow opened up in two enormous clamshell doors, and her hold was filled with agricultural vehicles destined for Havana. Her stack, like those of the *Krasnogvardyesk* and *Fyodor Bredkin*, showed the red and gold hammer and sickle.

Of the towline there was no hint at all.

Aznabaev had radioed in the American submarine's aggressive actions to Moscow. Britanov could easily imagine the turmoil back in the Sardine Can, the Emergency Action Center in Moscow. Whenever politics and sense collided, the High Command froze like a deer caught in the beam of a headlight.

It was no wonder they'd taken over an hour to reply, and even then their reply was not surprising: Stop. Do nothing while we think and argue.

In the end, Moscow lost its taste for adventure and ordered towing attempts abandoned. Now all five vessels, four surface ships and *K-219*, drifted silently north in the grip of the Gulf Stream current.

No, thought Britanov. *Not five. Six.* He was certain the American submarine was close by, even if its periscope could no longer be seen.

The American tugboat had drifted closer, so gradually it didn't register on Britanov until it startled him. In the dimming light he could see men walking about her flat afterdecks, even recognize their faces. Britanov was sure that they would be only too glad to offer help towing his submarine. The minute everyone was off, they would swarm aboard. He was sure of it, just as he was sure that he would never permit it.

"At least we're not sinking," said Krasilnikov.

That could become a problem, thought Britanov. He said to his chief engineer, "I think there's nothing more to be done tonight. It's time for you to take off."

"Me? What about you, Captain?"

Britanov took the handheld radio and pressed the transmit bar. "Zhenya?"

"Go ahead, Captain," came the familiar voice of his navigator from aboard the *Fyodor Bredkin.*

"Have the master of the *Bredkin* send over one last launch. I'm sending the code materials with the damage control party. Put the bags under guard when they arrive. They will be your responsibility until they can be accepted by proper authorities."

"Understood, Captain, but won't you be here to keep an eye on them?"

"No," said Britanov. "I'm staying."

The radio was filled with static for a few seconds, then Aznabaev said, "Understood, Comrade Captain."

"You're sure about this?" asked Krasilnikov. "What if something happens? It would be a miracle if all those fires were really out."

"I'll stay in touch by radio. You get the work party together and load the bags when the launch comes. Who knows?" said Britanov with a shrug. "Believing in miracles is against Party doctrine. But we're far from the Party, Igor. We're sailors on the sea, and the sea is a big place. It's large enough to hold a lot of things we don't understand."

Krasilnikov didn't answer. Instead he said, "It's the Americans. You don't want to leave the boat because you think they might try to steal it. I know that you wouldn't—"

"Do I have to throw rocks? I want those bags moved while there's still light enough to see. Understood?"

"Understood. But Captain—"

"What is it now, Grandfather?"

"Don't stay too long. Speaking theoretically, a sailor shouldn't count on miracles."

"Speaking theoretically, I thank you. Now go."

Krasilnikov rounded up the other nine men of the work party and had them form a chain from the open bridge down to the bow of the sub. The sea was just a short step down. Krasilnikov felt the hair on his neck rise. Had the waves always come up so high against the black hull of the submarine? Was that high-pressure vent opening always so close to the waterline?

He turned back and saw the last code bag lifted from the open bridge.

Britanov waved, the bright spot of his cigarette a falling star against an indigo sky.

The launch from the *Bredkin* muttered back across the flat sea. It thumped against the hull. The code bags were tossed in, the nine "volunteers" followed them. The launch wallowed low under all the weight. Krasilnikov was last. He saw a last puff of cigarette smoke rise from the open bridge, then Britanov waved, then nothing.

"Come on, Comrade Engineer," said the coxswain from the *Bredkin*. "The cook is preparing *pelmenyi* for dinner." They were Siberian ravioli, a delicacy the submariners had not seen in more than a month.

Krasilnikov found a place to sit in the launch. The coxswain used a boat hook to push off. When they were clear, he gunned the motor and the overloaded launch wallowed in the direction of the waiting freighter, and dinner.

———————

Britanov stood alone on the open bridge, watching as the last launch left for the *Fyodor Bredkin*. The twilight cool made his skin shiver. He was the last man alive on board *K-219*. Once the code bags were safely on board the freighter, the value of his submarine would be reduced to the sub itself and the nuclear weapons it carried. The boat, his command, had become a coffin bearing the bodies of four of his crew. Preminin, Petrachkov, the two missilemen. A poisonous, smoking coffin. What had it cost to build? Ninety, one hundred million rubles? Whatever the sum, it wasn't worth what it had already cost.

Not that the hull, the weapons on board, her secrets, were worthless. One look at the nearby American tugboat convinced Britanov of that.

He thought of Preminin going in and cranking those reactors safe by his own hand. He thought of the tapping on the intercom, Preminin too weak to speak. And then no tapping at all. It was amazing to think that he had simply and willingly given his life to keep the reactors from melting, from exploding. What harm would have come to the fatherland if they had? The radioactivity would have washed up on American beaches, not Russian. And yet Preminin had done it, not for glory, not for pay, not for anything more than because he had been asked to, he was there, and he alone knew how.

Well, if the Americans tried to board his submarine, Britanov would do the same. Like Preminin, he would do his job not for glory, not for pay, but because he was here, because he knew how.

The launch was halfway to the freighter now. Britanov was about to flick the half-smoked cigarette over the side when he saw a sudden commotion, a boiling of the sea a hundred meters to the northeast.

He took his binoculars out and trained them on the disturbance. It was the periscope, the American submarine. It was once again slicing the sea at high speed.

It was heading straight for the launch.

He dropped the glasses and switched on the radio. "Zhenya!" he shouted. "Are you able to contact the launch?"

"No," Aznabaev answered. "They don't have a radio. Why? They're almost back, Comrade Captain. Did you want to speak with—"

"Signal them to turn back! Can you fire a flare?"

"What's wrong?" Aznabaev thought that *K-219* was in danger of sinking.

"The American submarine! He can't see it! It's heading for the launch!"

From up atop the conning tower Britanov could see the periscope, he could see the white wake thrown to either side as it sliced the sea. But down in the stern of that heavily loaded motor launch, low to the water, it would be invisible until it was almost on them.

Britanov reached down and pulled out a flare pistol from a locker. He cocked it, held it over his head and fired.

One second, two, three. Finally a white star burst over the launch.

Krasilnikov swung and looked back at the submarine. "Captain's in trouble. Turn us back."

"They'll send another boat. There's no room for—"

Krasilnikov shoved the coxswain hard in the chest. "I said turn us back or else we'll give your seat to the captain!"

The coxswain leaned against the tiller and the bow of the launch slowly swung in an arc. As it did, he saw something strange, something terrifying, rising from the sea directly ahead.

A tall green cylinder sliced the black sea. Two fans of white water sprayed to either side.

He stood up in his seat. The launch rocked alarmingly. Now he could see the way the surface of the ocean was humped, where it flowed over the curved hull of a submerged sub. It was running fast and true like a giant torpedo, straight for them.

He threw open the throttle and bent all his weight against the rudder. The turn was dangerously sharp. The boat heeled alarmingly.

The huddled men yelled as water sloshed over the low side. The coxswain could hear the throb of the submarine's engines as it came at them, a submerged train rumbling on tracks that seemed to converge in the pit of his stomach. He could hear the waterfall rush as the waves of spray rose, then fell from the speeding periscope.

He straightened the rudder as the launch steadied on a new heading ninety degrees off from their previous course. The periscope rocketed by so close that its hooded cobra's head could be seen to swing in the launch's new direction, the glassy eye following them as the submerged attack sub roared by just beneath the waves.

The splash of its spray wet them as it fell. The launch rocked in the wake, taking on more water into the bilge and soaking the men as well as the canvas code bags. The coxswain bent the rudder back and made straight for the *Fyodor Bredkin* as fast as the overloaded boat could go. The calm sea had seemed peaceful enough, but it was an illusion. Like the old mariner's charts that showed spouting, razor-toothed beasts and grappling tentacles, there were monsters swimming in these waters, too.

USS *AUGUSTA*

The attack center went dead silent, waiting for Von Suskil's next command.

"We came awful close to that whaleboat," said the XO.

"Had to if we were going to film the code bags," said the captain. "We got that run on tape? The low light camera feed worked?"

"Aye aye," said a petty officer, the disgust in his voice plain. "It worked just fine."

"Good. You see," the captain said to the XO, "now we know what Ivan's code bags look like. Might help when we pick them up off the bottom."

Everyone in the attack center knew, and soon everyone on board

Augusta would know, that the launch they'd nearly rammed had been filled with more than just code bags.

Von Suskil walked away from the scope, then turned. "Let me know if anything starts to happen. I'm taking a rest. You have the conn."

The sonar operator knew that they'd received some hairy orders from Norfolk. But Von Suskil was not only playing a little rough with his billion-dollar boat, he was coming damned close to violating some sacred tenets of the sea; you don't run survivors down. Ever. Acting as if there were a war seemed to the sonar operator like a damned good way to start one. If it came to it, they weren't going to blame him. He began to keep copies of all his acoustic tapes. It was strictly against the books, but then, he wasn't going down in those books as the guy who let World War III start on his watch.

EMERGENCY ACTION CENTER, MOSCOW

The watch team was all but hidden by a dense haze of smoldering cigarettes. The polished table was strewn with overflowing ashtrays, half-eaten sandwiches, and glasses of tea gone cold. They'd been up all night working on a response to the cutting of the *K-219*'s towline by an American warship. On the one hand it was an incredible provocation; on the other, everyone knew that Gorbachev wanted the big summit in Reykjavík to go smoothly. Pushed one way, pulled another, the staff bickered, debated, and ultimately offered nothing useful to Britanov or his men.

The lights were all burning up in Admiral Makarov's offices, too. He had the unenviable job of keeping Admiral of the Fleet Chernavin up to date as events unfolded five hundred miles north of Bermuda. Chernavin, an old-line submariner, was running around with his hair on fire over *K-219*. His subordinates kept telling him what he wanted to hear, that everything in the considerable power of the Soviet Union was being done to save the crippled sub, yet each new communiqué from the scene was worse than the last. Surely someone, somewhere, was lying. Chernavin was getting ready to cast his net, and no one wanted to be caught in it when he did.

Captain Antonov bore much of the brunt of passing on the bad news. He was handling communications traffic between Moscow and the various Soviet-bloc ships on the scene. He had smoked his way through his fifth pack of Belomars, a strong tobacco much favored by Northern Fleet sailors for the flush of warmth it gave your skin. He'd spoken directly, and not exactly legally, with Captain Britanov's wife, Natalia. She'd listened, remained silent so long that Antonov wondered whether she'd fainted, but then, in a calm voice, Natalia asked whether any of the other wives could be told. Antonov had yelled, *"No!"*

In the end Natalia Britanov promised to keep it to herself, but Antonov guessed it was a matter of hours before all of Gadzhievo would know about the explosion aboard one of their subs. If Natalia didn't leak it, it would surely come in through the Voice of America, whose programs were officially forbidden and so rarely missed.

His secure telephone rang. "Antonov. *Slushayu.*"

A communications specialist read the latest of Aznabaev's increasingly dire messages. This, however, was in a different sphere altogether. This was something a hotheaded officer might well call an act of war.

He took careful notes for Admiral Makarov, but he thought, First they cut the towline, now they try to ram a whaleboat. What will the Americans try next?

It was against all the rules of the sea. What kind of a sailor was this American captain? Trying to swamp a lifeboat with survivors. The Americans were acting as though there were no summit next week at all. They were behaving like cowboys, and at sea, with men trained for war, such behavior could have unexpected consequences.

After a few brushes between Soviet and American naval forces, a quiet understanding had been reached by the two superpowers; a sort of under-the-table treaty aimed at accidents that could escalate uncontrollably to war. Apparently, the captain of the American *Los Angeles* was choosing to ignore it.

Captain Antonov hung up. And that airdrop of OBA units. No parachutes, no flotation collars. It was hard to understand. Admiral Novoystev was either criminally stupid, or criminally devious. Either was possible. He wouldn't put it by the admiral in charge of operations to see to it that Britanov had no tools to work with to save his submarine. Britanov's neck was already in the noose. It was easier to hang him than to find someone else to mount the gallows. And with Cheinavin on a rampage, it wouldn't be long before Admiral Novoystev's name floated to the top of the list. After all, as operations chief it was his order that sent ill-prepared submarines out on patrol. It was Novoystev who ordered leaves shortened and yard time eliminated in favor of less reliable field repairs.

It wouldn't harm Novoystev if *K-219* went down. It might well harm him more if it stayed afloat. Maybe he meant for his mistakes to be buried, or in this case, sunk.

Antonov called Makarov, Novoystev's boss, and was told to be prepared to brief the admiral in five minutes. Things had to calm down out there in the Atlantic, or else events would begin to develop a momentum of their own; a momentum that might carry *K-219,* the American *Los Angeles,* maybe the world, over the edge of the abyss.

Antonov finished the cigarette and lit a new one from the smoldering stub. He knew another missile submarine, a DELTA, had been ordered to make all speed to the scene in order to accept code materials from *K-219.* The DELTA was a fast nuclear boat commanded by Boris Apanasenko. Apanasenko was an aggressive young captain who would not take kindly to being pushed by an American *Los Angeles.*

Apanasenko wouldn't ask Moscow for permission. He wouldn't dither. He would push back, and hard. Then what would happen?

He gathered his papers and left the Sardine Can, taking the elevator up to the rarefied realm of the top brass. When he was admitted to Admiral Makarov's chambers, he found Novoystev already there, the short, overstuffed admiral sitting in a large overstuffed chair.

"So," said Novoystev with a sly look, "your friend Britanov not only sends his messages out in the clear, but now he's transferred his code materials to an unsecure freighter. Does he know Apanasenko is on the way to take them?"

"That has been communicated, Admiral," said Captain Antonov.

"And Britanov ignores it. Absolutely illegal. What regulations is he not prepared to break?"

"What's the latest, Captain?" asked Makarov. He was seated at his desk. Makarov had the noncommittal look of a man who had a close eye on the tide; the look of a man who did not intend to get wet.

"Admiral, all tow attempts have been suspended by your order. The entire crew of *K-219* has been transferred to the *Fyodor Bredkin* except for Captain Britanov."

"And the code materials?" asked Makarov, though he surely knew the answer.

"To the *Bredkin* as well. But there has been an incident. The launch containing the code bags, plus the last of the damage control party, was nearly rammed."

This got Makarov's attention. "Rammed? By whom?"

"By a submerged submarine, Admiral. It came very close to swamping them."

"That's—"

"You say the damage control party is no longer on board?" said Novoystev. "No one is trying to keep her afloat?"

"Captain Britanov is still on board, Admiral."

"Pah!" snorted Novoystev. "We're playing games in the Americans' backyard. None of this should be happening. Britanov should have dealt with the problems decisively and firmly. You see what halfway measures buy? This American submarine, he senses blood. He senses weakness. The whole world laughs while Britanov plays games."

"He's not playing games. He's got four dead already and we don't know about the injured. *K-219* is dead in the water," said Antonov. "He's got a hole in his missile deck and a hull full of poison. What would you have Britanov do?"

"His sacred duty. Fix his problems and get under way like an officer of the Soviet Navy. Instead he sends off all his engineers, his experts, and expects his problems to go away by themselves. If I were less forgiving I'd suspect he was trying to hand that submarine over to the Americans. I don't suppose any of you have wondered at the chances of this so-called accident taking place right where there is an American tugboat standing by? Is all of this just coincidence, or is it a plan?"

"It's near enough to their bases—" Antonov began, but Makarov broke in.

"A dark possibility, indeed," said Makarov gravely.

Now even Antonov could see the run of the tide. It was flowing strongly against Britanov, and anyone who sided with him. It wasn't right. It wasn't fair. But there was no mistaking it. *K-219*'s captain, like his command, was in danger of sinking in deep water.

Makarov said, "Captain Antonov, this ramming incident only proves the futility of continuing as we have. We've discussed this affair in great detail with Admiral Chernavin. He has in turn discussed it with General Secretary Gorbachev. Needless to say, Admiral Chernavin is concerned and confused about why more hasn't been done to save *K-219* and its nuclear materials."

You could try dropping OBA units with floats, thought Antonov, though he had the good sense not to say it.

Makarov continued. "Obviously, the affair presents political complications at a time when they are not welcome. We have come to the conclusion that not enough is being done by Captain Britanov to save *K-219*. That must end before events are permitted to go too far."

"Sir?"

"Britanov is too concerned for his crew and cares too little for his ship," Novoystev blurted out. "A commander must sometimes spend lives to win wars. The people entrusted Britanov with his command. The people paid with their blood so that our best scientists, our best designers, could create that submarine, those missiles. And all Britanov can do is bob in the sea like a wine cork while it sinks."

"The admiral has a point," said Makarov. "Admiral Chernavin has demanded results. We will give him results. You're in communication with the *Bredkin*?"

"Yes, Admiral," Antonov replied. "*K-219*'s navigator has assumed comm duty. His name is Aznabaev."

"Have this sent to Aznabaev immediately." Makarov handed a paper to the young captain. "That's all."

Antonov saluted and left. Out in the hall he read the new set of orders. They were addressed to the *K-219*'s KGB officer, Valery Pshenichny. Britanov was being sidestepped.

As Antonov read the paper, he stopped and stood in the quiet, plush corridor.

The survivors of *K-219* were to be shuttled back to the submarine at first light. Using the OBA units airdropped this afternoon, they were to make all efforts necessary to save the submarine and return it to service.

What OBA units? It was as though that fiasco had never happened! But then Antonov stopped. He'd seen these orders before.

They were very nearly the same ones that had gone out to the crew of the *K-8* back in 1970. That sub had caught fire and surfaced just west of the Bay of Biscay. Like Britanov, the captain got all his men off onto friendly ships. He expected the *K-8* to sink at any moment, but the stubborn sub wallowed in the low swells, refusing to go down.

Moscow became desperate and ordered the crew back. The captain obeyed, and the next day fifty of his crew followed him back onto the submarine. Then water began to suddenly pour in, and it proved impossible to get all fifty men out through the three small hatches available. They all went down in eight thousand feet of water.

It was happening again. To the letter. It was better to die while trying to save the sub than to bring back as many men as possible while losing the boat. Captain Antonov knew that Britanov would remember the story of the *K-8*. So, in a way, did Admiral Makarov.

The orders to Security Officer Pshenichny were explicit: if Britanov argued, if he delayed, if he resisted letting the crew back on board *K-219*, Pshenichny was authorized to use force to remove him from his command.

CHAPTER 14

Moscow wanted us to go back at first light.
Pshenichny told me to pick eight men to go back
into compartments eight, nine, and ten.
I knew what those compartments were like. To tell
you the truth, I was more frightened than during
the explosion. I knew what had happened to other submarines
in the same shape. I really didn't want morning to come.

—Gennady Kapitulsky,
Propulsion Engineer

Aznabaev made them repeat the orders twice, not because he had trouble copying them, but because they made no sense. Reboard with new OBA units? There *were* no OBA units left, not on any of the freighters, not in *K-219,* and if they thought that farce of an airdrop left them with something useful, then Moscow was not just misinformed. They were insane.

Vladmirov, the *K-219*'s executive officer, took the microphone after Aznabaev showed him the wording of the new orders. "This is Executive Officer Vladmirov," he said. "There are no OBA canisters. Repeat, there are no OBA canisters to distribute, over."

The voice on the other end merely repeated the standing orders; it was as though Vladmirov had not said a word.

"Listen," he said, frustrated, "there's an American ship standing by with OBA units. Are we authorized to accept American help?"

The answer was immediate. "Negative. Use what you have been given."

He looked at Aznabaev. "Are they serious?"

"You'd better tell the captain." He held out the microphone again.

Britanov rested in the open bridge, huddled down beneath the sides of the cockpit to shelter against the spray. The brighter stars showed through an indigo sky. The swells were building again, five to six feet from the northeast, rocking the half-submerged sub and sending sheets of water across her punctured missile deck.

Now and again the orbiting patrol plane swept low and ruined his night vision with its searchlight. The American tugboat was close enough to hear the voices of sailors on her deck. The three friendly ships looked like galaxies of light against the night. He could smell dinner cooking, wafted over by the strengthening wind.

The submarine was riding lower, Britanov could see that for himself. How many waves could she take over that hole in the missile deck before she no longer had enough buoyancy to float? Would it be a gradual slipping beneath the waves, or would it be more sudden?

It was ironic but it took a great deal of effort to force ten thousand tons of steel to sink. Compartment four was open to the sea and slowly flooding, and that was *K-219*'s largest space. But Soviet designers built their submarines tough and resilient. Not fireproof, not poisonproof, but they were devilishly tough to sink.

He took a deep breath of clean sea air. There was a harsh, metallic taste at the back of his tongue. The stink rising from the open hatch to central command carried with it stronger whiffs of poison. He was about to check his last OBA canister when the handheld radio squawked. He picked it up and turned the volume high enough to hear.

"Britanov. Listening."

"Captain, this is Vladmirov. Aznabaev is here and so is Security Officer Pshenichny."

"You'll be late for dinner. I can smell it from here. What's wrong, Volodiya? Is it Kochergin?"

"No. He's the same. Captain," the exec said uneasily, "we received new orders from Moscow."

"So?"

"They want me to form up teams of ten men each. They want us to reboard at first light. They want us to save the submarine, sir."

Britanov laughed. "You can't reboard. There aren't any OBAs."

"I told them. They don't seem to understand. What shall we do?"

Britanov thought about it for no more than a second. "Tell them they don't understand the situation."

There was an uncomfortable silence, then Security Officer Pshenichny came on. "Captain? It's Pshenichny."

"I hear you, Valery. How are the injured doing?"

"Dr. Kochergin is still unconscious. But four others who were out seem to be coming around. They're all breathing through rags soaked in vodka. It cools their lungs. Markov is even talking."

"Well, that's good news for a change."

"Sir, about Moscow. The orders say that if you don't allow the crew back on, you're to be taken off." He paused, then said, "By force if necessary."

A wave rolled over the missile deck. Britanov listened to the seep and gurgle of water down the ripped-open silo.

"Captain? Are you there?"

"It's *K-8* again. You know that, Valery," said Britanov. "They don't care if *we* go down so long as *they* can say they did their best. It's impossible. There's poison now in central command. What are the men supposed to do? Reboard with rags soaked in vodka in their teeth?"

"I know. What do you want us to do?"

Another wave, larger than the others, pitched the conning tower over ten, then fifteen degrees. The sub slowly, sluggishly righted.

"Captain?"

"All right. You can't disobey. You're KGB. You know what would happen."

"Yes. But what do you want us to say?"

Another wave rolled over the missile deck. Britanov watched the foam form a whirlpool over the open silo, then drain down into his submarine. "Listen to me," said Britanov. "Stay where you are. Make sure the men are fed and rested and the injured are cared for. That's your responsibility."

"But what about Moscow, sir? We have to tell them—"

"Tell Moscow I'm countermanding their orders. That responsibility," said Britanov, "is mine."

EMERGENCY ACTION CENTER, MOSCOW

"He's *what?*" Makarov shouted.

Captain Antonov had to hold the secure phone away from his ear. He was back at his chair in the Sardine Can. When the eruption subsided, he said, "The message from Aznabaev says he's countermanding orders to reboard. Britanov feels the situation is too dangerous. Apparently they're short on rescue equipment. Maybe if we can drop some more supplies, this time with parachutes and flotation gear, they might—"

"Britanov can't do this. It's treason."

Antonov remained silent.

Makarov cursed, then said, "All right. We've been very patient. Too patient. But at the end of patience Britanov will find a great anger. Tell them to stand by for a personal message."

"From, you, Admiral?"

"No," said Makarov. "I think we've gone well beyond that, Captain." With that, the line went dead.

Antonov lit another cigarette. Who was going to take off Britanov's head? Not Makarov alone, apparently. Novoystev? That would be a travesty, given that it was Novoystev who fouled up on the OBA drop. Or perhaps it would be the Northern Fleet commander, Admiral Kapitanets. One way or the other, there was a firing squad forming up. Despite the fact that Britanov had made things worse for himself, Antonov still admired him for his stand. He'd made a decision that, if not by the book, was surely courageous. He was probably even right, not that it was going to help. Indeed, it would only make what was going to happen to Britanov that much worse. He took a long, soothing drag, then dialed the communications watch officer. "Stand by for a flash message from Admiral Makarov to the *Fyodor Bredkin,*" he said.

FYODOR BREDKIN

"Standing by," said Aznabaev. He put the old microphone back onto its stand and clicked a switch to put Moscow over a loudspeaker so that everyone could hear.

The freighter's small radio room was crammed with officers from *K-219.* Security Officer Pshenichny, Grandfather Krasilnikov, the executive Vladmirov, even Sergiyenko, the sub's *zampolit,* was there. Aznabaev scanned their faces one by one. Sergiyenko was the only one who didn't seem appalled at the orders. His mouth was frozen in a strange, crooked smile. *Maybe he's as terrified as the rest of us,* thought

Aznabaev. Some people screamed, some panicked and ran in circles, maybe Sergiyenko smiled.

The link to the High Command net squealed, crashed with static, then suddenly cleared.

"Who is this?" demanded a deep, bass voice.

"Senior Navigator Aznabaev, listening."

"Who is in command, Aznabaev?"

The voice was familiar. It dripped with authority.

Vladmirov stepped up to the small desk. "Executive Officer Vladmirov, listening."

"Do you know who this is, Vladmirov?"

"No, sir." It had to be someone big. Someone big and angry. He looked at Pshenichny. The security officer shook his head.

"Then let me introduce myself. This is Admiral of the Fleet Chernavin. I imagine you've heard of me. I am your commander in chief."

Vladmirov's eyes went wide. He snapped to attention as though Chernavin might leap from the loudspeaker. The radio room was dead silent except for the crackle of static.

"Now that we know each other, patch me through to Britanov."

"Yest, Comrade Commander!" He looked at Aznabaev.

Aznabaev turned the rotary switch to the second, ship-to-ship frequency. "Captain?" he whispered into the microphone, praying that he'd activated the proper circuits. "Captain! It's Chernavin on the horn! He wants to speak to you!"

There was no reply.

"Well?" boomed Chernavin. "Is there a problem, Aznabaev? Are you perhaps waiting for orders from some higher authority, or can't you navigate your way around a radio?"

"Yes, Comrade Commander! I mean, no. Please stand by. We're raising Captain Britanov now." He turned the selector switch on the transmitter. "Captain! This is Aznabaev! Answer! Captain Britanov! Answer!"

". . . Britanov! Answer! It really is *Chernavin!*"

Britanov had fallen asleep huddled in the corner of the exposed bridge. The sudden voices made him start. He'd been dreaming, that he was back in his chair down in central command, with the usual chaos going on around him.

"Captain? This is Aznabaev! Answer!"

Next, Pshenichny's voice came over the radio. "Captain, they're going crazy back in Moscow. Chernavin demands to speak with you. He wants you off the sub right away. Captain? Are you there? It's . . . wait. Admiral Chernavin says that he is your commander in chief."

Chernavin! Britanov stiffened despite himself.

"Sir? Admiral Chernavin orders you to relinquish command to me," said Pshenichny. "He wants you to acknowledge."

The waves rocked the sub, the patrol plane roared overhead, then banked for yet another pass. Water gurgled from below. Britanov stayed silent. He took a drink of lukewarm mineral water, then spat it out.

"Captain?" said Pshenichny. "Chernavin is ordering you off the submarine. He says to stop this nonsense now and don't drag your officers down with you."

Don't drag your officers down? What the devil did Chernavin think would happen if they came back on board? What had happened before to the men of the *K-8?* Don't drag them down? He swore to himself, almost reached for the radio to tell Chernavin to stuff it, but he held himself in check.

"Captain?" It was Aznabaev again. "Are you there? Captain? Answer if you're there."

A new voice could be heard in the background. It sounded like Vladmirov.

". . . radio batteries dead?"

"How should I know?" Aznabaev snapped back.

"...signal?"

Dead batteries. He looked at the small handheld radio. Why not? It was a good enough excuse. Britanov switched off the radio just as a bright green flare arced up from the *Fyodor Bredkin*. An instant later it was followed by a red flare. Together they slowly descended under their little party-favor parachutes to the black sea. There they burned for a while, then winked out.

A searchlight lanced across from the *Bredkin*. Britanov ducked below the rim of the bridge as its scalding white light swept overhead.

More and more now, seas rolled over the missile deck. The stern was definitely down by a noticeable amount. The weight of the water inside her hull made *K-219* roll out of synch with the waves. The sub lurched and pitched in unfamiliar, dangerous ways. Would she last until morning?

There was no way to know. Not for certain. Submarines could be hard to sink. Another crippled boat, the *K-19,* suffered an explosion that trapped a number of her crew in the stern. She surfaced into the teeth of an Arctic gale; winds of nearly a hundred miles an hour, seas to fifty, sixty feet. The sub, and the men trapped inside her, were doomed. Waves rolled her over and over as the gale howled. Then, three weeks later, after the storm was spent, a rescue ship found her still afloat. They had to cut a hole in her plates to get in, and when they did, they found the trapped crewmen, alive.

No, there was no guarantee that *K-219* would sink before dawn. Before his crew would try to reboard her breathing through rags soaked in vodka. *Idiots!* Moscow would kill them all.

The searchlight from the *Bredkin* was joined by a beam from the *Krasnogvardyesk*. They poured light over the open bridge with an almost liquid intensity. He snatched the radio and turned it back on.

"Get those damned lights out of my eyes!" he told Aznabaev, then switched the radio off again.

First one, then the other light went out.

Britanov stood and looked back over the missile deck, gauging how much lower she seemed than when he'd first come up. The boat would sink, surely. But when?

He'd spent his whole career mastering this big black machine, how to operate its cranky systems, to command it in time of war. To survive. Now he found himself dwelling on ways to kill it before it could kill the rest of his crew.

The automatic scuttling charges were an obvious and an impossible choice. They demanded electricity, and there was no electricity. Even if there were, the wires were all eaten away by acid.

The missiles all had destruct packages in their warheads, pencil-thin thermite charges designed to set off a low-order, nonnuclear blast. Detonating one of those would surely do it, but that required power and wires, too.

He had to do it with his own two hands. Britanov knew there were just two avenues left: the manual scuttle valves at the bottom of compartment three, or the torpedo tubes. Open the first and the boat would slowly settle. Open a torpedo tube with the inner breech also open, and flooding would be rapid and catastrophic. With a stream of water as big as an oak tree and just as solid bursting in through the open tube, the boat would go down so fast he might well not get out. He looked forward and saw the bow escape hatch appear, then disappear under the waves. He'd have to run for it. To run all the way back through compartment two back into three, to climb the ladder leading back up here to the bridge. He'd have to do it in the darkness, chased by a tidal wave of black water. It might be a solution, but it was surely a nightmare.

Britanov took a final drink of mineral water, got to his feet, and tossed the bottle over the side. He listened for the splash, but he couldn't hear it over the roar of the patrol plane's engines. It was coming around for another low pass, its searchlight on. It made him furious. He waited for it to sweep over him, then walked back to the main trunk hatch and put on his OBA mask. Then, without thinking, he descended the ladder. First to the enclosed bridge where he opened an equipment locker and pulled out a heavy, awkward bundle of rubber. He hauled it back up the ladder and carefully laid it out flat across the deck of the open bridge.

It was a yellow life raft. Built for six, it could be inflated with a tug on a light painter tied to a CO_2 canister. He uncoiled the line. Who knew? A sailor shouldn't count on miracles, but what if they're all that's left?

Britanov glanced at the stars; there were millions of them now, bright as diamonds on velvet. Below them was a landscape of rolling sea, the glittering lights of the friendly merchantmen, the dim outline of the American tugboat. Moscow was crazy, the Americans, too. But it was still a beautiful world. He was starting to think of it with nostalgia, like his last view of Gadzhievo.

Odds were excellent he'd never see it again. But his men, they would. They were his responsibility, and he wasn't going to sacrifice them to Moscow's idiocy.

He took a last breath of clean night air, then pulled his mask back over his face and climbed down through the hatch to the dark spaces below.

He climbed down hand over hand through the enclosed bridge and on to the most familiar place in all the world, except for his flat back in Gadzhievo. Maybe, he thought as he dropped to the deck of the dim central command post, this was even more familiar.

He'd spent the better part of his adult life in submarines of one description or another. *K-219* didn't belong to anyone but him. Not to Moscow. Not to the Americans who were waiting to pounce, to steal it. It was Britanov's boat. His command, and he was, for the moment, alone.

Central command was dim in the failing battle lamps. They cast his shadow around the empty compartment; ghosts of the men who used to work here, men who would never see this place again. Men, his men, who were now safe less than half a kilometer away. Men who would surely die if Moscow had its way.

He paused for a moment and glanced up at the bulkhead where he'd posted the small sign that read

SUBMARINE LIFE IS NOT A SERVICE, BUT A RELIGION.

He reached up and took the small framed plaque off the hook and tucked it into his jacket. He turned and came face-to-face with his chair, the place that knew his body's contours, its weight, its smell. His proud seat of command. He touched the armrests, caressing them.

Submarine service was a religion that demanded much of its adherents. Their time, their expertise, their courage. And sometimes it demanded more. Sometimes it demanded their lives.

CHAPTER 15

I was standing on deck just staring out into space.
All of a sudden I saw something moving.
I ordered a spotlight aimed. I saw the stern
of the submarine rise out of the water. There was
a roar like a jet taking off. I realized
she was going down fast by the bow.

—*Alexei Gakkel,*
First Mate, Anatoly Vasiliyev

The radio room was filled with the stink of unwashed uniforms mixed with the sharp odor of hot electronics. Pshenichny stood with Vladmirov, arguing over how, or if, they could obey Moscow. Other officers clustered nearby, hoping to catch some useful information.

"How could you let them think we could go back in there?" Kapitulsky shouted at Aznabaev.

"I didn't let them think anything! It was *Chernavin*."

"I don't care if it was Lenin calling from his crypt," Kapitulsky argued. "There are no more OBA canisters. None. Zero. Just because Moscow—"

"*Chernavin.*"

"*I don't care.* Just because Moscow can't find its ass with both hands doesn't mean we have to go along!"

After so many hours awake, fighting for survival, everyone's nerves were badly frayed.

"Listen," said the propulsion engineer. "I know what those compartments look like. There's no way we can go back in there without OBA canisters. You find me OBA canisters and I'll be the first to go back in."

"*I* know that. *You* know that," said Aznabaev. "It's *Moscow* that doesn't realize it."

"The only OBA canisters around are over on that American tugboat," said the executive officer, Vladmirov.

"That's impossible."

They all looked over at Sergiyenko, the political officer. Somehow the *zampolit* had gone off and found a way to clean his white uniform; the one he'd put on to deliver his talk about *perestroika* in the armed forces. His hair was neatly combed, his face shaved, and there was the distinct aroma of lotion coming from him.

Now Kapitulsky had a better target for his frustration than Aznabaev. "What are you doing, getting ready to go to the dance?" he said with a sneer. "Or are you planning to find some cruise ship to run off to?"

Sergiyenko turned his back to the angry propulsion engineer and faced Vladmirov and Pshenichny. "I'm reminding you that accepting help from NATO forces is not approved," Sergiyenko said. "I speak for the Party in this. You know that I'm right."

Everyone glanced at the security officer. He was KGB after all. He knew submarines, but he also knew politics.

"He's right," said Pshenichny. "If we use their OBAs, they'll hang us for sure."

"If we don't use them we'll suffocate," said Vladmirov. "Is that what they want?"

Pshenichny sighed, then said, "There's no choice."

Kapitulsky stepped close. "You can't be serious. You know——"

Just then the first mate of the *Vasiliyev* burst into the crowded radio room. "The sub! She's going down! Down by the bow!" yelled First Mate Gakkel, then ran back out on deck.

Gennady Kapitulsky bolted after Gakkel.

Kapitulsky saw the stern rise up, surrounded by heaving waves, turbulence, and exploding bursts of air. Spotlights from all three freighters were now on the submarine, making the foam even brighter against the nighttime sea.

"The captain!" he yelled, then ran after Gakkel to the ladder leading down the freighter's sheer sides. At the bottom was a launch.

Gakkel was already in the boat; a coxswain had a hook around the ladder to keep it from drifting away, pulled by the steep swells. Kapitulsky jumped and fell into the bottom of the wooden boat.

"Go!" Gakkel yelled, and the coxswain dropped the hook and gunned the engine.

K-219

The whole world was tilting; a tremendous waterfall roar thundered from all around as Britanov scrambled up the ladder to the exposed bridge. He slipped, found his footing, and hauled himself up to the air, to the sea. The view aft was terrifying.

It looked like a huge, breaking wave. A solid sheet of water roaring down the missile deck, breaking around the sail. The air was filled with spray. Tons of water cascaded down the sloping deck. The stern rose majestically out of the sea even as the bow slipped deeper. The water was already to the base of the conning tower. The bronze screws at the stern emerged from a boil of whitewater.

Britanov started for the raft, then stopped. He went back to the forward end of the bridge, now the low end, and clambered up the short mast to cut away *K-219*'s flag. It was white and blue, with a red star, a red hammer and sickle. He stuffed it into his jacket, grabbed the line to the raft and tied it to his belt, then gave it a sharp jerk.

The raft hissed and inflated, but not completely. A loud horn blasted from one of the freighters, though it could scarcely be heard above the thunder of water cascading down the missile deck and a deeper rumbling coming from within *K-219*'s flooding hull.

She was settling fast, accelerating as she went. By the time Britanov tossed the raft over the side of the bridge and made ready to jump, it was just a short step down to the sea.

He fell into the limp raft, but a wave tossed him out. The water was warmer than he expected. He was still connected to the raft by the line at his belt. He hauled it back hand over hand until he could grab the half-inflated sides. The stern of the submarine rose higher and higher, the rumbling now a deafening thunder. Water rushing down the decks inundated him and filled the yellow raft.

Dazzling spotlights erupted like lightning. Britanov stared up at the black hull. It was close enough to touch. He had to get away or else it would pull him down. He struggled to climb into the raft again but once more he was tossed away to the very limit of the lifeline.

The conning tower disappeared. A huge burst of air and foam exploded above it. Britanov surfed the wave away from the sinking sub, but a black whirlpool sucked him right back. He struggled to swim away from it, but the raft was caught. Round and round, the limp yellow shape swirled, dragging Britanov after it. Then it disappeared, sucked down by the vortex of turbulence. It pulled him by its leash straight into the center of the whirlpool. He took a long deep breath just as his head went under.

Igor Britanov looked up as he was drawn down into the sea. He was being sucked down, deeper, he could feel the pressure of the water build against his ears. Underwater, he could see the play of lights on the surface as his dying submarine pulled him down, down into the blackness.

The coxswain steered the launch directly for the place where all three searchlights overlapped. A knot of turbulence, the whirlpool, the belching bubbles coming up from the plummeting sub. Kapitulsky stood in the bow. The sea churned. There was no sign of Britanov.

The coxswain slowed, leery of the whirlpool, of the powerful suction.

"Igor!" called Kapitulsky. He could hardly hear his own voice for the blast of the freighters' horns and the steady underwater rumble that shook the sea like an earthquake. He put his hands to his mouth and shouted again, *"Igor!"*

"Something's over there!" Gakkel pointed and Kapitulsky aimed a small light in its direction.

A half-sunk yellow raft bobbed, glistening against the black sea.

They motored over to it, and as they got closer, Kapitulsky's heart sank. Water sloshed over the raft from inside. The bottom of it was hidden in shadow. He swept the light around the raft. "Igor!"

"He's gone," said Gakkel. "He went down. No one could have gotten off."

Closer now, Kapitulsky stood at the bow, ready to jump. The waves were running to six feet and he nearly lost his footing. The raft was filled almost to the gunwales with water.

First Mate Gakkel grabbed Kapitulsky by the collar. "He's not there! Don't—"

Kapitulsky sprang. He landed in the middle of the drowned raft with a splash. He dropped his light. It bounced on the rubber side and disappeared. He cursed as he saw the beam fade into the depths, yellow to green, green to black. As he scrambled to stand in the limp raft, his leg struck something hard. He splashed around in the dark and felt a face, a mustache, a man.

"Captain?" He cradled Britanov on his knee. The captain was unconscious. "Get over here fast!" he called to the launch.

As the launch approached, the American P-3 roared overhead, its white light stabbing down. In its glare Kapitulsky saw Britanov's eyes flutter, then open.

"Captain?"

"I knew I could count on you, Gennady," said Britanov. "Well done."

Kapitulsky carried him to the launch. The coxswain gunned the motor and leaned against the tiller. The launch surged across the rolling swells in the direction of the closest ship, the big RO-RO freighter *Vasiliyev*. First Mate Gakkel knew there was little in the way of medical care on the *Bredkin,* and what there was had been all but used up by the badly injured submariners. He looked at Britanov's waxy, pale face. The man was in deep shock, it didn't take an expert to see that. He was shaking uncontrollably, his face contorted, shifting between tears and wild laughter.

USS *AUGUSTA*

"Conn, sonar. Red Two's still accelerating in the dive. I estimate four zero knots. She's passing through five hundred feet now, shearing off to the east."

"Mark the spot," said Captain Von Suskil. He didn't need sonar to hear the groans, the shrieks, the seismic rumbles of the sinking sub. The eerie noises came right through the hull. The sounds were almost alive. *Forty knots straight down,* he thought. The bottom lay three and a half miles deep. *Take her five minutes to hit.*

"Fifty knots now, sir. Through one thousand feet. Still accelerating."

Make that four minutes if she doesn't blow. "Sonar, I want your best estimate when she crushes. Might be useful information to someone."

"She's gone vertical. Through two thousand feet."

Any minute now, thought Captain Von Suskil. The sea would crush Red Two's hull like a cheap beer can and any air left inside would compress, catch fire, and explode. Anyone left inside, too. The debris would rain to the bottom, and someone might well find some of *that* interesting, too. A low heavy thud shook the submarine.

"Through three thousand, sir. Something just blew."

The sounds faded as the dying missile sub dropped away into the Hatteras Abyss.

"Sir, I don't think she crushed."

"She has to."

"Through four thousand. Still intact. And I'm picking up a new contact now, bearing zero eight five. Evaluate as Red One. Making turns for twenty-eight knots."

"Our friend the DELTA," said Von Suskil. He was hoping the death of this old YANKEE might chum the sea and bring in something interesting in from surrounding waters. A DELTA was a more modern nuclear boat. A more worthy opponent for *Augusta.* He smiled. *Hell. Maybe that one will kill herself, too.* Then he could sail back to New London with two red stars painted on his sail. Not that they'd let him. But the Russians would know. They'd have to realize that here off America they were far from home, sailing in hostile waters.

Von Suskil stayed quiet. So did the whole crew. Three minutes, four, five. Finally another thud shook the hull.

"Conn, Sonar. That was impact. It looks like she made it down in one piece."

Eighteen thousand feet! "Well, people," said the captain. "Ivan doesn't build them smart, but he sure does build them strong. Comm?

Get off a report. Tell them we're resuming covert trailing of Red One."

"Aye aye."

"Helm, turns for twenty knots. Course zero four zero. First we'll sprint, then we'll drift off to one side and let this DELTA come charging through. Then we'll have some fun with him."

The executive officer shivered. The sounds of the dying YANKEE had barely stopped. For all he knew she went down with some of her crew on board, down to eighteen thousand feet. Would it be worse to die in a flash of compressed, burning air, or to slowly suffocate at the bottom of a deep, cold sea? It was a nightmare. From their close encounter, the cutting of the tow, the ramming. The distant thunder as *K-219* struck the abyssal plain three and a half miles below them. A nightmare. All of it. If this was fun, the XO wondered what Von Suskil had in mind for the DELTA.

GADZHIEVO

Irina Kapitulsky was finishing setting up the kitchen table as a buffet for dinner. The wives of officers out on patrol often gathered for meals. It helped them endure the isolation and worry. Tonight Irina contributed her kitchen, a few bottles of a sweet fruity drink known as *sok,* and a tinned ham mailed to Gadzhievo from her sister in Tallinn, Estonia. The ham was a real prize. Nothing remotely like it was available in Gadzhievo. The other wives would each contribute a dish, and together they would have something like a family dinner.

The television was on in the next room, the volume turned up enough so Irina could catch the evening news show *Vremya.* She took a sharp knife and began slicing paper-thin sheets of succulent meat. A ham like this had to go a long way.

She heard the announcer's deep voice say the word *NAVAGA.* She stopped, looked up, and listened for a moment. The knife clattered to the floor, and she ran to the next room.

The screen showed a submarine on the surface with smoke billowing from a hole in its back. The announcer said that the footage came from an American airplane, that the scene had been taken from an American news broadcast. He said the submarine was in trouble, on fire off the American coast.

Irina's head felt pressurized, like a balloon ready to burst. She knew Gennady was on a NAVAGA off the American coast. How many could there be? Was it his submarine on fire? Was he alive? Was he dying some horrible death even as she sliced some damned Polish ham? She felt sick to her stomach. She realized she was hyperventilating. She calmed herself and walked to the phone.

The scene on the television changed to another story. In a daze she waited for Natalia Britanov to answer the phone, anxious to hear her say *don't worry,* and terrified that she wouldn't.

ANATOLY VASILIYEV

At first light, all 115 survivors were shuttled over to the big Baltic Steamship Company freighter, the *Anatoly Vasiliyev*. The injured sailors and the white canvas code bags were both carried in stretchers. Despite a night spent breathing through a vodka-soaked rag, Dr. Kochergin was still in bad shape; he still coughed up flecks of green acid foam from his seared lungs.

The deck of the *Vasiliyev* was piled high with big containers, leaving only a small area free for the men to gather. As word spread that the captain was on the way, the officers assembled them into formal ranks. The low buzz of constant conversation competed with the throb of the freighter's idling engines and the occasional low pass by the pesky American patrol plane.

"We were supposed to go back on. He saved us," said one of the seamen-engineers who'd been assigned to *K-219*'s engine room. "The captain pulled the plug and saved us."

"He didn't have to. It was going to sink anyway."

"Don't be an idiot. Of course he pulled the plug."

"How do you know so much?"

"I heard the officers talking in the radio room."

"That proves it isn't so. And if it is, they'll crucify him for it. Wait and see."

"Attention!" shouted Valery Pshenichny. "Captain's on deck!"

All eyes turned to see a stooped figure emerge from a hatch in the *Vasiliyev* wheelhouse. Britanov stood there for a moment, squinting in the bright morning light. He was normally a tall man with regal bearing. None of that showed today. He was still in his soaking-wet uniform. When he saw the crew standing at attention, he broke into a weary grin. "It's good to see you all."

"Greetings, Comrade Captain!" the crew roared back in unison.

Britanov worked his way down the long line, shaking hands with every man. At the end he came to Security Officer Pshenichny. There were tears rolling down Pshenichny's face. "What's wrong with you, Valery?"

"We thought you were dead, Comrade Captain."

"Not yet, but it's early." He embraced Pshenichny and then stood back to address the entire crew. He called out each of their names from memory, not missing a single man.

"Petrachkov."

Gennady Kapitulsky answered for the dead missile officer. "Still on patrol, Captain."

"Pshenichny."

"Present, Comrade Captain!"

"Preminin."

A short pause, then Chief Engineer Krasilnikov said, "Still on patrol, Comrade Captain."

Four dead. More that will die from breathing poison. How many would have gone if they'd come back aboard? he wondered. He finished the roll call, then said at the end, "I'm proud of you and I know the Navy is proud of you, too. To each and every one of you, well done."

With that he turned and went back to the freighter's bridge to radio Moscow. He didn't see the murderous look Gennady Kapitulsky gave *Zampolit* Sergiyenko, nor Sergiyenko's innocent, satisfied smile.

Someone pointed to the east. "Look!"

"Our ship! It came back up!"

The men rushed to the rails.

A black shape rose from the sea. At first they were stunned, thinking that *K-219* had somehow answered Britanov's roll call, that Preminin, Petrachkov, and the two other dead were coming back, riding the sunken sub one last time. But it wasn't a NAVAGA. The missile deck was humped higher, the details wrong.

"None of you see that submarine," warned Pshenichny.

It was Boris Apanasenko in his DELTA, come to relieve the merchant ship of all classified material.

Once more the code bags were handed down the line, over the side, and into launches. The bags went over, the launches returned. In under a half hour, the black ship hissed as she blew ballast, tooted her horn in final salute, and slowly slipped back beneath the waves.

SKORNYAKOVO

Anatoly Yefimovich Preminin was home alone when he received the summons from the village community council. Like Irina Kapitulsky, the tall, gangly mill worker had seen the report on *Vremya* the night before. He'd also listened to a more detailed account on the Voice of

America. He was beside himself with worry over his son Sergei. It was his submarine, no doubt about it. On fire, in trouble. And Sergei an engineer! Probably in the middle of things, if he knew him. Why couldn't he have stayed in Skornyakovo and gone to work in the mill like all his friends? What possessed his son to leave home for a life under the ocean? He was a boy, not a fish!

At least I'll know, he thought as he rode the wheezy old bus from his little farming village to the gray, concrete community council building.

Waiting for him inside was a man in naval uniform. A man with an envelope gray as the concrete, gray as the heaviness in Anatoly's heart. He handed it to Anatoly and said nothing.

Preminin's hands were rough, his fingers thick and scarred. He'd worked with machines all his life. He knew what they could do when the devil got in them. Was Sergei injured? Had he lost an arm, a leg? His hands shook as he ripped open the paper and unfolded a letter.

DEAR ANATOLY YEFIMOVICH PREMININ: IT IS WITH GREAT SORROW I INFORM YOU THAT YOUR SON, SEAMAN SERGEI AN-ATOLYEVICH PREMININ, BORN 1965, DIED WHILE FULFILLING HIS SWORN MILITARY DUTY.

He quickly folded the gray paper, put it into his work jacket and left. The Skornyakovo bus came to the stop, but he ignored it. Instead, Preminin started walking back to his home village along the narrow, rutted road. One foot after the next, through icy puddles, over drifts of new snow, he walked like a robot that saw nothing, felt nothing.

He came to a tall snow bank and paused, teetering the way a man standing at the lip of a canyon sways, feeling the strange gravity of empty space. He leaned, then fell to the snow, clutching his heart and sobbing.

A villager in a cart came by, recognized him, scooped him up and brought him home.

THE PENTAGON

The VIP dining room was empty except for two men; an admiral in dark navy blue and a United States Air Force general in a slightly lighter shade of the same color. Their lunches were set down before them by a Navy steward. Lieutenant General Richard Burpee had a bacon, lettuce, and tomato sandwich. Admiral Bill Crowe, the chairman of the Joint Chiefs of Staff, was on a diet. His plate contained only raw vegetables.

"Sir, I keep wondering if I'm the right guy to brief the press on K-219," said Burpee. "I mean, it's an all-Navy deal."

"You'll do just fine," said Admiral Crowe.

"How will I know where the line is drawn on this? I could overstep it and not even know."

"Don't worry so much. Powell Carter is a good Joint Staff man. And the submariners are sending Hank Chiles. They'll be there to backstop you. How's your sandwich? You haven't touched it."

"Fine, sir." Burpee wasn't feeling very hungry. As the J3/Operations officer for the Joint Chiefs, he had been on watch during the K 219 incident. But he was a pilot, not a submariner, and the whole affair had a smell to it he didn't like. That was why Hank Chiles was showing up at the brief; he was the submariner's number one watchdog. If Burpee said something wrong, it would quickly come back to haunt him. And he was convinced there was something more to the story than he'd been let in on.

The submarine mafia was hiding something from him, maybe even from Crowe, too. In the minds of the submarine community, Crowe wasn't really one of them; he'd been a diesel sub skipper a long time ago and he wore a navy blue uniform, but as Chairman of the JCS he was more of a purple-suiter. A quasi-political post with too many ties outside the submarine world.

A news conference was scheduled to take place at noon in the briefing room. The journalists would all know from Cap Weinberger's little leak that an American sub was out there, watching *K-219*. The press would come in armed, and Burpee had no intention of getting ambushed.

Crowe picked up a carrot stick, then dropped it, eyeing General Burpee's sandwich. "Just steer 'em off anything that feels too hot. Make a few jokes, and tell them they'll be let in on anything that develops."

"Steering them only gets them more interested, sir," said Burpee glumly. "What if they want to know if we hit that boat?"

"Tell 'em we didn't." Crowe picked up a stalk of celery and eyed it suspiciously.

"Is that the case, Admiral?"

"Damned if I know." The admiral tossed the celery down to the plate. "Listen, Dick. You're perfect for the brief. You're not Navy. They wouldn't believe an old submariner like me. They think we're all sneaky."

They aren't the only ones, thought Burpee.

"You'll do fine. Just relax and look stupid. That's the trick in handling the press. You have to convince them you're too damned dumb to know anything good."

"The SecDef didn't help us out."

"Didn't help? Cap Weinberger peed in the grits," Crowe huffed. Even with his Princeton education, Crowe's speech was sprinkled with as much salt as any common sailor. "On the other hand, there are a lot of folks in this country who were mighty surprised to have a Red boomer with sixteen missiles come up off Hatteras. Hell, a lot of folks in this town had no idea they were running missile patrols so close. Be good for them to realize it."

"I just have a problem going in there without knowing the whole story." Burpee picked up half his sandwich. A piece of crisp bacon fell to the plate.

Crowe's eyes followed it. "Admiral Carter will catch any curve balls they throw at you. He knows he's got a lot at stake. If they want to go down there and play with that sub, they're going to have to keep things smooth on this end. They'll carry the ball."

"Play with it?"

"The word from our unit in trail is the boat went down more or less intact. Reactors. Missiles. Who the hell knows what all."

"The *Glomar Explorer* coming out of retirement, Admiral?"

"Stranger things have happened." Then Crowe said, "It's about time for the briefing. You sure you're not hungry?"

The Air Force surrendered to the Navy, and Burpee pushed the plate over.

When the noon conference finally began it was after one in the afternoon. Vice Admiral Powell Carter took the question Burpee had dreaded.

"Was there a collision?" asked a reporter.

General Burpee smiled and glanced at the admiral.

"No," said Carter. "Definitely not. As you know there's an agreement between our forces and the Soviets. We try to avoid complications like collisions. Especially the week before a summit."

The journalists laughed.

"I thought that agreement on incidents at sea governed surface ships only," someone called up.

"That's true," said the admiral. "The *K-219* became a surface ship when she blew a hole in her hull."

Then, a reporter from *Newsweek* stood up.

"Admiral, will there be an effort made to go down and take a look at the Soviet sub? I mean, for intelligence purposes?"

"To be honest, I doubt that," said Carter. "The boat's twenty years old. I don't think we'd learn enough to warrant the costs."

"What about the crew? Where will they go now?"

"Gentlemen, that's a Soviet Navy problem," said Burpee, happy to step in and appear accommodating. "But just between you and me, I think the crew can look forward to a little tropical vacation."

"Vacation?"

"Havana."

CHAPTER 16

For most of us, it was hard to accept
the reality of Havana. But then,
the closer we got to home, the worse they treated us.

—Gennady Kapitulsky,
Propulsion Engineer

HAVANA

Three days after the *K-219* went down, four shipwrecked officers stood together on the starboard wing of the *Anatoly Vasiliyev*'s bridge. Britanov, Grandfather Krasilnikov, Aznabaev, and Gennady Kapitulsky. All except Kapitulsky chain-smoked as the master of the *Vasiliyev* guided the ship into Havana's inner harbor. It was a bright morning, the powerful tropic sun beat down on the red tile and brown tin roofs of the city. It felt good on their backs.

"I thought the next land I'd see would be covered in snow," said Britanov as the big ship nosed into its berth. The esplanade beyond the docks swarmed with lightly dressed brown men and women carrying unimaginable riches: fresh fruits, vegetables, things you couldn't find in Gadzhievo in the *summer,* much less in mid-October. It was almost surreal to men accustomed to the bleak fjords and rocky coast-line of northern Russia.

"We might as well enjoy it," said Aznabaev. "It won't be this warm back home."

Britanov took a long drag, then slowly let the smoke out. "It's sweet. Can you smell it?"

"All I smell is rotting fruit," groused Krasilnikov.

"It smells better than you do," said Kapitulsky.

"We all stink like goats grazing on a chemical dump," Aznabaev added, and he was right. There was no real laundry aboard the *Vasiliyev*. Other than Sergiyenko, all the men stank of burned rubber, chemicals, smoke, and poison gas. They'd washed as best they could, but it was like a stain that wouldn't go away.

"Better get the men on deck," said Britanov. "Assign a detail to sick bay. Kochergin still can't walk." With that he turned and went back inside the freighter's bridge to thank her master for his help.

"He looks bad," said Aznabaev.

"Tight as a drum," said Kapitulsky.

"That's because he knows we're all going to get it in the neck," said Krasilnikov. He tossed his cigarette over the side. The three officers joined Britanov at the bridge.

As the ship moored, a string of tourist buses pulled out onto the pier. At the head of the line was a black Mercedes limousine flanked by motorcycle police. A boarding ramp was nudged up to the ship, and almost before it was made fast to the freighter's deck, a group of uniformed VIPs got out of the Mercedes and walked on board, making for the bridge.

The VIPs coming up the brow were all dressed in light green jungle fatigues, perfectly pressed and bedecked with medals. They looked as if they'd never been worn in the garden, much less a jungle. The guards who came along were heavily armed with bandoliers of ammunition slung over their chests. With their berets and beards, they looked more like terrorists than soldiers.

The VIPs came onto the freighter's bridge. The shortest one of the group, and the one with the most medals on his battle jacket, said, "Welcome to Cuba, comrades. I am Defense Minister Raoul Castro." He was a small man, much shorter and thinner than his more famous brother. His beard was prematurely gray, and his face was almost wizened. "Which one of you is Captain Britanov?"

Britanov stepped forward. He towered over the smaller Cuban. "I am."

Castro reached to shake Britanov's hand, then to the Russian's surprise, drew him into an awkward embrace. He then stepped back and welcomed the other submarine officers in perfect Russian.

"You will find a warm welcome here in Cuba, comrades," he said. "Nothing will be spared. You will have excellent medical attention and the best rest facilities for your recovery. Now, what about the injured? How many are there?"

"Fourteen," said Britanov. "One badly."

"Let's go see them now."

The group filed after the defense minister, down to the freighter's small sick bay. Three men lay in bunks; the air smelled of bitter almond and chemical smoke. Dr. Kochergin's eyes were yellow, but open. A rag stuffed into his mouth was flecked with green mucus. Green rivulets streaked down from the corners of his mouth. His bright red hair and pale, waxy pallor and poison-yellow eyes gave him the look of a ghoul, a frightening Halloween pumpkin. The other two men in sick bay were much improved. They sat up to watch the spectacle.

Castro stepped up to Kochergin's bed. "Young man, you'll soon be on your feet. You'd better, because we're giving you all the run of Havana and you won't want to miss anything."

The other two men grinned, but Kochergin just gazed up.

"We'll find you a nice brown-eyed Cuban girl," Castro said to the doctor, "and then we'll see what your Russian red hair and our dark-skinned beauties can make together."

Kochergin spat out the rag and coughed, then wiped away the mucus from his mouth. In a small, croaking voice, a rasp, he said, "Thank you, but I'm married."

Britanov cheered silently. Castro seemed nonplussed. He patted Kochergin on the shoulder, turned to Britanov and said, "Get your men on the buses. We'll take care of them now." With that he turned on his heel and left.

Britanov gave Kochergin a wink.

Up on the sun-drenched main deck, the men of the *K-219* were assembled in a motley array of uniforms; some wore striped jerseys, others their blue submariner's coveralls, others nothing more than what they'd been wearing when they'd been roused from their bunks on board the sub. Bare skin pale as polar light was exposed to the bright, hot sun. Castro paused, made a short speech to the crew, then hustled back down to the Mercedes and roared off in a cloud of blue exhaust smoke.

"His car needs a tune-up," said Krasilnikov.

"Not as much as I do," Kapitulsky quipped. "Ever taste Cuban rum?"

Krasilnikov huffed. "I've pissed more Cuban rum than you've swallowed."

"We'll see."

The crew filed down and onto the waiting buses. They were fancy Hungarian Ikarus models, air-conditioned with plush seats and tinted glass. The men put their noses to the windows, gawking at the sight of pretty, dark-haired Cuban girls going about their normal morning routines. In their light, tropical dresses they seemed nearly naked.

The tour buses made their way through the crowds to an Army

rest center just outside the city. It had a magnificent view of the sparkling Caribbean, palm trees shading a broad veranda, a swimming
pool, and best of all, rooms with just two beds in them. Each Russian
was given a pair of new cotton shorts, some sandals, and a fresh shirt.
The men disappeared into the hostel as though they were entering a
dream. Only Britanov still seemed troubled.

That afternoon, showered, rested, Aznabaev, Kapitulsky, and Krasilnikov gathered in a communal dining room. A big, impossibly exotic
buffet was being set out on a long table. It was filled with pineapples,
oranges, meats, cheeses, bread, and fresh vegetables.

"How do you think he did it?" asked Aznabaev in a low whisper.

"Who?" said Krasilnikov as he eyed a plate of hard-boiled eggs go
by. "What?"

Aznabaev leaned closer. "The captain. He scuttled the boat somehow."

Just then Britanov entered the dining hall. He still had the same
haunted look he'd worn ever since Kapitulsky had found him in the
bottom of the yellow life raft. The three officers stood.

"Relax," said Britanov. He eyed the buffet. "Everything is all right
in here?"

"Everything except the vodka," Kapitulsky said glumly. He nodded
at a row of bottles. All mineral water.

One of the servers heard him and understood. He went to a bam-
boo-covered bar and opened a double door. Behind the wooden slats
was a walk-in refrigerator, stocked to overflowing with beer, champagne, and bottles of ice-cold Russian vodka.

"Long live the fraternal socialist state of Cuba!" Krasilnikov
grabbed a handful of boiled eggs and popped one into his mouth.

"I'm dying of thirst," said Kapitulsky and made straight for the bar.
But before he could get there, a man dressed in the uniform of rear
admiral of the Soviet Navy appeared at the door.

"Attention!" shouted Britanov. "Admiral on deck!"

Rear Admiral Koslov marched in along with the *K-219*'s political officer, *Zampolit* Sergiyenko. It was no coincidence; Koslov came from the Navy's Main Political Branch. Sergiyenko, in a way, was his boy.

Grandfather Krasilnikov spat out the egg into his hand and stood at attention.

"As you were," said Koslov. "I've just arrived from Moscow. After you've had a chance to rest, you and your men will accompany me back." He gave a cold stare to Kapitulsky. "There will be some questions asked of you in the next few days and weeks. Experts are ready to help you remember the necessary details."

Kapitulsky gave a knowing look to Aznabaev. *Experts* had a distinctly ominous ring to it.

"In the meantime, alcohol should be consumed only in moderation. Overindulgence will not be tolerated." Koslov turned to Britanov. "Your captain will see to it." With that, Koslov and Sergiyenko left. The rest of the sub's officers came in, led by Security Officer Pshenichny.

"Sergiyenko. That shit," growled Kapitulsky, then spat. He hadn't told anyone yet that Sergiyenko had panicked, that he'd jumped off the stern of the sub into a launch when only the injured were supposed to go.

Britanov waited until the admiral was well gone, then said, "I hereby delegate authority on the consumption of alcohol to Zhenya Aznabaev," he said with a sly look. "As navigator, he will be responsible for making sure no one gets lost returning to their rooms. Understood?"

"Understood, Comrade Captain!" came the answer in a shout.

Britanov walked to the bar and took down a bottle of frosted Stolichnaya vodka. He filled a row of tumblers, then handed them out to the officers. He got up on a stool and held his arm out straight, the brimming glass extended. "Gentlemen, officers of crew number one of the Northern Fleet submarine *K-219*, my friends, my comrades. I propose to begin in the traditional manner with the first toast of the night."

The room fell silent.

Britanov's hands shook. Crystal vodka drops spilled down the tumbler and to the floor like tears. "I drink to those we left behind at the bottom...at the bottom of the sea." His eyes glistened. His body swayed as though an invisible wind buffeted him. He downed his vodka, then, as he tried to get down off the stool, he fell.

Aznabaev and Kapitulsky caught him. Britanov sobbed uncontrollably, his shoulders heaving. They took him back to his room and put him down onto his cot. A medic was called, but by the time he arrived, Britanov was asleep.

Around midnight, all the vodka had been consumed, much of the beer, and even the champagne was getting low. The buffet was a shambles. Aznabaev, Krasilnikov, and Kapitulsky sat huddled together at a table, basking in the unfamiliar feeling of plenty.

"They know," said Kapitulsky.

"Of course they know, I told them," said Aznabaev. "The captain said, 'I countermand the orders to reboard.' That's balls. They won't forget something like that."

"Or forgive it," said Krasilnikov. He turned to Kapitulsky. "What happened with you and Sergiyenko? You looked ready to bite him when he came strutting in with the admiral."

Kapitulsky said, "What he did was also unforgivable." Then, as the other two sat close, the propulsion engineer explained exactly what he meant.

GADZHIEVO

It was cold and gray, with a low, woolly sky spitting ice pellets. A typical October day in northern Russia. A member of the Submarine Flotilla's Political Directorate walked up the concrete steps of the naval headquarters building. His heavy greatcoat made the pudgy officer look like a *matryoshka,* one of the wide-beamed, bottom-heavy nesting dolls. A small crowd of women gathered at the base of the steps. Wives of the crew of the *K-219,* they'd been summoned by the Political Directorate for "an announcement of great importance."

Of course they all knew by now what it was about, just not what he would have to say. Natalia Britanov and Irina Kapitulsky had called nearly everyone who needed to know, and those who had been away found out soon thereafter. Irina had even received a covert message from Gennady. He'd sent it to her sister in Estonia, routed through a merchant marine communications center in Tallinn.

"Your sister's husband is coming home to Shermetyovo."

Shermetyovo was the name of the big Moscow airport.

Natalia Britanov even knew the name of the naval rest center the crew would return to, thanks to a kind officer at the Emergency Action Center in Moscow. Still, they all hoped that the political officer would have more details, though none of the women trusted him. After all, it was men like him who'd been exchanging travel passes, nylon stockings, and medicines for sexual favors.

At the top of the stairs he stopped and turned. "Rumors have been circulating around Gadzhievo," he said sternly. "It's time to put them to rest."

"More than he knows," whispered Irina Kapitulsky.

"I'm here to set the record straight and inform you to the maximum degree possible. Of course, it concerns matters of state security, so we shall have to speak cautiously." He let his words hang, making sure the women all knew that he knew something they didn't, and perhaps he knew more than he would say up here and now. Later, in private, was another story.

"There's been an accident aboard your husbands' submarine," the *zampolit* intoned. "While the submarine was lost, our crew will be returning very soon."

At that the women all breathed a sigh of relief. They thought this meant there had been no deaths.

"They will need warm clothes. Please go back to your homes and pack your husbands' winter uniforms, underwear, and shoes. Say nothing to your neighbors and bring the clothes back here quickly. If there is more information, the Political Directorate will be sure that it is properly distributed."

"He means *traded*," whispered Irina as the women dispersed. She really hated them all.

Lyudmilla Petrachkov walked back to her flat in a daze. Even though she had filed for divorce from Alexei, he was still the father of their son. His clothes were still in the apartment, though she now lived there with another man.

She ran up the dark, grimy stairs rather than wait for the unreliable elevator. Thankfully, her new boyfriend, a *michman* on another sub, was not around. She didn't want to see him just now. In a small, inexplicable way, she felt strangely guilty, as though the accident had happened out off Bermuda because she had kicked Alexei out.

She went through his boxed things, grabbing heavy wools and sturdy boots, underwear and a hat, and tossing them into an old battered brown suitcase. She'd meant to pack all his things into storage for when he returned. She had to sit on the bag to lock it. As she pulled the heavy suitcase to the door, her eight-year-old son, Alexei, appeared, back from hockey practice.

"Where are you going, Mother?"

"It's your father's things. He needs them. Help me carry this back to the Flotilla building."

They each grabbed the handle and, between them, hauled the case all the way back through icy, muddy streets to the gray concrete naval headquarters. Other wives had already come with their suitcases, some had only cardboard boxes. The belongings were lined up in a row at the top of the stairs.

The *zampolit* was there with a clipboard. Lyudmilla and Alexei heaved the heavy suitcase up and set it down at his feet.

"Lyudmilla Petrachkov," she said, barely catching her breath.

The officer hardly glanced up from the clipboard. "Go back home," he said. "Your husband no longer needs them."

"What . . . what do you mean?"

He looked up and said, "He died fulfilling his patriotic duty."

"But you said they'd all be coming home—"

"Be proud for what he has done." He looked back to his clipboard.

She stood there, her mouth open, then blinked. Alexei started to cry. The other wives moved away from them as though they might have a contagious disease.

"Next."

Lyudmilla and her son picked up the heavy case and dragged it back down the stairs as the other wives watched.

Galina Kochergin stepped up next. She'd left their eight-month-old son back in the apartment with her mother. "What about Igor?"

The *zampolit* looked at the doctor's wife. She was a pretty woman, and a defiant one. He'd heard she'd had the nerve to laugh at Romanov when he suggested they meet and get to know each other better. Worse, as the wife of a medical officer, she had access to travel passes the other wives did not. She didn't need to beg for permission to visit other towns. She was not in his debt, his power.

The officer said, "I'm very sorry. Your husband died fulfilling his patriotic duty. You can take his things home. Next." The women cried out their husband's names.

"What about Sergei?"

". . . Viktor Petrovich? Is he alive?"

He held up a hand and said, "One at a time." He ignored the doctor's wife.

In shock, Galina Kochergin walked back down the steps. Natalia

Britanov put her arms around her, yet she had never felt more alone in her life.

HAVANA

The crew boarded the same luxurious buses for the trip out to the military airfield. They drove through a guarded gate and went directly to the side of the VIP Illyushin 62 waiting to fly them home. Two days of rest had cured almost everything that ailed the healthy, and except for Dr. Kochergin, even the injured were on their feet.

Kochergin was still confined to a stretcher, his skin still too pale, his eyes too yellow. He'd been severely poisoned when he'd given his OBA mask to Pshenichny, and now Pshenichny hovered next to the doctor, making sure no effort was spared to keep him comfortable.

The crew filed out onto the warm tarmac. They wore their new tropical khaki shorts, sandals, and lightweight shirts.

The men filled the VIP cabin from rear to front; lowest ranks to highest. Britanov sat with Kapitulsky and Aznabaev, two rows behind Admiral Koslov. The admiral sat alone in the forwardmost row on the right, ignoring the crew and officers. He made it clear he didn't want to be too close to the men of the lost submarine; as though they too possessed a deadly, contagious disease.

Word had traveled fast. No one sat next to *Zampolit* Sergiyenko.

The hatch was sealed, the loud turbojet engines started, and soon the long-range jet was airborne, climbing out over the light blue Caribbean. The men watched Cuba recede as though it were a lost paradise.

The ocean grew darker and colder as they flew northeast. As the jet began its approach to Shannon, Ireland, for a fuel stop, Admiral Koslov stood and addressed the crew at last.

"Comrades," he said into a microphone the cabin attendant had provided, "we have new uniforms for you in the hold. While refueling is under way, they will be passed among you. Take your size and change into proper attire. There will be a party of senior officers waiting for you when we land in Moscow. Also, while we are on the ground, all window shades will be pulled down for security reasons." He handed the microphone back and sat back down.

"What security reasons?" said Kapitulsky.

"His," said Britanov. "I hear you have something to say about Sergiyenko?"

The propulsion engineer told the story of how the *zampolit* had panicked out on the stern of the wallowing sub, how he'd jumped into a launch meant only for the injured.

Britanov felt his stomach turn as he listened.

"You know, they'll probably give him a medal for heroically providing his weight to ballast that lifeboat."

Britanov didn't find it funny. Instead he said, "From now on, Sergiyenko does not exist. He's not part of this crew." With that he turned and stared out the porthole as Ireland appeared on the cold blue horizon, rising from the sea.

On the ground, the boxes were unloaded from the belly of the blue and white jet. They were opened and passed through the cabin.

The men quickly discovered that they were all one size. Almost none of them fit and there were no insignia on them.

"This is a prisoner's outfit!" someone complained.

Suddenly uniforms began sailing through the cabin as the crew laughed and cut loose from the tension that was building in direct proportion to their proximity to Moscow. Chaos erupted. Britanov tried to stop it, but he couldn't. Finally Admiral Koslov walked slowly down the aisle, glaring at the men to settle them back down.

The plane took off again, heading north by northeast. The sea disappeared behind them, and below the ground became bare brown, then white.

Someone had their face to the porthole and shouted, "Moscow!"

Britanov looked. Where were they landing? The city was on the wrong side of the jet.

"Captain," said Kapitulsky. "We aren't landing at the main airport."

"I can see that."

"It must be Vnukovo," said the propulsion engineer. Vnukovo was an airport reserved for VIPs southwest of the city. There was no way a normal Soviet citizen could go there. Kapitulsky was worried because his secret message to Irina mentioned a different airport. Now she would not be there to greet him.

The jet circled, then descended. The pilot executed a smooth, flawless landing, but then he was used to flying around VIPs. They taxied to a distant ramp where six battered buses, two ambulances, and three distinct clusters of officers waited. Britanov saw representatives from the Naval Counterintelligence and Security in one group, officers from the Main Political Branch in another, and between them a team from the Fleet Medical Service.

The buses were yellow where they weren't rusty, and half of them had windows plated over with metal.

They'd come down a long way from how they'd been treated in Havana.

The hatch opened and Admiral Koslov hurried down the ramp. He disappeared into a black Volga waiting nearby, and without waiting, left.

Valery Pshenichny followed Britanov down the steps. He was welcomed by his fellow KGB men and hustled off into another black Volga. *Zampolit* Sergiyenko was met by the Political Branch officers. No one looked at Britanov.

A new car appeared. A black Zil flanked by a Volga sedan with the markings of the Military Police on it. It stopped in front of the boarding ramp. Out came a three-star admiral. Britanov recognized him at once: it was Medvedev, head of the Navy's Political Branch.

Admiral Medvedev approached Britanov. He shook his hand limply, but did not return his salute.

"Admiral, the number one crew of *K-219* is returning for—" Britanov began, but Medvedev cut him off.

"I must inform you that you are being charged for losing your ship," he said to the captain. "You and your crew will be confined at Gorky Rest Center until we figure out what to do. An official inquiry is under way." The admiral turned on his heel and opened the door to his car. But before he got in he looked at Britanov and said, "The charges against you are serious, Captain. But you're lucky."

"Sir?"

"In the old days you would have been shot." With that he got in and slammed the door.

"Welcome home," whispered Kapitulsky.

Britanov stood on the ramp as his men filed off into the buses. For a moment, he wondered whether the joke about prison uniforms might not be such a joke at all, then realized there was nothing he could do about it now. They were home, and what they might want to do, who they might want to see, where they might wish to go, mattered very little.

The buses wheezed off in the direction of Moscow, but they never arrived. Instead, they took a turnoff from the Outer Ring Road that led to an area still heavily forested in birch and pine. There, at an unmarked exit, the buses left the main road and clattered into the woods down a narrow lane. The buses swayed as they negotiated the twisty road. Designed for twelve, each of them carried twenty, and the men swayed with them, packed as tightly as tinned fish. One bus broke down, but a seaman from *K-219* got the motor going again.

Finally the first bus ground to a stop at a guard booth. Two soldiers in the uniform of the naval infantry pulled wide a high steel gate and let them through. The gate shut behind.

It was a naval rest facility called Gorky, a word that can also mean *bitter*. It was a cluster of drab brick buildings surrounding a central courtyard. Dirty snow had been pushed to the side of the yard, there to melt and send sheets of ice across the walkways.

Britanov hopped down from the bus and walked into the somber brick building marked as the administration center. Inside at the desk, the staff handed out room assignments and keys.

He found his on the third floor. It was a tiny cubicle without a window, as small and even less homey than his cabin aboard the lost submarine.

Political Officer Sergiyenko had arrived ahead of the crew. He'd been assigned a double room to himself. It had two windows looking down on the drab courtyard.

The significance of the snub was not lost on Britanov, nor on his crew. They grew quiet, guarded even with one another. All of them, but most especially the officers, began to realize that escaping the burning, poisonous sub had been the easy part of the journey home.

CHAPTER 17

We were forbidden to go to Moscow,
but we found our own way.
What was the first thing I did when I saw Gennady
at the Gorky Rest Center? Well, I won't say.
But the second thing I did was put down my suitcase.

—*Irina Kapitulsky*

OFF BERMUDA

With *K-219* on the bottom, there was no need to rush radiation specialists to the site. The American destroyer racing from Norfolk turned around and returned to base. The USNS *Powhatan* remained over the sunken sub, taking air and water samples until a task force of Soviet ships shooed it away. The nuclear-powered cruiser *Kirov,* her escorts, and several fast attack submarines scoured the sea looking for floating pieces of the wrecked *K-219* as well as sanitizing the area of American forces. There was little to find of the lost sub; a few pieces of floating insulation, some pickle bottles from her mess, a magazine over a month old.

With the Reagan-Gorbachev summit in Reykjavík ready to begin, the political as well as the financial costs of maintaining the units so far from home quickly outweighed the benefits. The Soviet Navy departed, though not without plans to return and visit the wreck on the bottom. Farther east, Boris Apanasenko's DELTA-1 ran submerged for home at high speed. She carried with her the twelve code bags recovered from *K-219* and, perhaps, some of their bad luck as well.

Jim Von Suskil in the *Augusta* was right behind him, following him as he sped across the Mid-Atlantic for Gadzhievo.

Unknown to Von Suskil, the Soviets were sure he'd caused the sinking of the *K-219*. They were furious, and so they set a trap: as *Augusta* trailed the DELTA, a nuclear-powered VICTOR III attack boat was silently trailing *him*.

At their speed, the acoustic sensitivity of even the vaunted American sonar was badly degraded. Von Suskil had not picked up the VICTOR; the Soviet boat was lost in the white noise of water streaming by his hull.

When Apanasenko ordered a Crazy Ivan, the same sharp veering turn that had doomed *K-219, Augusta* was forced to back down to avoid running over the Soviet boomer. Both submarines were 396 feet under the waves.

It was only then, as *Augusta* turned and slowed, that Von Suskil's sonar chief detected the VICTOR hiding in his baffles.

Now there were *three* subs rocketing along at wildly different angles and ranges. In the ensuing scramble, Von Suskil lost situational awareness; he no longer had a good mental picture of where *Augusta*, the VICTOR, and Apanasenko's DELTA were to be found.

In the confusion, *Augusta* and the DELTA collided.

As Britanov had done just days before, Apanasenko blew his ballast tanks and surfaced to see what had happened. His foredeck, from the sail to the bow, was smashed in badly. It looked as though someone had taken a giant hammer and pounded the hull. There were no leaks, but Apanasenko knew that if the collision had taken place aft of the sail, over his missile hatches, the story would have come out very differently.

After the collision, *Augusta* remained absolutely silent. Her bow sonar sphere was smashed and some equipment bays flooded. When Von Suskil was convinced the two Soviet boats were no longer a threat, he limped back to New London. It took a week to make it home. He arrived on 27 October. There the most modern attack sub in the fleet would spend nearly a year, and millions of dollars, having the damage repaired.

Repairing Von Suskil's career would prove more difficult.

The duplicate acoustic tapes kept by members of *Augusta's* crew managed to find their way up the chain of command in the submarine community. The allegations of overly aggressive behavior were winked at, the reports buried. Aggression was what an attack skipper was paid for.

In frustration, some of the crew leaked their allegations to the press. Much to the dismay of the submarine community, this brought on an official inquiry.

Their final report was classified. The flap subsided. The findings remain classified to this day. But Jim Von Suskil was never given command of another ship. After failing selection for promotion to admiral, he retired from the Navy.

GORKY NAVAL REST CENTER, MOSCOW

When the flight from Havana failed to show up at the appointed place, Irina Kapitulsky nearly panicked. She didn't trust anything about submarines, the submarine service, or for that matter the Navy. If it suited them to lie to her, they would. If it suited them that her husband, Gennady, should die, or disappear, that too would happen. She hailed a cab and got in. As her panic became fury, she said to the driver, "Gorky Naval Rest Center."

The driver turned. "Where is it?"

"Drive. We'll find it together."

She had only a sketchy description of the place, gleaned from other wives and a cryptic note from Gennady. But if her husband could find his way back from the bottom of the sea, she could find Gorky Rest Center.

They wandered through the outskirts of the capital for hours, and then, finally, more out of exhaustion than hope, she told the driver to turn down an unremarkable one-lane road. It plunged into a deep birch forest that made the night come early. The driver switched on his lights and saw a sign warning that they were approaching a closed military area. Then, at the end of a drive, a barricade appeared in the headlights.

"That's it," he said as he stopped and made ready to turn.

"Wait." Irina Kapitulsky had seen something move. "Drive closer."

"This is a closed military zone. They'll shoot me."

"All right. I'll go myself." She grabbed the heavy suitcase containing Gennady's winter uniform and got out, slamming the car door as she left.

The cab backed up, swung around, and departed, leaving her stranded. Irina had no place to go but forward, and she walked to the barricade and saw a guard with a rifle. He was dressed in the uniform of the naval infantry.

"Forbidden," he said and started to turn away to go back into his heated booth.

"I'm Irina Kapitulsky," she said. "Wife of Chief Propulsion Engineer Gennady Kapitulsky. You will let me in or you will hear about it from my husband."

The guard paused, then went into his kiosk. He came back with a clipboard. "Kapitulsky?" he said.

"Captain Third Rank Gennady Yakovlevich Kapitulsky, crew number one, *K-219*," she said. "Is that enough or do you want to hear from the Flotilla commander, too?"

The barricade lock was opened. The chain rattled in the cold night air. Irina smiled and walked into the compound. Victory was sweet.

She hauled the heavy suitcase down the access road, found the administration building, and got them to give her Gennady's room number. No one offered to help carry her bag. She couldn't have cared less. She sailed up the steps to his room, knocked on the door and stood back.

Gennady was groggy from sleep. The entire crew had found it impossible to concentrate on anything for more than a few moments. Even their interrogations, attended by recorders, security people, and representatives from the Flotilla, were not enough to keep them from yawning uncontrollably. It was dangerous to act so unconcerned, but their nerves were worn down too badly. Gennady Kapitulsky got up from his bed and answered the knock. He opened the door and stared, not sure he was completely awake.

"I've come a long way. Aren't you going to invite me in?" she said as she dropped the suitcase and ran into Gennady's open arms.

The next morning Gennady put on some fresh, warm clothes. He'd hidden five hundred rubles in his wool overcoat back home. When he put his hand into the pocket he found only two hundred fifty, and a note: *Half for you, half for us.*

Galina Kochergin sat alone in her cold, empty apartment, listening to the sound of an old windup clock. Snow drifted by the only window. The day faded from gray to black, matching the empty feeling in her heart. She stood up to switch on a light when the telephone rang. She thought about answering it. Many of her friends, wives of other crewmen, had called to offer her sympathy. Could she stand another one? Could she take hearing the words *I'm so sorry!* one more time? No.

The phone buzzed again. She looked at a picture of her husband in his dress uniform. Whoever was calling was being very persistent.

She looked at the phone, wishing it would stop. She had nothing more
to say, nothing more to give.

When it didn't stop, she sighed, then picked it up. "Yes?"

But it wasn't one of the other Gadzhievo wives. It was a captain
from Moscow calling. His name was unknown to her: Antonov.

"This is Captain Antonov. I'm calling from the Emergency Action
Center."

"I already know what happened. You don't have to call, Captain."

"I don't understand."

"The *zampolit* told me. My husband is dead. What more do you
want from me? What else can I give you? You want one of our
children? They're still too young. I can give you blood, but I'm afraid
it's very thin just now."

"I'm calling because what you were told is not the case."

Her heart tripped over itself. "What do you mean?"

"Dr. Kochergin was hurt badly. But he's coming home."

"Igor is   "

"Alive."

The formal investigation began in earnest the next morning. Britanov
was taken to a small, isolated house deep in the forest surrounding
the main building. There, apart from his crew, he was grilled by officers from Chernavin's staff, the Flotilla, the Main Political Directorate, and more worrisome, the KGB. They sat behind a long table,
smoking. A model of a NAVAGA submarine sat in a cradle.

Britanov was given no place to sit. He stood before them, forced to
repeat the story of the sinking again and again. The interrogators
clearly hoped to trip him up in some small way that would reveal their
darkest suspicions to be true.

"Did you know the American submarine was there?"

"I suspected it."

"And the tugboat?"

"No. That was a surprise."

"I wonder," said a captain from Admiral Medvedev's staff. "Tell us again. How did you sabotage your ship?"

"It was sinking. Sabotage was hardly necessary."

The political officer jabbed a thumb down on the tail of the little submarine model. "You did something. What?"

"You have my statement," Britanov answered.

"Did you open a torpedo tube? Set off the scuttling charges? How did you sink your ship, Captain? Please inform us."

"You have my statement."

"We aren't interested in your statement!" blurted the officer from the Main Political Directorate. "Your words only condemn you. We've already learned of your attitude toward higher authority from your *zampolit*. We know about your habit of posting anti-Party sayings around the submarine."

"Sayings?" Britanov asked.

"Submarine Life Is Not a Service, But a Religion! That alone should have been a sign of mental inadequacy. If service was a religion, what did that make you? A priest? God? What were your plans, Captain? To hand over your submarine to the enemy? To defect and use the *K-219* as your calling card? No one would dare countermand Admiral Chernavin unless he was sure he'd never come back to the Soviet Union. You had some treachery in mind!"

"I lost my submarine but I saved my crew. That's not treachery."

At that the KGB officer leaned forward in his chair. He'd kept silent during the interrogation. "You lost your submarine *and* thirty nuclear warheads, all of them dropped into the laps of the Americans. Most probably they have some of them now. They'll have all of them soon enough. You didn't consider this?"

"What they do or don't do is no longer my concern. I did my duty. It was enough."

"I don't think so, Captain," said the man from Medvedev's staff. "I don't think so at all. You have nothing more you wish to tell us? It could be your last chance."

"You have my statement."

Four days later, Captain First Rank Igor Britanov and Chief Engineer Krasilnikov were ordered to travel to Moscow in civilian clothes. Their Party cards were confiscated.

The crew knew their captain was being set up by the high command for the loss of the submarine and its nuclear weapons. That he'd saved their lives meant nothing; indeed, it seemed to count heavily against Britanov. Rumors, some even true, flew through the narrow, ill-lit dormitory halls late into the night. All they knew for certain was that Britanov and his chief engineer were being sent away early the next morning to an unknown, but clearly unenviable, fate.

Before dawn, a black Volga sedan drove up the narrow access road to the Gorky Naval Rest Center. Its lights swept the dark windows of the dormitories, its tires crunched gravel spread atop a layer of refrozen slush.

Britanov was already up. For the first time in weeks, he'd found it hard to sleep. He was dressed in a civilian suit and long overcoat. Grandfather Krasilnikov knocked on the door. The engineer had a leather jacket on against the cold. They both carried small canvas bags with their uniforms neatly folded within.

"You're ready, Captain?" said the gruff-voiced engineer.

"They shoot prisoners at dawn, don't they?" said the captain.

"Not anymore. Or at least, not so much."

Britanov picked up his cloth bag. "In that case, let's go."

Britanov closed the door to his tiny room. It had been a steady progression downhill: from his sea cabin to the incredible hotel on the Caribbean beach to this bare monk's cubicle. What was the next logical step if not a cell?

They walked down the silent corridor to the lobby. There was no sign of his crew. They were all still in their rooms. He'd avoided saying good-bye to them, although now he wished he'd done so.

They'd been a good team, crew number one of *K-219*. Not always, and not uniformly; Petrachkov had been a suicidal fool, and *Zampolit* Sergiyenko, well, he didn't belong before the accident and had even less claim now. But they'd come to rely on one another, and it was a real shame they'd now be broken up and sent to the far corners of the Soviet Navy.

If, thought Britanov, *they're lucky.* He'd encouraged them to be truthful during their interrogations, but even he hinted that they could say what they wanted to say in order to survive. Any convenient lie would do. Anything. It didn't have to be true. The High Command had already convicted him. It was only sensible for the others to try and save themselves.

As for himself and Grandfather Krasilnikov, well, Moscow needed someone to blame. It was a shame about the chief engineer. But for himself, Britanov was ready to accept the responsibilities of command.

The two officers who had driven in to collect Britanov were already by the door, waiting. One looked at his watch and said, "Time."

Britanov looked around the empty lobby. He knew he was leaving Navy life now, that this would be his last exit. He wished he'd been permitted to wear his uniform.

"Let's go," said the other officer. He opened the front door and Britanov and his engineer followed.

There was a hint of light in the sky, the barest white frosting of pale sunrise. Britanov took two steps in the direction of the idling Volga sedan, and stopped.

Two long ranks of men had assembled in the courtyard. They extended halfway out to the barricades. His men. His crew.

"Attention!" cried Kapitulsky. "Captain on deck!"

From the ranks came the roar of ninety men shouting in one voice:

"Ooh-rah BRIT-anov!"

Britanov stood rooted in place as he searched their faces. Krasilnikov took the captain's bag and loaded it into the car. Britanov walked to the center of the courtyard and faced his crew. "Men," he said, his voice breaking, "I want you to know that regardless of how this all comes out, I am proud of every one of you. Regardless of my fate, my greatest regret after the loss of our ship and the death of our four comrades, is that crew number one of *K-219* will be disbanded. I wish each of you the best." Britanov then stiffened to attention, and saluted the men.

Once more they roared:

"Ooh-rah BRIT-anov!"

Aznabaev stepped forward and presented a small paper bundle to the captain.

"What is it, Zhenya?" he asked.

"Open it, sir."

Britanov was embarrassed, but he did as Aznabaev asked. Inside the paper wrapping was a flag; a blue and white flag with a red star. The very flag he'd taken down from *K-219* as she slipped beneath the sea.

And a plaque:

SUBMARINE LIFE IS NOT A SERVICE, BUT A RELIGION.

Britanov's eyes glistened with emotion as he carefully folded the flag and the plaque into his jacket, repeating the same motions he'd made in the exposed bridge of the *K-219* as she went down. He turned away from his crew and got into the waiting Volga.

As the car drove down the narrow road, he could hear their cheer echo, then fade in the gray, frosty dawn:

"Ooh-rah BRIT-anov!"

"They know what you did, you did for them," said Krasilnikov as he got a cigarette lit. He offered one to Britanov.

"Thanks." Britanov took it. He could hear their proud shout long after the Volga had left Gorky behind. He felt honored to be associated with the young men of crew number one of the *K-219*. Some of them barely old enough to leave their mothers. Honored even if his commanders had looked and found him wanting. He'd done the right thing, he'd kept faith with his men, and perhaps that was enough.

The Volga sped downtown in the center lane reserved for official traffic. It turned right onto Yanesheva Street, by the guard post, and on into the parking lot of the Ministry of Defense. They stopped and the two escorts got out. Britanov and Krasilnikov followed, though the captain noticed the Volga's engine was still running. Apparently, what was in store for them inside was not going to take very long.

Their two escorts hurried them through an arched tunnel, by a pair of guards dressed in fancy, high-topped boots and white leather belts, and inside. It wasn't terribly cold for Moscow, but Britanov was numb, frozen, almost immobilized the way a prisoner going to execution must feel. Resigned to fate.

They were ushered down a long, carpeted corridor to the cavernous office of the deputy minister for political affairs.

Inside, a stuffy-looking colonel wearing the insignia of the tank corps looked up, grunted something, then opened up an inner door. Britanov and Krasilnikov walked in without their two escorts.

Inside was a stocky general with the red-veined nose of a serious drinker. To his side was Admiral Medvedev, the man who'd greeted Britanov at the airfield. As they filed in, the clock on the general's desk chimed 0900.

"*Zdorovye zhelayu,* Comrade General," said Britanov as he came to attention. The general grunted something, but did not respond.

He left Britanov and his engineer standing as he launched into a twenty-minute lecture on the responsibilities a commander has to secure nuclear weapons from falling into enemy hands.

"As such," he concluded, "the results of our investigation show that you and your engineer are to be charged with negligence. I myself believe your worst crime is in giving the Americans thirty nuclear weapons. The maximum penalty for these crimes is twenty years hard labor. Your questionable actions as the last man on board your ship have given rise to an additional charge of sabotage. If that charge is proven, you will both be court-martialed for treason against the state. The penalty for that is death. Personally, I believe this charge is accurate. You will both be sent back to Gadzhievo pending final decisions." The general nodded, dismissing them from his office.

Britanov filed out, still numb. The black Volga was where they'd left it. He got in, stiff as a man who'd half frozen.

Inside the layers of numbness, underneath the ice, he could still feel the beat of a single, glowing truth: he'd done the right thing for his men. He'd taken responsibility for them at Gadzhievo the day they sailed for patrol. He'd done all in his power to bring them home again.

Fate had made him their commander. Now it was splitting them apart. Perhaps for twenty years. Maybe for all eternity.

It would be five more months before he found out that his own future, and that of Chief Engineer Krasilnikov, was in the hands of a German boy even younger than the men of *K-219:* a student pilot named Matthius Rust.

CHAPTER 18

Everyone was afraid of making Moscow unhappy.
This is not just the tragedy behind our accident.
It's the tragedy behind nearly everything that's
wrong with Russia today.

—*Gennady Kapitulsky*

The Reagan-Gorbachev summit in Reykjavík went on despite grumblings over the *K-219* incident. Not everyone was happy about it. Many believed the two leaders became too friendly and too willing to give up everything in the name of peace. The total elimination of all nuclear weapons was on the table, though aides to the two leaders quickly backpedaled away from it.

Caspar Weinberger was sure that the Soviet leader was offering worthless concessions in exchange for real cuts in the American nuclear arsenal. His feelings were echoed on the opposite side of the negotiating table.

The Soviet minister of defense, Marshal Sergei Sokolov, was against anything that diminished the power and prestige of the Soviet Union. A tank officer from the very old school, he had no use for politicians who used his military forces as bargaining chips. They were there to fight and win wars. Period.

Below the topmost layer of diplomacy the world went on much as it had. The following June, Admiral Novoystev traveled to Washington to meet with his counterparts in the U.S. Navy. Still smarting over the loss of *K-219*, the only nuclear ballistic-missile sub ever lost by either side, he delivered a blunt warning: if American submarines continued to behave aggressively, then Soviet forces would have no choice but to counter them. He lodged an official protest over American interference in the *K-219* incident. Even though the Soviet's own internal investigation revealed the leak in silo six, Novoystev hinted the tragedy was the result of a collision with the American submarine in trail: the USS *Augusta*.

Of leaky missile silos, divorced weapons officers, and nuclear safety systems that failed when most needed, Novoystev was mute.

Nor was the fate of her captain and chief engineer discussed.

Britanov and his wife, Natalia, were forced off the base at Gadzhievo pending sentencing for his crimes against the State. They packed their apartment up and left for his parents' house in the town of Sverdlovsk, forty-eight hours away by train. Krasilnikov moved to nearby Murmansk. The two officers remained with their families that long, dark winter as they waited to hear what punishment Moscow would send their way. The final disposition of the case awaited only Defense Minister Sokolov's signature.

It was never to come.

On the afternoon of May 28, 1987, Matthius Rust took off in a rented Cessna 172 from a small civilian airport outside Helsinki, Finland. He flew low over the Gulf of Finland, and then turned southeast. He crossed into Soviet territory near Irina Kapitulsky's sister's house in Tallinn, Estonia. He kept on flying until the smudged skies of Moscow appeared in his windshield. It was a national holiday in honor of the Soviet Union's Border Guards.

Whether Rust chose the day for that reason or not, it was high irony even for a land that overflows with it. Perhaps the Border Guards were too busy celebrating to notice, or perhaps they were too unwilling to question the business of an aircraft approaching Moscow. In any case, Rust and his little Cessna successfully penetrated some of the most heavily guarded airspace on earth.

By seven in the evening, Rust had flown more than five hundred fifty miles. He was almost out of fuel, circling over the heart of Moscow, looking for a place to land. He missed a small grass airfield in the middle of the city, and chose, instead, Red Square.

Then, as now, nothing happened in Moscow without political echoes, and the one that followed the little white Cessna's arrival was deafening: Defense Minister Sokolov was out, and Dmitri Yazov, an Army general and Gorbachev man, was in.

The results of the investigation into the sinking of the *K-219,* as well as the recommended punishment to be meted out to Britanov and Krasilnikov, now lay on Yazov's desk. So did the investigation into the penetration of Soviet airspace by the German teenager.

Dmitri Yazov was a deeply political general in a byzantine political system. He read both reports in great detail, not only seeking the truth behind the words, but for the likely fallout of his decision.

One investigation recommended severe punishment for a captain whose acts, though rash, were made in the interests of his crew. He was, at least in the eyes of the world, a kind of hero. More, he could be seen as a man who had adopted the "New Thinking" Gorbachev was espousing; a style of thinking that put a human face on the gray, granite façade of old-style Communism.

On the other hand, there were several air defense generals whose failure to stop Rust made the Soviet Union a laughingstock to the world. This was clearly less forgivable. To Russians, nothing, not even losing a submarine filled with atomic warheads on the doorstep of the United States, was as bad as being laughed at.

More, Gorbachev had issued a directive to all his ministers to submit names of political prisoners, dissidents, and victims of repression for a general amnesty he planned to declare. Analyzed in this way, Yazov's choice was clear.

He tore up the orders mandating punishment of Britanov and Krasilnikov, and drafted a new set for the admirals in the Main Political Branch to carry out:

20.7.1987   DECLARATION OF SUSPENSION

OF CRIMINAL CHARGES

INVESTIGATION INTO THE

MAJOR MILITARY CASE BY

THE MAIN MILITARY PROSECUTOR

COLONEL YEROFEEV

In consideration of the extraordinary and unusual conditions surrounding the accident with a missile weapon system which resulted in the loss of the submarine, it is determined that the crew and those operationally responsible, BRITANOV, I. A., and KRASILNIKOV, I. P., could not have prevented, without abnormal actions, the explosion and subsequent leak into their submarine compartments of elements of missile fuel. Their actions taken to thwart the effects of the accident were blameless and positive in nature such to release them from charges of misconduct in accordance with Article 1 of Chapters 208 and 209 of the Statutes of the Communist Party, USSR. The accused are released from charges of criminal responsibility and all criminal acts under Basic Article 6 of the Laws of the Communist Party, USSR, in accordance with the investigation into the charges.

Although the expulsion from the Party would be upheld, Britanov and his engineer were permitted to remain officers in the Naval Reserve.

They were even allowed a small pension, though after the fall of the USSR, runaway inflation made it almost worthless. Still, he had his head, and Britanov knew how fragile the defense minister's mercy might be. It had come as an accident; it could be revoked at a whim.

As for *Zampolit* Sergiyenko, when word came out of his behavior that day on the burning *K-219,* he was expelled from the submarine service forever. No one took away his Party card, though the same forces that swept away the value of the ruble soon made it just as worthless.

But for Britanov, Yazov's mercy was not the same as forgiveness, or acceptance. Expelled from Navy society, his name whispered among officers as the captain who defied Chernavin, Britanov brooded for years. He refused to meet with any of his old crew members. He was a man freed from the threat of prison, but locked up by his memories.

Krasilnikov found work in Murmansk on the big, and troublesome, nuclear-powered icebreakers based there. The story of the lost submarine and a captain who refused to obey Moscow's orders to leave his submarine, who had sacrificed himself for his crew, quietly circulated through the Soviet Navy. The ordeal of the *K-219* was not forgotten by the men of the Russian Navy.

Neither had the Americans overlooked it.

In 1988, the Soviet hydrographic research ship *Keldesh* positioned itself over the wreck. It sent down a pair of remote-controlled cameras to take a look at what was left of the *K-219.* What they found under eighteen thousand feet of water was this:

The submarine was sitting upright on the sandy bottom. It had broken in two aft of the conning tower. Several missile silo hatches had been forced open, and the missiles, along with the nuclear warheads they contained, were gone.

Sergei Preminin, the young sailor who had gone into a live nuclear reactor and shut it down with a steel crank and his iron will, was posthumously awarded the Red Star for his bravery. His parents were given a somewhat larger apartment in their village and a telephone.

The only survivor of the sinking to be honored was Senior Lieutenant Sergei Voroblev, the damage control officer who had been smoking in the bottom level of the missile room when silo six blew up in his face. He received the Red Star for carrying Markov, the injured communications officer, out of the burning, flooding compartment in his arms.

The *K-219* sank in October 1986, but the chain of events set off by a leaky missile silo hatch continues to kill more than a decade later. Acid-seared lungs yield to pneumonia; livers poisoned with nitric fumes fail. Memories haunt men to desperation, to suicide. Each year the sunken sub, rifled for her secrets and left to be buried by the Gulf Stream's steady snow of silt, claims new victims. Of the 115 survivors of the explosion, the flooding, and the fires, four have since perished from their injuries. Eleven more are crippled. Many of those still alive have no access to special medical care from a bankrupt Navy, nor money to pay for care at the new private hospitals.

In 1996, Chief Engineer Igor Krasilnikov's lungs began to fail him, the acid he'd breathed going into compartment four finally taking its toll.

GADZHIEVO, ARMED FORCES DAY, 1995

The town of Gadzhievo is nicknamed Rocky because of its rugged setting. Officially known as Murmansk-130, it has not aged well in the post-Soviet era. Its slab-sided apartment flats are unpainted and crumbling. The docks tilt alarmingly into the icy fjord and the roads have potholes deep enough to bear the names of their unlucky discoverers. Electricity is cut off for days at a time, even to critical base areas, for nonpayment of bills to the local, and now privately owned, utility.

Many of the Flotilla's submarines have not left port in years, nor are they even safe to board. Some have sunk outright, still tethered to the pier.

Winter, for all its harshness, covers the raw bones of the military town with a clean white blanket. It was on such a winter day, February 13, 1995, that a ceremony was held honoring Gadzhievo submariners who had been lost at sea. Britanov had been invited. His friend Gennady Kapitulsky begged him to come. No one knew whether he would.

The day was clear and bright, the low sun sparkling on the snow, as officers and their families gathered outside one of the drab apartment flats. On a corner of the building was a shrouded plaque. A band played martial tunes that the deep cold and empty blue sky swallowed whole.

Two guards flanked the memorial. After a short speech by the mayor of Murmansk, a rope was pulled and the shroud fell away.

It was a monument to Seaman Sergei Preminin. As the military band played a slow funeral dirge, his friends and family stepped up to touch the cold bronze and to place bright, fresh flowers at its base. Survivors of the *K-219* crew were there in force. All those still healthy enough to travel, except for *Zampolit* Sergiyenko, were there. A banquet was scheduled to be held that evening in their honor at the Gadzhievo Officers' Club. After nearly a decade, their harrowing ordeal, their bravery, their endurance, would be recognized by the brotherhood of submariners.

Grandfather Krasilnikov was one of the last to put a spray of flowers at the memorial. As he turned away he stopped and stared at a lone figure walking down the snowy road from the main gate.

He stiffened to attention as the crowd erupted in whispers, then fell silent.

Igor Britanov, his bearing tall and erect, his face determined, his bare head covered by a cloth beret, walked by the ranks of his former crew as well as serving submariners. He carried a bouquet he'd brought with him on the long train ride from Sverdlovsk.

Kapitulsky shouted, "Attention!" and the veterans of *K-219* responded by bracing themselves as their former commander walked by. Britanov placed the flowers at Preminin's memorial, then turned.

Kapitulsky was grinning. So, in his way, was Krasilnikov. Zhenya Aznabaev came to him. He was heavier than when he'd served as *K-219*'s navigator, and he'd lost a lot of his hair. But his smile was the same.

"Welcome back, Captain," he said, then embraced Britanov with both arms.

Aznabaev held him close. Soon he was joined by Kapitulsky. As Britanov was embraced by his officers, the cry from the crowd was spontaneous and loud:

"Ooh-RAH! BRIT-anov!"

"Ooh-RAH! BRIT-anov!"

"Ooh-RAH! BRIT-anov!"

The three-month patrol had become almost ten years, but Captain Igor Britanov had come back to Gadzhievo. He'd returned to the men he'd sacrificed a decade and his command for. Britanov had come back from the abyssal plains where monsters prowled and surfaced into the light. Standing here, with their cheers echoing from the drab concrete apartment buildings, it was possible to believe that his long ordeal was over. That even with his old country dead and his new one struggling to find its way in the world, Britanov's own life could begin again.

APPENDIX

PROJECT NAVAGA *K-219*: SUBMARINE'S COMPLEMENT

Died 3 October 1986

Petrachkov, Alexandr V.	Captain Third Rank	Weapons Officer
Kharchenko, Igor K.	Seaman	Machinist
Smaglyuk, Nikolai L.	Seaman	Weapons Division
Preminin, Sergei A.	Seaman	Reactor Team

Survived

OFFICERS

Britanov, Igor A.	Captain Second Rank	Commanding Officer
Krasilnikov, Igor P.	Captain Second Rank	Chief Engineer
Vladimirov, Sergei V.	Captain Third Rank	Executive Officer
Aznabaev, Yevgeny R.	Captain Third Rank	Navigator
Pshenichny, Valery I.	Captain Third Rank	Security Officer
Sergiyenko, Yuri O.	Captain Third Rank	Political Officer
Kapitulsky, Gennady Ya.	Captain Third Rank	Main Propulsion Assistant
Lysenko, Oleg M.	Captain Third Rank	Damage Control Officer
Gordeev, Vladimir D.	Captain Third Rank	Torpedo Mine Officer

Osipov, Vladimir A.	Captain Lieutenant	Commander Hull Group
Prikhunov, Sergei A.	Captain Lieutenant	Electronics Officer
Kretov, Igor O.	Captain Lieutenant	Engineer Officer
Vishtalenko, Aleksandr V.	Captain Lieutenant	Engineer Officer
Babenko, Yuri V.	Captain Lieutenant	Electrical Officer
Kiselev, Vyacheslav V.	Captain Lieutenant	Radio Electronic Officer
Ryasanov, Sergei N.	Captain Lieutenant	Sonar Officer
Simakov, Aleksandr I.	Captain Lieutenant	Commander Third Compartment
Vorobyev, Sergei V.	Captain Lieutenant	Chief Chemical Detachment
Cherkasov, Sergei A.	Senior Lieutenant	Assistant Navigator
Gus'kov, Oleg V.	Senior Lieutenant	Assistant Navigator
Kuz'menko, Oleg P.	Senior Lieutenant	Assistant Weapons Officer
Dem'yan, Yuri, M.	Senior Lieutenant	Engineering Officer
Belikov, Nikolai N.	Senior Lieutenant	Reactor Officer
Konoplev, Aleksei K.	Senior Lieutenant	Commander Eighth Compartment
Skryabin, Sergei G.	Senior Lieutenant	Commander Sixth Compartment
Dolmatov, Roman M.	Senior Lieutenant	Electronics Officer
Kochergin, Igor A.	Lieutenant Medical Service	Doctor
Sergienko, Vladimir N.	Lieutenant	Commander Second Compartment
Pasechnik, Anatoli I.	Lieutenant	Commander Tenth Compartment

WARRANT OFFICERS

Baidin, A. I.; Bednosheev, S. V.; Bondarenko, A. F.; Borunov, S. M.;
Budalov, A. A.; Buryak, V. V.; Chepishenko, V. V.; Chudakov, Yu. I.;
Demchenko, V. M.; Dmitrievskii, V. A.; Dyachkov, Y. A.;
Gasparyan, A. Kh.; Gridin, A. D.; Gurshal, V. V.; Kalychenko, V. A.;
Ketov, N. M.; Kusov, A. Yu.; Linskii, V. V.; Lyutikov, I. V.;
Medyanik, A. P.; Morozov, P. N.; Povarov, S. V.; Pungin, S. V.;

Ryzkin, N. I.; Samorokovskii, V. P.; Sergeev, V. V.; Shcherbakov, A. A.; Shpakov, N. T.; Shvidun, V. V.; Smolev, V. P.; Syich, V. N.; Taran, V. V.; Vashchenko, Yu. I.; Vasil'chuk, A. D.; Yezhov, V. N.; Yurin, A. A.; Zastavnyi, P. F.; Zhdanov, A. E.

SEAMEN

Almonaitis, B. V.; Ananenko, A. S.; Banders, A. Ya.; Banyzhkov, M. A.; Beskier, S. M.; Burunov, Yu. G.; Butkus, V. P.; Butnaru, I. A.; Bystrov, V. G.; Derkach, A. A.; Dolotii, A. A.; Gekalo, S. N.; Griyasnov, A. A.; Ivanov, D. N.; Khaidarov, N. G.; Kuchkarov, U. Kh.; Maikan, A. N.; Maiorov, V. L.; Marchukov, S. A.; Melynikov, S. A.; Mingliev, A. T.; Mukharryamov, F. Kh.; Musyakevich, A. N.; Muzharyakov, A. A.; Nedely, A. M.; Popov, N. N.; Postnikov, S. A.; Rakulytsev, I. G.; Roman, L. P.; Sadauskas, R. V.; Salikhov, V. I.; Savchik, V. V.; Savin, V. N.; Solovei, A. F.; Solovyev, I. V.; Tarasov, S. A.; Tatarenko, V. N.; Timashkov, S. V.; Vanyushkov, M. A.; Vasilev, N. B.; Velientienko, S. I.; Vyugin, V. G.; Yegorov, V. A.; Yesipov, V. V.; Zakharutin, I. N.; Zakruzhnii, A. Ya.; Zubov, Yu. V.

Died Later of Health Complications Resulting from the Incident

Karpachev, Vladimir N. Captain Lieutenant Commander's Deputy
Markov, Vladimir P. Captain Third Rank Communications Officer

BIBLIOGRAPHY

PRIMARY SOURCES

Interviews, Memoranda of Conversation

Andreev, Gennady Aleksievich, Captain First Rank. Former CO YANKEE SSBN, Flag Missile Specialist, Gadzhievo Division. Interview. St. Petersburg, 2 October 1995.

Antonov, Gennady Nikolaievich, Rear Admiral. Former CO DELTA-class SSBN, Chief Naval Missile Directorate, On-Site Inspection Directorate, Russian Defense Ministry. Interview. St. Petersburg, 2 October 1995.

Aznabaev, Yevgeny, Captain Third Rank. Former *K-219* navigator. Interview. St. Petersburg, 27 September 1995.

Bohn, Michael, K., Captain, U.S. Navy retired. Former director of the White House Situation Room. Telephone interview. Washington, D.C., 11 January 1995.

Britanov, Igor A., Captain First Rank. Former commanding officer and survivor of YANKEE class SSBN *K-219*. Interviews: Moscow, 8–9 November 1994; telephone, 15 February 1995; Yekaterinburg, 4 March 1995.

Brooks, Thomas A., Rear Admiral retired. Chief Intelligence Center,

JCS. Telephone interview. Greensboro, North Carolina, 10 January 1995.

Burpee, Richard, Lieutenant General USAF retired. J3/Operations on the U.S. Joint Staff, JCS. Interview. Alexandria, Virginia, 9 January 1995.

Bush, James, Captain, U.S. Navy retired. Center for Defense Information. Interview. Washington, D.C., 12 January 1995.

Carter, Powell N., Admiral U.S. Navy retired. Former director of the Joint Staff, JCS. Telephone interview. West Virginia, 10 January 1995.

Chernavin, Vladimir Nikolaievich, Admiral of the Fleet. Former commander in chief, Soviet Navy. Interview. St. Petersburg, 29 July 1996.

Chifonov, Rear Admiral. Deputy chief of board of investigation on the sinking of SSBN YANKEE *K-219,* Commanding Officer DELTA-IV class SSBN. Interview. Moscow, 8 November 1994.

Combs, Richard E., Foreign Service Officer. Former deputy chief of mission, U.S. Embassy, Moscow. Interview. Washington, D.C., 12 January 1995.

Federov, George, Russian Naval Specialist. Naval Intelligence Command. Interviews. Washington, D.C., 11 January 1995 and 5 February 1997.

Herrington, David L., Captain, U.S. Navy retired. Former director of Chief of Naval Intelligence Plot, IP. Interview. Arlington, Virginia, 10 January 1995.

Ivanov, Vladimir Petrovich, Kontr Admiral Russian Navy retired. Former chief, Soviet Navy Security and Counter-Intelligence. Interview. St. Petersburg, 1 August 1996.

Kalistratov, Nikolai Yakoblevich, General Director, Scientific Production Director. SVEZDOCHKA (Little Star) Nuclear Submarine Construction and Repair Yard, Severodvinsk, Russia (yard that built and repaired YANKEE-1 class SSBN *K-219*). Interview. Moscow, 30 July 1996.

Kapitanets, I. M., Admiral, First Deputy CinC Soviet Fleet. Former, Northern Fleet Commander during *K-219* sinking. Memcon. Moscow, 10 July 1989.

Kapitulsky, Gennady Ya., Captain Third Rank. Former main propulsion engineer, survivor of SSBN YANKEE *K-219*. Interviews. St. Petersburg: 15 November 1994, 26 September 1995, and 30 July 1996.

Kapitulsky, Irina Yurevna, wife of former main propulsion engineer and survivor of SSBN YANKEE *K-219*. Interviews. St. Petersburg: 15 November 1994, 26 September 1995, and 30 July 1996.

Kipyatkova, Anna I., Director, Underwater Shipbuilding History. Central Design Bureau for Marine Engineering, RUBIN. Interview. St. Petersburg, 26 September 1995.

Kochergin, Igor N., Captain Third Rank. Former medical officer and survivor of SSBN YANKEE *K-219*. Interviews. St. Petersburg: 15 November 1994 and 1 August 1996.

Krause, Vladimir Alexeievich, Captain First Rank, GRU. Former assistant Soviet naval attaché, Ottawa and Washington, D.C., 1986–1990. Interviews. 8–13 November 1994.

Kurdin, Igor, K., Captain First Rank. Former executive officer, SSBN YANKEE *K-219,* and CO SSBN YANKEE-1 class *K-241* and DELTA-IV class *K-84.* Interviews. St. Petersburg: 15 November 1994, 18 September–2 October 1995, and 28–31 July 1996.

———, Letters to author dated 15 February 1995, 13 November 1995, 10 and 27 December 1995, giving accounts of debriefings with the former crew members of *K-219.*

———, Video and audio recording of interviews with former officers of *K-219*: Navigator Yevgeny Aznabaev, Chief Engineer Igor Krasilnikov, Executive Officer Vladimir Vladimirov. Severomorsk, 23 February 1995.

———, Audio recording of interview with former *K-219* officers and survivors Vladimirov, Pshenichny, Aznabaev, and Krasilnikov, concerning the radio communications between merchant ship *Krasnog-vardyesk* and Moscow Soviet Naval High Command, 5–6 October 1986.

———, Audio recording of interview with First Mate Aleksei Gakkel of the *Anatoly Vasiliyev,* who recovered Commanding Officer Britanov from the life raft on 6 October 1986.

———, Video recording of interviews with former *K-219* crewmen, commanding officer and wives, filmed by "Adam's Apple," produced by Kiril Nabutov. LenTV, 4 October 1996.

Kurdin, Irina, wife of the former executive officer, SSBN K-219 and resident of Gadzhievo. Interviews. St. Petersburg, 18 September–2 October 1995, 28–31 July 1996.

Loikanen, Gary Genrikovich, Rear Admiral. Former commander of a Northern Fleet YANKEE Flotilla. Interview. St. Petersburg, 27 September 1995.

Makhonin, Admiral. Former first deputy chief of Soviet Main Navy Staff for Logistics 1988–1991. Interview. Moscow, 14 November 1994.

Moiseev, Mikhail, General of the Army. Former chief of Soviet General Staff, 1988–1991. Interview. Moscow, 14 November 1994.

Musatenko, Roman Ivanovich, Captain First Rank. Former YANKEE SSBN CO. Director, Weapons Faculty, War College. Interview. St. Petersburg, 28 September 1995.

Navoytsev, Petr Nikolaevich, Admiral. Former first deputy chief of Main Navy Staff for Operations, 1975–1987. Interview. Washington, D.C., 18–24 June 1987, while escorting Soviet Delegation U.S./Soviet Annual Incidents at Sea Talks.

Nikitin, Yu. Captain Second Rank. Author. Interview. Moscow, 8 November 1994.

Northup, Donn, Commander, U.S. Navy retired. Former NOIC watch officer. Telephone interview. Springfield, Virginia, 9 January 1995.

Paroshin, Vladimir I., Vice Admiral. Former First Deputy Commander in Chief, Northern Fleet, during sinking of *K-219*. Interview with Captain Kurdin. St. Petersburg, 3 June 1996.

Petrachkov, Alexei A. Cadet at Nakhimov Naval Preparatory School and son of Captain Third Rank Petrachkov, former weapons officer, killed during incident aboard SSBN YANKEE *K-219*. Interview. St. Petersburg, 15 November 1994.

Poindexter, John M., Vice Admiral retired. Former assistant to President Reagan for National Security Affairs. Interview. Rockville, Maryland, 11 January 1995.

Ponikarovskiy, Valentin Nikolaevich, Admiral. Former CO NOVEMBER SSN, Deputy Northern Fleet Commander for Submarine Operations, Superintendent, St. Petersburg Naval War College. Interview. St. Petersburg, 29 September 1995.

Pshenichny, Valery, Captain Second Rank. Former *K-219* security officer. Interview. St. Petersburg, 15 November 1994.

Ramee, Mark, Foreign Service Officer. Former political counsellor, U.S. Embassy Moscow. Interview. Washington, D.C., 11 January 1995.

Selivanov, Ye. V., Admiral. Chief of Russian Main Navy Staff, Interview. 20 September 1995.

Sheafer, E. D., Rear Admiral, U.S. Navy retired. Former J2/Fleet Intelligence Officer, Staff Commander-in-Chief Atlantic Fleet, Norfolk, Virginia. Interview. McLean, Virginia, 12 January 1995, and by telephone 3 February 1997.

Shevardnadze, Eduard, Former Foreign Minister, USSR. Interviews. Moscow, 20 June and 5 September 1991.

Skryabin, Sergei, Senior Lieutenant. Former commander of compartment six aboard *K-219*. Letter account of the events he witnessed aboard *K-219*, 3–6 October 1986, written to Captain First Rank Igor K. Kurdin in December 1995.

Tarasenko, Vladimir Ivanovich, Captain First Rank, Russian Navy. Former *starpom* (executive officer) DELTA-1 class SSBN *K-279*, which collided with USS *Augusta* (SSN-710) in the eastern Atlantic, 20 October 1986.

Toporikov, Viktor Viktorovich, Captain First Rank. Former aide to Admiral Navoytsev. Interviews: Washington, D.C., 18–24 June 1987 during Annual U.S./USSR Incidents at Sea Meeting; Moscow, 8 July 1988 and 20 July 1989.

Volkova, Yelena Petrovna, wife of former *K-219* officer and resident of Gadzhievo. Interview. St. Petersburg, 15 November 1994.

Voroblev, Sergei, Captain-Lieutenant. *K-219* chemical officer. Interview with Captain Kurdin. Murmansk, 23 February 1995.

Weinberger, Caspar, former Secretary of Defense. Interview Arlington, Virginia, 6 January 1995.

Yazov, Dimitry Timofeevich, Marshal. Defense Minister, USSR, July 1987–August 1991. Interview. Sevastopol, 9 August 1988.

Zadorin, Captain First Rank. Former executive assistant to the CinC Soviet Fleet, V. N. Chernavin, 1985–1991. Interview. Moscow, 8 November 1994.

Private and Government Documents and Studies

Bellona Report, vol. 2. "The Russian Northern Fleet, Sources of Radioactive Contamination," Thomas Nilsen, Igor Kudrik, and Alexander Nikitin. Oslo, 1996.

Crew list of NAVAGA Class Project 667 SSBN *K-219*.

Decree of the Main Military Prosecutor, Soviet Ministry of Defense, dismissing criminal charges against Igor A. Britanov and Igor P. Krasilnikov, 20 July 1987.

Greenpeace Trip Report. "Radioactive Waste Situation in the Russian Pacific Fleet, Nuclear Waste Disposal Problems, Submarine Decommissioning, Submarine Safety, and Security of Naval Fuel." Joshua Handler, Research Coordinator, Disarmament Campaign, 27 October 1994.

Greenpeace Working Paper. "Soviet Submarine Accidents and Submarine Safety." Joshua Handler, Research Coordinator, Greenpeace Nuclear Free Seas Campaign, Washington, D.C., 4 September 1991.

Greenpeace. "Soviet/Russian Submarine Accidents: 1956–94." Joshua Handler, Research Coordinator, Greenpeace International Disarmament Campaign, 9 October 1994.

Log of the NAVAGA (YANKEE 1) Class Project 667 *K-219*, portions for 3–6 October 1986.

Neptune Papers No. 3. "Naval Accidents 1945–1988." William M. Arkin and Joshua Handler, Greenpeace, Institute for Policy Studies, June 1989.

Nikitin, Yevgeni. "Rokov'e Bermudi" (Murmurs off Bermuda). Unpublished manuscript account of the loss of YANKEE Class SSBN *K-219.*

U.S. Council for Energy Awareness. Study Source Book: *Soviet-Designed Nuclear Power Plants in the Former Soviet Republics and Czechoslovakia, Hungary and Bulgaria.* Washington, D.C., 1992.

Yablokov Report. *Facts and Problems Related to Radioactive Waste Disposal in Seas Adjacent to the Territory of the Russian Federation* (Materials for a Report by the Government Commission on Matters Related to Radioactive Waste Disposal at Sea, Created by Decree No. 613 of the Russian Federation President, 24 October 1992). Office of the President of the Russian Federation. Moscow, 1993.

Autobiographies, Memoirs, and Firsthand Accounts

Chernavin, Vladimir N., Admiral of the Fleet. *Vakhtenn'i Zhurnal (The Log); Flot V Sud'be Rossii (The Fleet and the Destiny of Russia).* Moscow: Andreevski Flag, 1993.

Mikhailovski, Arkadi P., Admiral. *Vertikalnoye Vspl'itie (Blow to the Surface).* St. Petersburg: Nauka, 1995.

Romanov, D. A. *Tragediya Podvodnoi Lodki "Komsomolets," Argumenti Konstruktura (Tragedy of the Submarine Komsomolets, Arguments of the*

Constructors). St. Petersburg: Peasant and Humanitarian Institute Press, 1995.

Samoylov, V., Admiral (reserve), "Semnadst Sotni Meterov Vniz Na Bortu Komsomolets" (Seventeen Hundred Meters Down Aboard the Komsomolets), *Morskoi Sbornik* 4 (September 1992): 33–36.

Zhiltsov, Lev, Nicolai Mormoul, and Leonid Ossipenko. *La Dramatique Histoire des Sous-marins Nucleaires Sous-marins Nucleaires Sovietiques: Des exploits, des echecs et des catastrophes cachées pendant trente ans.* Paris: Robert Laffont, 1992.

———. *Atomnaya Podvodnaya Epopeya: Podvigi, Neudachi, Katastrofi* (Nuclear Submarine Epochs: (Exploits, Misfortune, Catastrophe). Moscow: A/O "Borgee," 1994.

Newspaper Articles

Alekseev, Vladimir, "Vrazhdebn'ie Vod'i" (Hostile Waters), K 10-letiyu gibeli atomnoi podvodnoi lodki '*K-219*' (Tenth Anniversary of the Sinking of Nuclear Submarine *K-219*), *Smena* (St. Petersburg), 4 October 1996, no. 223.

———, "B Oktyabre 1986 Sovetskie Podvodniki Spasli Ameriku" (Soviet Submariners Saved America in 1986), *Smena* (St. Petersburg), 11 September 1996, no. 204.

Atlas, Terry, "Old Russian Nuclear Subs Pose Environmental Threat, Study Says," *Chicago Tribune,* 26 February 1993, sec. 1, p. 5.

Bivens, Matt, "Soviet Captain Recounts Tale of a 'Chernobyl' Under Sea," *The Nation* (Bangkok, Thailand), 21 May 1993, p 1.

Black, Norman, "*Augusta* Likely Hit Soviet Sub," *The Day* (New London, Connecticut), 2 March 1987.

Bohlen, Celestine, "Soviet A-Sub Blaze Off Bermuda Kills Three," *Washington Post,* 5 October 1986.

Broad, William J., "Navy Has Long Had Secret Subs," *The New York Times,* 7 February 1994, pp. A1, B7.

————, "Russians Seal Nuclear Sub on Ocean Floor," *The New York Times,* 9 September 1994.

————, "Disasters with Nuclear Subs in Moscow's Fleet Reported," *The New York Times,* international, 26 February 1993.

————, "Sunken Soviet Sub Leaks Radioactivity in Atlantic," *The New York Times,* 8 February 1994, p. A13.

Drew, Christopher, and Michael L. Millenson, "For the U.S. and Soviets, an Intricate Undersea Minuet," *Chicago Tribune*, 8 January 1991, p. C1.

Fagin, Steve, and Maria Hileman, "Navy Admits Sub Hit Object," *The Day* (Groton, Connecticut), 4 November 1986, p. A16.

Gundarov, Vladimir, "Narushitel Pravil Podvodnovo Dvizheniya C Mesta Proisshestviya Skrilsya" (Violation of Rules of Submarine Operations, Together with an Incident of Concealment; Collision of a Russian Atomic Submarine with an American Nuclear Sub in the Eyes of Witnesses), *Krasnaya Zvesda* (Moscow), 27 March 1993, no. 69–70, p. 1.

Gwertzman, Bernard, "Moscow Reports Fire on Atomic Sub in North Atlantic," *The New York Times,* 5 October 1986, pp. A1, A14.

————, "Soviet Submarine Crippled by Fire on Her Way Home," *The New York Times,* 6 October 1986, pp. A1, A6.

————, "Soviet Atomic Sub Sinks in Atlantic 3 Days After Fire," *The New York Times,* 7 October 1986, pp. A1, A21.

Khraptovich, Albert, "M'i Naklepali Sotni Plavayushikh Mishenei" (We Riveted Hundreds of Floating Targets), *Rossiskovo Gazetta* (Moscow), 19 October 1996.

Kolton, Ilya, "Vspl'itie Pokazhet" (Surface and Show); "Sovershenno Sekret'ie Dokument'i O Sostoyani Podvon'ik Lodok Rossiskovo Flota" (Top Secret Documents About the Condition of Submarines in the Russian Fleet), *Sobesednik* 12, Moscow (June 1992): 1–3.

Krikunov, Konstantin, "Katasrof'i Veka, Taina Gibeli Yadernoi Sub-

marin' *K-219*" (Catastrophes of the Century, the Secret Sinking of Nuclear Submarine *K-219*) *Izvestiya*, (Moscow), 4 October 1996, no. 147.

Kondratev, V., "Chem Zhivet Ckalist'i Gorod?" (Why Live In Rocky-
Gadzhievo?), *Murmanski Vestnik*, 30 August 1994, no. 171.

McNish, Thomas, "USNS *Powhatan* Sails on Eventful Voyage," *Sealift*,
(Norfolk), 1 November 1986, p. 1.

Nikitin, Yevgeni, "Bez Grifa 'Sekretno' " (Without the Secret Caveat:
The Secret of Submarine 'YANKEE'), *Rossiskaya Gazeta* (Moscow),
2 September 1994, p. 6.

Rensberger, Boyce, "Soviet Sub Fire Seems to Be Out," *Washington
Post*, 6 October 1986, pp. A1, A21.

Sokirko, Viktor, "Kak Dva Russki Podvodnika Spacli Ameriky ot
Yadernoi Katastrof'i" (How Two Russian Submariners Saved
America from a Nuclear Catastrophe), *Komsomolskaya Pravda* (Mos-
cow), 4 October 1996.

Wilson, George C., "Soviet Sub Skipper Balked at Rescue," *Washington
Post*, 9 October 1986, p. A3.

Yakimets, Vladimir, "Razcheplenn'i Atom Perv'ie Polveka" (Splitting
the Atom, the First Half-Century), *Sobesednik*, Moscow (1994): 3–7.

Yemelyanekov, Aleksander, "Voenno-morskoi flot: U Tragedii V
More-Prichin'y Naberegu" (The Navy: In Tragedies at Sea-
Conditions Ashore. Unsinkable, From Notes Under the Caveat
'Secret'), *Sobesednik* 14, Moscow (April 1992): 4–5.

Secondary Sources and Periodicals

Aleksin, V. Kontr, Admiral, "Po Sledam Operatsii 'Jennifer' " (The
Case of Operation Jennifer), *Morskoi Sbornik* (Moscow), 5 June 1992,
p. 79–83.

———, "Incident na Berentsova More" (Incident in the Barents Sea),
Morskoi Sbornik (Moscow), 5 June 1992, pp. 21–22.

———, "Flot i Avariinost' " (The Fleet's Accident Rate), *Morskoi Sbornik* 10, Moscow (1992): 37–42.

———, "Oni Pogibli Ha Boebom Postu" (They Died At Action Stations), *Morskoi Sbornik* 12, Moscow (1993): 12–14.

Bukan', S. P. "Po Sledam Podvodn'ikh Katastratof" (On the Trail of Underwater Catastrophes). Moscow: Guild Master "Rus,' " 1992.

Burov, Viktor N. *Otechestvennoye Voennoe Korablestroenie V Tret'em Stoletii Svoei Istorii* (Patriotic Naval Shipbuilding in the 300th Year of Our History) St. Petersburg: Sudostroenie, 1995.

Clancy, Tom. *Submarine: A Guided Tour Inside a Nuclear Warship.* Berkley Books: New York, 1993.

Chaze, William, and Robert Kayler, "Silent War Beneath the Waves," *U.S. News and World Report,* 15 June 1987, pp. 36–43.

Cherkashin, Nicolai. "Requiem Linkora" (Requiem for a Battleship). In *The Secret Bond that Destines All Seagoing.* Moscow: Voenizdat, 1990.

———. "Hiroshima: Vspl'ivaet v Polden" (Surface at Noon). In *Vakhteni Dzhurnal* (The Log). Moscow: Andreevsky Flag, 1993.

——— "Kak Pogibaet Submarin'i" (How Submarines Die). In *Vakhteni Dzhurnal (The Log).* Moscow: Andreevsky Flag, 1995.

Dubski, Kiril, "Sekret Toma No. 33" (The Secret of Volume No. 33) *Chest Imayu* 7, Moscow (1994): 16–19.

Handler, Joshua, "No Sleep In the Deep for Russian Subs," *Bulletin of the Atomic Scientists* (April 1993): 7–9.

———, "Submarine Safety—The Soviet/Russian Record," *Jane's Intelligence Review,* int. ed. (July 1992): 328–332.

Huchthausen, Peter, "Russian Navy in Distress," *U.S. Naval Institute Proceedings*, Annapolis (May 1993): 77–80.

———, "Sabotage or Espionage; The Secret Sinking of Battleship NOVOROSSISK," *U.S. Naval Institute Naval History,* Annapolis (February 1996): 19–23.

Kessler, Ronald. *Moscow Station: How the KGB Penetrated the American Embassy.* New York: Simon and Schuster, 1989.

Kobchikov, E. Yu., "Nesostoyavshisya 'Chernobyl'/K 10-Letiyu Gibeli Atomnoi Podvodnoi Lodi *K-219*" (A Chernobyl Which Didn't

Happen/On the 10th Anniversary of the Loss of *K-219*). *Pamyat* (St. Petersburg), 10 September 1996.

Kravtsov, Anatoli, "Rassledovanie: Podvodnaya Chernobyl?" (Investigating An Underwater Chernobyl?) *Ogonyok*, Moscow (December 1993): 44–45.

Mikhailov, A., "Odna Tain Bermudskovo Treugl'nika" (A Secret of the Bermuda Triangle), *Severn'i Rabochii* (Murmansk), 20 October 1994.

Minchenko, S., Captain First Rank, "Operatsya Glubina" (Operation Depth), *Morskoi Sbornik*, Moscow (July 1994).

Mozgovoi, Aleksander, "Sekrete Pod Vole" (Secrets Concealed Beneath the Waves), *Echo of the Planet* 6 (February 1994): 22–27.

———, "Taran 'Hiroshima,'" *Morskoi Sbornik* 11, Moscow (1993): 48–50.

Nikitin, Ye., Captain First Rank, "Tragediya V Sargassovom More" (Tragedy in the Sargasso Sea), *Morskoi Sbornik,* Moscow (October 1991), pp. 45–51.

———, "Matros Kotor'i Spac Ameriku" (The Sailor Who Saved America) "Serezha Protiv Chernob'ila-2" (Sergei Verses Chernobyl-2) *Echo of the Planet* (Moscow) 4 October 1991, no. 40.

Oberg, James E. *Uncovering Soviet Disasters: The Limits of Glasnost.* New York: Random House, 1988.

Polmar, Norman, and Jurrien Noot. *Submarines of the Russian and Soviet Navies, 1918–1990.* Annapolis: U.S. Naval Institute Press, 1991.

Schoenfeld, Gabriel, "Underwatergate, A Submarine Chernobyl," *The New Republic,* 27 April 1993, pp. 20–21.

Shoumatoff, Alex, "The Silenced Love Song of Pvt. Clayton Lonetree," *Esquire* (November 1993): 105–112.

van Voors, Bruce, "Murky Waters for the Supersub," *Time,* 25 January 1988, p. 26.

Zavarin, V., "V Pamyati Zhivikh" (In Memory of the Living), *Morskoi Sbornik* 6, Moscow (1990): 42–46.

ACKNOWLEDGMENTS

The authors are grateful for the counsel of literary agent and friend Knox Burger, without whose kindness and advice this book could not have been produced as effectively.

The authors also thank Admiral Valentin Selivanov, former Chief of the Russian Main Navy Staff, who made it possible to interview many Russian naval officers still on active duty; and Rear Admiral Ted Sheafer for his help in tracking the sequence of events in the United States chain of military command during the *K-219* accident.

Special thanks to Tom Mangold of BBC and Bill Cran of InVision Productions, who made the entire research effort possible. The authors also acknowledge and are deeply thankful for the many kindnesses and advice provided by Stephanie Tepper, Bill Cran's wife and InVision partner, who lost a long battle with cancer in March 1997. Stephanie played a key part in telling this story.

Captain Igor Britanov and many of the officers, wives, and men of Crew Number One, YANKEE-1 Class SSBN *K-219*, provided most of the material describing their ordeal. Their willingness to tell their own story is appreciated.

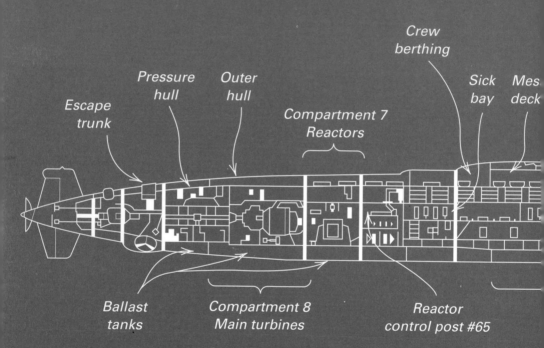

Escape
trunk

Pressure
hull

Outer
hull

Compartment 7
Reactors

Crew
berthing

Sick
bay

Mes.
deck

Ballast
tanks

Compartment 8
Main turbines

Reactor
control post #65